NEWSROOMS IN CONFLICT

Pitt Latin American Series

George Reid Andrews, General Editor

Catherine M. Conaghan, Associate Editor

Newsrooms in Conflict

Journalism and
the Democratization
of Mexico

SALLIE HUGHES

University of Pittsburgh Press

To my parents, my first and best teachers

*To those who practice civic journalism, and to those who want
to but can't*

Published by the University of Pittsburgh Press, Pittsburgh, PA 15260
Copyright © 2006, University of Pittsburgh Press
All rights reserved
Manufactured in the United States of America
Printed on acid-free paper
10 9 8 7 6 5 4 3 2 1

Library of Congress Cataloging-in-Publication Data

Hughes, Sallie.
   Newsrooms in conflict : journalism and the democratization of
Mexico / Sallie Hughes.
         p.   cm.
   Includes bibliographical references and index.
   ISBN 0-8229-5928-3 (cloth : alk. paper)
   1. Journalism—Political aspects—Mexico—History—20th century.
2. Journalism—Social aspects—Mexico—History—20th century.
3. Press and politics—Mexico—History—20th century.   I. Title.
   PN4974.P6H84 2006
   302.230972'0904--dc22   2006001962

CONTENTS

TABLES AND FIGURES

Tables

Figures

ACKNOWLEDGMENTS

I have amassed several debts of gratitude during the course of researching and writing this book. The largest is to the many journalists and others in Mexico who gave me their time and insights during interviews that sometimes took hours and touched sensitive subjects. To all of them go my sincere respect and thanks. Among those people were several who opened doors for me, either physical ones into their newsrooms or conceptual ones into areas that I might never have thought to include in the study. They are Claudia Fernández, Roberto Rock, Alejandro Junco, Lázaro Ríos, Michael Zamba, Juan Angulo, Maribel Gutiérrez, José Santiago Healy, Daniel Lund, Alejandro Moreno, Pedro Armendares, Marco Lara Klahr, and Alejandra Xanic. Another group that guided the development of the project is made up of several gifted scholars and mentors, who in some way informed this book either by directly commenting on earlier drafts or influencing the course of my own academic formation. I especially want to thank Roderic Ai Camp, Chappell Lawson, Daniel C. Hallin, W. Lance Bennett, Rosental Alves, Peter H. Smith, Timmons Roberts, Mary Clark, Leo Flynn, Richard Greenleaf, Thomas Reese, Leo Ferreira, and Sigman Splichal. Several graduate students offered able and much-needed assistance: Jesús Arroyave, (now Dr.) Roberto Domínguez, and Juliet Gill, all of the University of Miami.

I also gratefully acknowledge several institutions that saw the worth of the project and supported it financially over the years. The Goldsmith Research Award from the Joan Shorenstein Center for the Press, Politics and Public Policy at Harvard University funded part of the content analysis. The Center for U.S.-Mexico Studies at The University of California, San Diego, gave me a write-up fellowship and an incredible interdisciplinary atmosphere in which to develop the project. Tulane University's Roger Thayer Stone Center for Latin American Studies and The Institute for the Study of World Politics funded the initial year of field research. The Horowitz Foundation for Social Policy helped fund research on the country's new access-to-information law. The *Dallas Morning News* funded focus groups with political party press officers. The University of Miami's James W. McLamore Summer Research Award and Provost's Innovative Teaching Award, as well as Pomona College's Wig Summer Research Award, funded follow-up field work. Rosario Solórzano, Ada Pereyra, Blanca Guarneros, Maria Brindis, and Teresa Myscich influenced me with their deep knowledge of Mexico and supported me with their friendship, as well as a place to crash when the grant money ran out. Likewise, Miles, Cindy, Leigh Ann, Nic, Ragan, and Reece deserve my thanks for living with this project almost as much as I have, and two of them for their entire lives. Finally, I must thank Catherine M. Conaghan, Cynthia Miller, Peter Kracht, Deborah Meade, and everyone at University of Pittsburgh Press who took an interest in the project and improved the final result enormously.

Part I

THE INSTITUTIONAL DEVELOPMENT OF THE NEWS MEDIA

1

Civic Journalism and the Transformation of an Authoritarian Media Institution

When reporter Alejandra Xanic looked into the eyes of firefighters emerging from manholes all over Guadalajara, she could not believe government officials' assertion that the fumes from a gas leak had been successfully dispersed throughout the country's second-largest metropolis. While workmen from a nearby gas plant scurried about secretively, city emergency workers just looked puzzled. Instead of returning to her newsroom, Xanic stayed into the night and interviewed workers as they crawled up from the city's underground drainage system. Early the next day, April 22, 1992, twenty-six blocks of Guadalajara exploded. The blast killed more than two hundred people and left twenty thousand homeless. The explosion followed the very path Xanic's young newspaper, *Siglo 21*, had said it would on that morning's front page.[1] The Guadalajara gas explosion and the government's flimsy denial that the leak came from a state-owned plant—all reported in *Siglo 21*—became major issues in the next mayoral and gubernatorial elections. For the first time, the Partido Revolucionario Institutional (PRI, or Institutional Revolutionary Party), which had run Mexican politics with little challenge since 1929, lost both the city of Guadalajara and the state of Jalisco in the bellwether elections of 1995. Over the next five years, major city governments, congressional seats, and state governors' posts tumbled like dominoes to the opposition. In 2000, the PRI lost the epicenter of the authoritarian Mexican political system—the presidency. A new era of politics and journalism had been born, and reporters such as Xanic and newspapers such as *Siglo 21* had played an important part of how this came to pass. In the current democratic era, they hold the key to whether an autonomous, assertive, and citizen-focused form of journalism recedes with the country's political transition or survives as more than a limited and marginalized way to produce the news.

Even casual observers could see that the authoritarian political system was under increasing scrutiny by a more assertive, diverse, and autonomous component of the press in the mid-1990s. A cluster of publications within the Mexican press had forced open a space for public debate and deliberation in the mid-1980s, and then widened the public sphere in the 1990s as society became more participatory and demanding. By giving voice to oppositional messages that challenged the PRI's monologue, the civic-oriented press eroded autocrats' ability to shape political reality through the control of information and national symbols in the mass media. These journalists portrayed participation outside of state-sanctioned organizations as legitimate, offered information needed to form reasoned political opinions, and enabled participation that held government more accountable for its actions via elections, protests, and autonomous organization by crystallizing opposition values into alternative options for political behavior.

Clashing Models

My analysis of what happened to Mexico's media system is based on a conception of three models of journalism that existed in Mexico toward the end of the twentieth century: the civic, or civic-oriented, model, the authoritarian model, and the market-driven model.

In the civic model, news media provide information that helps citizens communicate their needs to government, hold government accountable, and foster deliberation and debate. This is accomplished by providing a two-way system of communication between government and citizens, acting as a monitor on governmental behavior, and providing information from many perspectives. To do this, newsrooms must demonstrate autonomy, diversity in the perspectives they present to the public, and assertiveness in news-gathering.

Alternatively, the authoritarian news model is characterized by the absence of newsroom autonomy, a representation of only points of view that support the positions of the current regime, and a passive approach to news-gathering. The model can be imposed from above (as in the case of repressive authoritarian regimes), by journalists themselves, when they believe in the mission of the regime or support it to further rent-seeking career strategies, or some mix of both.

The concept of market-driven journalism also involves the quid pro quo of news for material gain, but in a liberal political system and market-based economy. Market-driven newsrooms exhibit a lack of autonomy, monitor powerful actors only when commercial ends are advanced (or, at least, not threatened), and provide a diversity of viewpoints to the extent that the market demands it. News may be subordinated to market pressures, for example, by dramatizing news accounts in order to increase ratings. It may be attentive to political actors who control economic incentives, such as when news interviews are traded for advertising contracts during political campaigns. Finally, market-driven news may be conditioned by ratings or corporate interests, as when reform-minded legislators are vetoed from newscasts for supporting anti-monopoly regulation. Variants of the model thrive in electoral democracies characterized by market liberalism and journalism paradigms that legitimize the subordination of news to commercial forces (McChesney 2000; McManus 1994). Cross-country analysis in the 1990s found that the intensifying market imperative worldwide supported the proliferation of new news genres—such as attack, scandal, and crime-focused news—that are thought to lower participation by alienating potential participants and misdirecting attribution of responsibility to individual (over systemic) causation (Ansolobehere, Behr, and Iyengar 1993).

Civic Journalism *a la Mexicana*

Journalism as practiced in democratic societies has been called many things—democratic, liberal, libertarian, Western, public service, commercial, market-driven, etc.—reflecting variations in practice and conceptualizations of purposes, structures, ownership patterns, and methods to resist outside encroachment. I call the autonomous, assertive, and politically diverse form of journalism that emerged in Mexico to contrast authoritarian journalism "civic" because of its potential to enhance civic participation and government accountability to citizens, the civic objectives expressed by its principal practitioners, and its location in the upsurge of Mexican civil society and citizen participation. Mexico's civic journalism communicated information between citizens and governors, and monitored government like a "watchdog," thus facilitating two political dynamics of central importance to democracy: representation of citizens and government accountability to the public.[2] It accommodated news organizations and individual journalists who held ideological positions on the left, right, and center, and supported political competition in a democratic framework. From advocacy journalism, Mexico's civic journalism borrowed a general commitment to the establishment of democracy. Civic journalism thus aggregates elements of three theories of the press in a democratic society—watchdog, ideological, and advocacy—within its central mission of empowering participatory citizens.

Civic journalism *a la mexicana* did not utilize the same techniques, appear in the same formats, or have the same types of sponsors as the reform movement that appeared in late-twentieth-century U.S. journalism that sometimes calls itself "civic" or "public" journalism. Some of the philosophical foundations of the two forms are similar, but the specifics differ. While the United States movement arose in a context of declining civic participation and remained marginalized in smaller newspapers or specific projects, Mexico's civic journalism emerged as Mexican society challenged an authoritarian regime and became the dominant form of newspaper journalism in the country. Mexico's civic journalism was influenced by the awakening of civil society and simultaneously stimulated its development. This interactive notion of civic journalism and civil society better describes how journalism transformed during democratization in Mexico, at least momentarily.

The designation "civic" is mine; the participants in the transformation of Mexico's media institution sometimes used the terms "independent" or "democratic" to describe themselves. More typically, they acted without conceptualizing their behavior as part of a larger societal process. Consciously or not, however, they were part of a wider civic movement in several respects. First, the transformation of journalism had implications for the development of a robust public sphere and, through that, democracy. In the influential discussion by Habermas (1989a, 1989b), the public sphere is a space within which citizens share information, which allows them to form reasoned political opinions and communicate desires and demands to their governors. A vibrant public sphere includes diverse political information that is unencumbered by control from centers of political, economic, or cultural power. The quality of the public sphere in modern, complex societies depends in large part upon the performance of journalists and the news media. The media are increasingly recognized as "reality defining" institutions for the majority of citizens, who are not political or social activists (McNair 1998, 55).

Second, participants in civic journalism expressed the objectives of a larger movement. For instance, the executive editor of the newspaper *Reforma*, Lázaro Rios, connected his newspaper's informative mission directly to empowering citizen participation. When asked to select among various potential roles of the press in society, he chose "to inform." He explained: "I believe society itself monitors political activity and that the people are wise. That's why the role of informing is even more important than a monitoring role because with this focus the people are the ones who take the next step." Ignacio Rodríguez Reyna, a reporter in the 1990s who later directed a critical newsmagazine at the newspaper *El Universal*, believed the press should act as a counterweight to power in all forms to enforce the people's sovereignty. "Social groups should look to us, should use us, and we should get them to use us, as a way to constantly monitor power and through us to constantly express their impatience, their concerns, society's interests, or at least the interests of large groups in society, so that the people restrain power," he explained. Similarly, the managing editor of *La Jornada*, Josetxo Zaldúa, said the press "must monitor the behavior of the state, must maintain the attitude of a monitor of government . . . because the fundamental role of the press is to serve society, the citizen."[3]

Finally, the sweeping societal mobilization within which Mexico's new model of journalism arose underscores the civic essence of the approach. Clientelism, corporatism, and a state-centered ideology of social justice had attached most Mexican social, economic, and political organizations to the government or its party after the 1940s. The causes of the strength and durability of the PRI regime were many, including the legitimacy of the Mexican Revolution, constant economic growth for the urban middle classes until 1982, and the control of public space. Opposition behavior grew in the 1980s and 1990s because of economic stagnation, the increasing complexity of society, and changing international conditions.

In this context, autonomous social movements and nongovernmental organizations working on issues such as housing, debt relief, the environment, and neighborhood problems created a new discourse to press for solutions to concrete problems. Rather than oppositional political ideologies, these organizations demanded short-term, pragmatic solutions. They distanced themselves from the ideological movements of the past, which were easily repressed or co-opted by the Mexican regime (Olivera 1997; Avritzer 1997; Ochoa and Wilson 2001; Williams 2001). These activists anchored their oppositional discourse in a politics of citizenship rights and the rule of law, which undermined the regime's claim to be both originator and guarantor of social justice. From 1980 to 1990, 89 human rights groups formed, and another 161 formed in the 1990s. These groups focused on the rights of refugees, torture victims, indigenous people, women, gays, and other sufferers of government abuse or societal scorn. The majority of the members were young and university educated, and their leaders tended to be what Chand calls "institutional entrepreneurs," who capitalized on a more favorable domestic and international environment (Chand 2001, 205–6).

The work of the Mexican Academy of Human Rights illustrates how change advocates in the 1990s anchored pleas for participation and accountability in discourses of legality and citizenship rights. One of the academy's programs monitored television, which the activists argued had social responsibilities because of the use of public airwaves. Academy president Sergio Aguayo and researcher Patricia Cruz spoke in an educational video about bias in the two main television newscasts during the 1994 election:

> AGUAYO: The constitution guarantees us access to information. And because of the importance of the communications media in elections processes, the Mexican Academy of Human Rights has reviewed the respect of this right since 1991. The academy is a plural, nongovernmental organization that has promoted the respect of human rights in Mexico since 1984.
>
> CRUZ: The law is very clear. All of the news that is transmitted by the mass media, particularly by television, has to be truthful, objective, and not change or distort the facts. All of this stems from the right to free expression in Article Six of the Mexican Constitution. To obtain reliable data, we developed scientific research methods whose systematic application allows us to obtain data that clearly demonstrates the way that equality, truthfulness, and impartiality was violated in the more than fifteen elections that have taken place since 1991.
>
> AGUAYO: In this program we submit to you a selection of the manipulated images that the two main television networks transmitted about the presidential election of 1994. Our purpose is to offer you information to orient you in the art of viewing the newscasts.[4]

The group also distributed a *Guide for the Analysis of Electoral Content in the Electronic Media* before the 1994 election and, prior to the 2000 election, the educational pamphlets *The Communications Media and Citizen Education, Manual for Citizen Communication,* and *Ethical Practices in the Media.*

Like the human rights academy, autonomous civic groups of diverse origins had come together to press for free and fair elections as a solution to their problems by the mid-1990s. In response to the widespread electoral fraud of the 1980s, an umbrella group called the Alianza Civica (Civic Alliance) grouped seven large civic networks (over four hundred individual civic organizations) to mount the country's first citizen observation of a presidential election in 1994. Thousands of nonpartisan volunteers watched polls, monitored the vote count, statistically checked voter registration rolls, and documented biased coverage on television and in the press (Aguayo 1995).

The Ejército Zapatista de Liberación Nacional (EZLN, or Zapatista Army of National Liberation) also mobilized and aggregated the burgeoning civic sector in the 1990s, but through a military approach. The EZLN marched into four southern Mexican townships on January 1, 1994, demanding equality and justice for Mexico's indigenous peoples. The government responded by bombing nearby villages as the Zapatistas retreated. Then the public got involved.

About one hundred thousand people marched throughout the country within days of the uprising, demanding that the government halt the bombing and the two parties come together to negotiate. Hundreds of civic organizations sent representatives to monitor the ensuing peace talks and attend "civil society forums" that EZLN hosted over the next three years. Attendees wrote proposals on indigenous rights, citizen participation, political democracy, social democracy, and human rights. Subcommander Marcos, a spokesman for EZLN, explained how the unexpected response from civil society caused EZLN leaders to reassess their tactics: "Dawn, January 1, was a life-death coin toss. Life would require something radical, like the fall of the government and the onset of a transition government. Or death. They would destroy us. We never considered that the coin might not fall, that a new force would emerge, that society would dictate that neither side would destroy each other. We faced a situation where neither side could annihilate the other and we had to talk."[5]

As they reported on events like the EZLN uprising, many journalists in Mexico were pleased that their work supported social movements and activists in areas such as human rights, feminism, ethnic justice, and the environment. In the Guadalajara elections in 1995, radio reporters worked with civic election monitors, denouncing polling station irregularities on the air in real time. A reporter who helped found the civic newspaper *Reforma* in 1993 reflected, a decade later, that she was happiest when she covered civic activists.

> I am very much a defender of human rights. I have that as a vocation. So [my professional orientation] could have come from my family and, obviously, could have been cultivated more in my schooling and even more still by practicing my profession. But it's really a personal vocation of service. For example, I covered NGOs and human rights for a time, and this was the moment when I was the happiest I've ever been because I really felt that I was performing a service by denouncing abuses, or denouncing the systematic abuse of human rights and things like that.[6]

The newspaper *La Jornada* openly supported the Zapatista movement, but journalists for many other publications revealed that coverage of the uprising had a profound impact on their conception of journalism. Alejandro Paez, a young Mexican reporter, helped cover the EZLN for a U.S. newspaper before becoming an editor at several civic Mexican publications. A few years after the uprising, he reflected, "all of the journalists, Mexican and foreign, were affected emotionally upon seeing an underworld that had been so forgotten by everyone, including journalists, the government, NGOs. It changed us. There was a period of great enchantment with the movement. It was a moral debt paid for what we hadn't done before."[7]

A connection with civil society seemed to permeate civic journalists' professional identities during Mexico's political transition. When 126 journalists at fourteen of Mexico's more independent newspapers were asked in 1999 to identify with whom they felt most committed professionally, 1 percent said people of their own political values, 18 percent said their own publication, 19 percent said themselves, and 60 percent said "society, including those who have values different from myself."[8] In the same survey, a majority of journalists indicated that they felt least compelled to critique nongovernmental organizations (rather than political and cultural institutions), although they defended their autonomy from these groups.

The actors who propelled journalistic change in Mexico may not have envisioned themselves as members of a movement, but they were part of a multilayered process that was closely intertwined with the country's civic awakening. They were energized by society's movement toward democracy, and, through their innovative newsrooms, gave society back the information that citizens needed to end the seventy-one-year-old single-party regime.

From Media Institution to Hybrid System

Civic-oriented journalism was not the only innovation that arose from gradual democratization and incomplete market-based economic reform. As the authoritarian media institution disaggregated, it was replaced not with a new monolithic institution, but with a "hybrid" media system of organizational clusters responding to alternative models of belief and behavior. The hybrid media system is made up of civic, market-driven, and adaptive authoritarian media organizations.

The dominant form of journalism under Mexico's PRI regime was authoritarian from the 1940s until the 1990s. Most newsrooms produced news that exhibited a lack of autonomous, assertive, or diverse viewpoints of the regime. The PRI did not often overtly coerce newsrooms to ensure this kind of coverage because many owners' and journalists' self-interests were served by supporting the state (Fernández and Paxman 2000; Riva Palacio 1997).[9] The civic model evidenced itself as an alternative to the authoritarian form of journalism in the early 1980s, as a generation of journalists whose values opposed those of the PRI learned about more independent styles of journalism and, in some cases, obtained the organizational resources necessary to change subservient newsroom cultures. As politics and the economy liberalized in the 1990s, incentives for news production changed and the legitimacy of separating the newsroom from state domination increased. These two trends further diversified the mix of newsroom orientations, stimulating the diffusion of civic journalism through a second-wave of civic-oriented newsroom formation and creating the new, market-driven journalism model. In the late 1990s, market-driven journalism emerged in Mexico to challenge the PRI regime and the media system it created. Market-driven journalism, like civic journalism, was linked to changes in wider society, such as the shift from state protection and promotion of the economy to a greater, if uneven, role for market mechanisms in economic production. This market shift weakened state controls on news production, and simultaneously increased the power of private sector advertisers.

Market-driven journalism manifested itself most strongly in network television. Just two networks competed for national television audiences and advertisers in the late 1990s, and management believed the best way to increase ratings was by presenting more balanced electoral coverage while shifting the news agenda toward sensational topics such as crime and personal tragedy. Civic-oriented broadcast journalists had little choice if they wanted to work in television. They could absorb the hyper-commercial culture, limit their civic impulses to the reduced opportunities existing within network newsrooms, or leave to establish alternative projects in radio or independent television with smaller audience reach.

Like civic journalism, market-driven journalism in Mexico has its own particular traits and can also claim to have helped undermine authoritarian government by giving greater voice to the electoral opposition. The mere fact that the opposition was featured on network television in the late 1990s gave viewers more complete political information upon which to make electoral choices.[10] Yet market-driven journalism lacked the straightforward autonomy and assertiveness of civic journalism. In addition to more balanced electoral coverage, in the 2000s market-driven television became more tabloidized. Newscasts began to air political scandals when others uncovered them, especially when videotaped images were leaked and individual moral failures could be highlighted. Rarely, however, did broadcast television investigate powerful actors on its own. Moreover, market-driven broadcasting distorted the public agenda by focusing on conflict, drama, and a fragmented, event-oriented view of reality. At the same time, the networks used the news to promote or protect corporate interests. Usually the promotion had to do with highlighting the work of their corporate foundations. The most far-reaching instance of protecting corporate interests occurred in December 2005, when in just one week corporate lobbyists pushed an overhaul of the broadcast concessions system through the lower house of Congress that might have cemented a television duopoly into place for the next four decades. On the major newscasts, however, almost nothing was said about the enormous public response that stopped the effort in the Senate (Villamil 2005a, 2005b).

Authoritarian traits in Mexican journalism did not fade easily in the face of civic and market-driven innovation. Leaders of newsrooms that followed forms I call "inertial" or "adaptive" authoritarianism held to the tenets of the authoritarian press institution, even while more innovative newspapers followed civic-oriented approaches. Today, in many parts of the country, local commercial television stations, government-owned television stations, and local newspapers still trade journalistic autonomy for partisan or personal advantage. The causes are various. As electoral competition increased in the 1990s and the standards of journalism changed, some private sector media owners, newspaper editors, and station managers remained blind to the strength of new incentives or decided to profit by trading news for personal gain with new power holders. Directors of government-run television were named by state governors, who continued to use broadcast news as propaganda despite criticism from partisan opponents, academics, and civic groups.

Despite the continued presence of authoritarian journalism in some sectors, my interviews found that the normative orientations of rank-and-file journalists had shifted significantly toward civic journalism by the 2000s. Unfortunately, these journalists rarely had the professional autonomy that would have allowed them to openly combat authoritarian or market encroachment on civic journalism norms when mandated by owners or state directors. An absence of professional autonomy and conflicting norms and practices characterized the hybrid media system as Mexico headed for another presidential election in 2006.

The Study Design

Mexico in the 1990s was a fortuitous locale and epoch in which to study journalistic change in real time. I worked in Mexico between 1993 and 2005 in stays as long as three years and as short as a day. During this time, the world's longest single-party regime slowly crumbled, society and politics became much more participatory, and journalism changed profoundly. The relationships between journalists, media organizations, and societal-level transformations would have been difficult to discern had they not been gradual, visible, and measurable within media content.

Two central questions guided my inquiry. How did Mexican journalism change during the years of broad societal transformation? Why did Mexican journalism change? No single methodology could answer both of these questions. Strict hypothesis testing might have missed dynamics that had not come to light during previous research, especially since so little work has been done on the causes of journalistic change. Instead, I used a content analysis to detect patterns and directions of change in media messages and deeper ethnographic techniques to identify the incentives, tacit understandings, and inherent values guiding news production. This is similar to the approach that David Altheide recommends in his book *Qualitative Media Analysis* (1996). In the last chapter of this book, I apply the model constructed from the Mexican case to press systems in three Latin American countries that have undergone democratic transitions, in order to explore the generalizability of the model and look for clues about the fate of civic journalism in Mexico.

Content analysis provided a detailed snapshot of media behavior during the regime-ending 2000 presidential campaign, as well as a broader picture of the period, from before the political transition through the years of profound societal transformation. I studied newspapers in the greatest detail because they were the first mass media type to diverge from the passive, subordinate journalism of Mexican authoritarianism and became reference points for the politically active population during the transition. Moreover, it was only in the printed press that civic journalism manifested in a sustained and important manner. Television provided an important contrast to the direction and timing of change in the printed press, and was the primary source of political information for less active mass audiences. Comparing the transformation of newspapers and television revealed organizational dynamics that otherwise might have remained hidden.

I chose four newspapers for the content analysis because insider accounts suggested they represented the range of variation of news production in Mexico, and together reached 65 percent of newspaper readership in greater Mexico City, the country's largest and most influential media market. The newspaper *Excélsior* represents the authoritarian approach. Following government intervention in newsroom leadership in the 1970s, *Excélsior* was known for stenographic coverage, support of the PRI regime, and myriad relations compromising autonomy. *El Universal* represents a transitional case. In the late 1990s, the newspaper underwent a directed change project guided by outside consultants and a reformist editor. Finally, *Reforma* and *La Jornada* represent civic-oriented newsrooms. Despite ideological differences, both newspapers were known for assertiveness, autonomy, and presenting diverse viewpoints about the PRI regime.

To test for variation in news coverage, I defined alternative models of news production based on three elements found in scholarly studies of

Table 1.1 Central Elements of Alternative Press Models

	Diversity	Assertiveness	Autonomy
Civic	Yes	Yes	Yes
Authoritarian	No	No	No
Market-Driven	Variable	Variable	Variable

national press systems and types: newsroom autonomy from powerful actors, assertiveness in the search for news, and diversity in representations of the PRI regime. I chose depictions of the regime rather than partisanship or ideological orientation because a media organization's stance on regime change most distinguished Mexican news producers during the transition. Ideological differences became more important after the PRI lost power. Table 1.1 lays out the approach of each model of journalism to each element.

In civic newsrooms, journalism supports an informed and participatory citizenship, and all three characteristics are present. The authoritarian news model, however, does not display any of these characteristics. Rather, in this model, newsrooms present only the vision of the state and allied sources of power, passively transmit messages from the regime and its allies, and are subordinate to outside (primarily state) controls. News produced under the authoritarian model blocks both informed political deliberation and demands for accountability. Market-driven journalism reflects political pluralism and assertively seeks news when such behavior attracts audiences and advertisers. It is autonomous from the state as a political power, but not from advertisers (whether those advertisers are from the private sector, political parties, or government entities).

I relied upon ethnographic techniques to answer the question of why the media changed. I first went inside two Mexico City newspaper offices and conducted structured interviews and participant observation. One field site was the traditional newspaper *El Universal*, which attempted to transform its newsroom culture and behavior during my fieldwork. The other was a well-established, civic-oriented newspaper, *Reforma*. At each site, I interviewed all of the top editors and the majority of reporters who covered political beats. I also did more limited field work in the left-leaning civic newspaper *La Jornada* and its sister newspaper *El Sur* in Acapulco, Guerrero.

Successful field research sometimes requires a little luck, and I had that at Mexico City's oldest and largest newspaper, *El Universal*. I arrived there in 1999, just before the management gathered staff in the gargantuan press room and announced a project of transformation. This was the second time *El Universal*'s sole owner, Juan Francisco Ealy Ortiz, had flirted with such an idea. In the 1980s, he had contemplated a more-limited makeover but nixed

Figure 1.1 Study Participants

the project a day before its launch. This time, societal conditions, his personal break with the political regime, a different kind of competition, and the influence of a reformist editor convinced him that his newspaper had to change profoundly. Thanks to a receptive editor, Roberto Rock, I was not only able to interview journalists before and during the project, but also participate in retraining sessions and do follow-up interviews years later. The opportunity to observe and interview journalists across a decade was incredibly important to refining my arguments about the origin, direction, and reach of media transformation.

The second field site, *Reforma*, is the sister publication of *El Norte*, the newspaper credited with starting the civic trend in Mexico. Based in Monterrey, an industrial city near the border with Texas, *El Norte* sent editors and hired young, inexperienced reporters to staff *Reforma* when it opened in Mexico City in 1993. The new paper's style of journalism, graphic presentation, and autonomous relations with advertisers and government was a turning point in Mexico City journalism. In its premiere issue, *Reforma* led with a story about the launch of opposition party presidential campaigns and, the following year, chronicled a dispute with the PRI-linked union that monopolized newspaper distribution in the capital. Backed by opposition party leaders and intellectuals, the newspaper won the dispute and now is distributed through subscription and self-employed street-corner hawkers. Two of the important traits of the newspaper were its hard-hitting investigative unit in the 1990s and pioneering use of opinion polls, closely and obviously linked to increasing press assertiveness and connection to citizens.

In addition to studying how civic-oriented journalism was established, I wanted to explore the diffusion of the *Reforma* style, which was noticeable in *El Universal*'s transition, and gauge how far the transformation of journalism values and behavior reached beyond Mexico City. To do that, I conducted interviews and a survey on journalists' values at fourteen of the country's more independent newspapers. Figure 1.1 shows the location of 126 print journalists who participated in the survey in 1999 and 16 more who participated in follow-up interviews in 2003. One hundred and twenty-six top editors and reporters on politically relevant beats made up the non-random sample. Additionally, in 2002 and 2003 I interviewed journalists and news executives at the two national networks, Televisa and TV Azteca, as well as local commercial and state-owned television stations in four states.

An Institutional Model of Media Transformation

What explanations for journalistic change emerged from the study? As political economists would suggest, democratization and the rise of the free market in Mexico transformed the incentives for news production. These broad societal transformations lessened state controls on the media and changed financial incentives in favor of greater political pluralism in the news. However, these factors alone do not explain why some news organizations changed and others did not, or why newsrooms changed at different times and in different ways.

Mexican journalism until the 1980s was what sociologists would call an overdetermined institution. Incentives, values, and assumptions all acted as the glue holding together regularized patterns of journalistic thought and action that endured across decades and a field of similarly behaving news organizations. I found that alterations in one or more of these forms of institutional binding explained particular moments and directions of newsroom change. Then innovative newsrooms, once buttressed by the right environmental conditions, sparked change across the newsroom field. The diffusion of new journalistic forms was part of a process of institutional transformation that held across a range of organizational experiences.

I argue that journalistic change is a process that develops through exchange between four domains of institutional action: the environment,

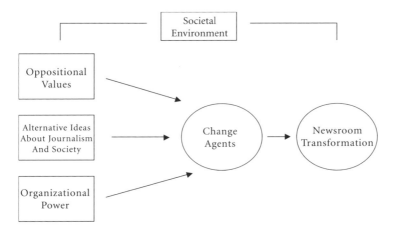

Figure 1.2 A Model of Civic Newsroom Transformation

the organizational field, the newsroom as an organization, and the social-psychological world of the individual journalist. The newsroom-level model of organizational change is depicted in figure 1.2. At the newsroom level, three variables influence journalists to become successful change agents who transform their organizations: oppositional political values, alternative ideas about journalism and society, and organizational power to set and enforce newsroom policy. Civic-oriented change agents opposed the regime on political, economic, or moral grounds; absorbed outside ideas about journalism as a facilitator of government accountability and citizen participation; and gained control of their newsrooms to direct change. Market-driven change agents held neutral political values. They placed profit generation above regime considerations; were happy with the status quo as long as it defended their interests; and assimilated ideas about journalism as a generator of commercial profit in a competitive environment. Once they gained control of their newsrooms, market-driven change agents implemented new policies and promoted new personnel.

A fourth variable contextualizes the model. The societal environment of news production shaped change agents' values and access to new ideas. For instance, civic-oriented change agents who appeared prior to political liberalization in northern Mexico were driven by political values that opposed the state-led economy and ideas about journalism that had disseminated from the United States. These values and ideas were more common in the northern part of the country than they were in central Mexico, where early journalistic innovators tended to hold leftist political values and be influenced by ideas about citizenship and journalism that came from Mexican academia and the Spanish political transition.

The societal context also set the political and economic parameters determining whether these ideas and values could manifest themselves as civic journalism. As Chand (2001) found with the emergence of civic organizations, civic innovators could barely hold on in the 1980s. By the 1990s, however, political and economic space had opened enough for institutional entrepreneurs to build on the foundations set a decade earlier. Civic participation flourished in many parts of the country. The experience was similar for the civic press. Repression after massacres of student protesters in Mexico City in 1968 and 1971 included a clampdown on the press. Only a few stand-out publications attempted assertive journalism in the 1970s and they did not survive the decade. It was not until the 1980s, when localized protests against the regime appeared along the northern border, that the first wave of civic-oriented newspapers could consolidate. They created an innovative core from which a second wave of civic journalists formed in the 1990s, when political and economic conditions liberalized even further.

Newsroom transformation occurs within a wider institution, which operates on distinctive planes and encompasses a trans-organizational field of news organizations. Sometimes innovative newsrooms spark change in the wider trans-organizational institution; other times they are responding to transformations that have started in other news organizations. My model of transformation for the wider media institution is derived from the Mexican context, but I believe it has applications elsewhere. The process begins with the creation of innovative civic newsrooms, which, in Mexico, occurred in the hostile environment of a state-led economy and authoritarian political system. In the media field, the authoritarian approach to journalism dominated, but began to face a sustained challenge from the new form. Once the wider environment opened, the civic model diffused to a wider population of newsrooms, driven by new political and financial incentives, mentoring and networks expansion, foreign influences, transformative shocks, and the growing prestige of the new approach.

In contrast to the civic innovators, inertial authoritarian newsrooms remained frozen when environmental conditions began to change because they were led by owners and editors whose mental models of reality, formed in previous eras, filtered information about changing instrumental cues and professional standards. In authoritarian pockets of the country where oligarchies controlled power after the PRI lost the presidency, adaptive authoritarian owners and propagandist governors used the news instrumentally to promote their personal and group interests with whatever faction held political power.

Other newsroom leaders responded to the new financial incentives of economic liberalization and absorbed ideas about how to commercialize news production. They transformed newsroom culture in reaction to the strengthening market. Market-driven newsrooms produced news about opposition political parties to maintain audiences; were assertive when such behavior generated profits; and offered limited protection to major advertisers, including political parties. As in civic transformations, control of decision-making power in the newsroom was essential to the adoption of market-driven journalism or the maintenance of authoritarian practices.

Mexican journalism currently exists within an economy of crisscrossed incentives of the market and cronyism, as well as a shallow democracy of competitive political parties that are, in many ways, disconnected from their constituencies. Mechanisms of representation and accountability, while much stronger than during the PRI regime, remain incomplete. Consolidating and deepening the practices of civic journalism remain as vital today as during the transition from authoritarian rule. But in postauthoritarian Mexico, civic journalism faces a complicated set of pressures: the concentrated structure of media ownership and the domestic advertising market, extra-state violence, holdover authoritarian press laws and practices, state media penetrated by political pressures, private media controlled by owners with varying degrees of commitment to newsroom autonomy, a weak community media sector, and hierarchically managed news organizations. The consolidation of civic journalism as a vibrant alternative to market-driven and holdover authoritarian news production depends upon further structural transformation to address these concerns. However, the survivability of civic journalism also depends upon the ability of civic-oriented journalists to anchor their professional identities in concepts of participatory citizenship and accountable government in the face of enormous social, economic, and political deficits.

Why Media Change Matters

This book looks to the Mexican experience to answer a question of central importance in democratic societies: How do we build news media that foster a robust form of citizenship? Understanding how media institutions break down and new systems are formed has important practical implications for new democracies attempting to consolidate mechanisms of participation, representation, and accountability.

Scholars and policy analysts have amassed evidence that news media can play important, affirmative roles during democratization and in deepening electoral democracy. At certain moments in Mexico's transition, for example, Lawson's analysis found that independent publications propelled political change by publishing scandals that delegitimized the PRI regime, and creating a new language for civil society groups that encouraged participation (2002, chaps. 7–9). Television news, when opened to opposition voices late in the transition, promoted better-informed voter decisions. Similarly, Western news coverage of protests against communism in Eastern Europe reaffirmed opposition values and dissolved the atomization of society that sustains authoritarian regimes (Bennett 1998).

The media also support citizen pressure for democratic representation and accountability once something resembling democracy is established. Politicians and policymakers in Latin America monitor news content closely and sometimes react to citizen demands presented through the media. In such circumstances, the press provides a link between public needs and government responses (Hughes 2006). For example, watchdog journalism helped increase accountability in South America's new democracies (Waisbord 2000). Smulovitz and Peruzzotti argue that media exposés are helping to redefine how citizens and politicians interact across the hemisphere: "Citizen action aimed at overseeing political authorities is becoming a fact of life and is redefining the traditional concept of the relationship between citizens and their elected representatives. The emergence of rights-oriented discourse and politics, media exposés of government scandals, and social movements organized around demands for due process are only some of this politics of societal accountability" (2000, 147).

But media effects are contradictory, in part because of the variations in how journalism is practiced across organizations, media types, and societal contexts. While journalism can enable citizenship, it can restrain it as well. Political bias in the news remains relatively common in Latin America today, and sustained political bias can distort participation and subvert accountability, especially when other sources of information are few. For example, biased electoral coverage in Latin America helped keep autocrats in power in authoritarian Mexico and Brazil, while contributing to the election of a neopopulist with authoritarian traits in Peru (Lawson 2002; Boas 2005; Straubhaar, Olsen, and Nunes 1992). Media owners also use their news organizations to take sides politically based on personal, class, or oligarchic interests. In Guatemala, Mexican mogul Ángel González used his television monopoly to back the eventual winner in the 1999 presidential election, Alfonso Portillo, who then made González's in-law and legal advisor the minister of communication. In Uruguay, family-owned groups that have controlled the country's three private networks since the 1950s gave advertising discounts of up to 95 percent to the long-ruling Colorado and National Parties. Perhaps in return, the government made Montevideo's cable market a closed shop jointly controlled by the three groups. The left-center National Front has been the only major political force to complain, perhaps because it has not been a recipient of media largesse (Zamora 2004; Rockwell and Janus 2003).

Likewise, market-driven journalism, which in Mexico and elsewhere has meant the encroachment of tabloidized techniques and content in mainstream television newscasts, can be problematic for participation. On one hand, use of personal stories and dramatic music helps media users connect with difficult issues, but only if the coverage makes the connection between the featured person or event and the wider social or historic context. On the other hand, concentrated focus on dramatic, tantalizing issues can distort the public agenda. In the Mexican congressional election of 2003, for example, tabloidization essentially pushed electoral politics out of the newscasts. Moreover, studies of political cynicism, mostly conducted in the United States, suggest that media may augment political alienation when they consistently bombard viewers with negative information about government without contextualization. News framing studies suggest episodic coverage of crime or corruption may increase the population's deception regarding individual politicians (Graber 2004; Iyengar 1991; Bennett 2003).

These criticisms of market-driven coverage do not mean that media should omit coverage of crime or corruption. On the contrary, both are important public issues that should receive ample press attention. However, whether context and potential solutions are included is extremely important. This may be especially so in Latin America, where mechanisms of representation and accountability are not institutionalized. Frustration sometimes has nowhere to go but the street. Protests against government corruption led to the removal of four Latin American presidents from office between 1992 and 1999 (Pérez-Liñán 2003). While the accountability inherent in presidential impeachment is obvious, only three of the four presidential removals followed constitutional procedures. Since 1999, angry crowds have forced unpopular presidents from office in Argentina, Ecuador, and Bolivia in constitutionally questionable circumstances.

Beyond practical urgency, the study of journalistic change is important on a theoretical level. News media are recognized as a necessary part of the institutional makeup of modern democratic systems, but academics have rarely addressed how and why media systems change (Lawson 2002, 2–3). Sociologists who study change in organizations and institutions have given us a good trail of breadcrumbs to follow, however. Using their lead, I have proposed a multilevel institutional approach. News organizations that share similar values and behavioral norms comprise a trans-organizational institution until a group of newsroom change agents disrupts uniformity. In permissive environments, these "outlaw entrepreneurs," as sociologist Walter Powell describes them, create innovative organizations that begin to influence "fields" of similarly behaving newsrooms. As the innovation spreads, the media institution breaks down. A struggle for hegemony occurs between the innovative and inertial organizations, as each battles for its own vision of journalism and society (Powell 1991, 198; Cook 1998, 69; Fligstein 1991; Scott 1995, 55–56; Scott 1998, 129–30; Singh, Tucker, and Meinhard 1991).

An institutional view of media transformation contrasts with approaches that look at the political economy of the media, the organizational imperatives of news work, or journalistic professionalism in isolation. Institutionalism tells us that efforts to explain media change should focus on the microlevel formation of professional identities, and shifts in organizational power as they interact with macrostructural conditions in the news environment. Civic journalists need space in the political and economic environment in which to operate, but they also need to maintain civic values and hold sufficient power in their organizations. The creation of assertive, autonomous, and politically diverse news media that foster governmental accountability and democratic deliberation depends on personal conviction and sustained risk-taking by a core of institutional entrepreneurs who gain control of their newsrooms and survive long enough to influence the rest of the media.

The rest of the book presents the story of the breakdown of an authoritarian media institution and creation of a new, hybrid media system. The first section describes the emergence, spread, and limitations of civic journalism. The second section describes the alternatives to civic journalism, including adaptive authoritarianism and market-driven journalism. The last section applies the model to other media transformations in Latin America and explores whether civic newsrooms in Mexico, Guatemala, Chile, and Argentina will survive as more than marginalized organizations.

The prospects for a vibrant, civic-oriented media in Latin America are not heartening given the disadvantageous environment of news production. Generalized weakness in the rule of law, holdover authoritarian laws, concentrated media ownership patterns, sporadic economic crises, and spotty journalistic professionalism chill autonomous, pluralistic, and assertive reporting in much of the region. Far from flourishing, press freedom actually eroded in Latin America as electoral democracy consolidated, power centers reconfigured, and participation levels fell in the late 1990s. According to Freedom House's survey of press systems in the region, the number of countries with a fully free press fell from ten systems in 1994 to just three in 2004. There were more Latin American media systems rated "not free" as of 2004—Cuba, Colombia, and Venezuela—than at any time since the height of the military rule in the mid-1980s (Sussman and Karlekar 2003; Karlekar 2003, 2004).

Latin America's "democratic vanguard" newspapers, identified by Alves (1997) in the late 1990s, have trajectories that resemble those of Mexico's civic newspapers, but have been overwhelmed by adverse environmental changes and resurgent ideological identities. I analyze three cases in chapter 10 and find that none could sustain their momentum. *Página/12* in Argentina became dependent on advertising from an ideologically compatible government administration during an extreme economic crisis in the early 2000s. It no longer displays the critical investigative edge that made it successful in the 1990s. *La Epoca* in Chile folded for financial reasons, but only after losing its innovative tendencies when a series of Christian Democratic presidents took office after the military regime departed. The journalists of *Siglo Veintiuno* in Guatemala quit en masse when the editor was fired for challenging the armed forces. They reopened as *elPeriódico*, but their reconstituted newsroom survives under serious physical and financial pressure.

On a brighter note, the institutional legacies of each of these civic projects survives, at least marginally, within journalists' transformed professional identities. Hence Argentine journalist Martín Rodríguez, who grew up reading the exposés of *Página/12*'s muckraking columnist Horacio Verbitsky, laments the decline of investigative journalism in his country and practices it when he can. A group of critical journalists from *La Epoca* in Chile, including award-winning author Alejandra Matus, bounce from project to project looking for an open space in which to report. They eventually open a smaller-scale newsmagazine called *Plan B*, and when that failed financially, they continued to look for outside funding to revive the project. In many countries, investigative journalists have turned to book publishing rather than relying only on newspaper reporting, where owners' interests, financial pressures, and narrow news agendas interfere with long-term investigative projects.[11] Where journalists retain the professional values and identities of civic journalism, they look for the space in which to practice it, if only in a limited way. Should Latin America's press environments and organizational structures reopen, journalists' civic identities would again reassert themselves more clearly in the news.

2 Media Transformation through Institutional Lenses

El Universal editor Roberto Rock moved through his newsroom like a man on a mission. His objectives were twofold: keep his job and use his position to transform Mexico City's largest newspaper. If he was successful, his newspaper would not only survive, but also contribute to the creation of a more democratic Mexico. Rock's task was complicated, but not impossible. Nor was he the first to attempt such a feat. Forty years old when he took the helm of Mexico City's oldest and largest newspaper in 1996, Rock followed a string of other journalists and media owners who, by the late 1990s, had gained control of newsrooms across Mexico and transformed the way they produced the news. Because of change agents like Rock, the Mexican media had profoundly altered the way it conceptualized and produced the news by the end of the twentieth century.

Newsrooms were the focal point for this transformation, becoming crucibles in which changing professional identities, organizational cultures, and incentives from the macroenvironment met, mixed, and together created a new style of reporting, writing, and editing. The newsroom, as envisioned here, is a multilayered phenomenon. It is an organization, in that it has limited entrance and is goal-oriented. It creates an organizational culture, since its members typically share values, expectations, and norms of behavior. Finally, the newsroom can become an institution, when values, expectations, and norms of conduct become widely shared across space and endure across time. When an agreement about newsroom values, expectations, and behaviors transcends organizational boundaries and spreads across a "field" of similar organizations such as newspapers or broadcast stations, then the press or the news media as a whole can be considered a trans-organizational institution similar to state legislatures, art museums, or community colleges.[1]

Newsrooms are not just any organization, of course. News media are centrally important to democratic politics as intermediaries—like political parties, interest groups, and social movements—that help ensure political leaders take popular preferences into account and allow citizens to demand accountability from politicians. In a newsroom, the daily interaction of media owners, journalists, advertisers, politicians, and news sources produce the texts that help set a robust agenda of public discussion and debate, or, in the case of authoritarian states and shallow electoral democracies, diminish the prospects for government by the people.

Scholars are just beginning to understand how newsrooms construct the news in transitional societies and new democracies. Academics interested in democratization largely ignored news media, for various reasons, as the advance of democracy's third wave of nations in the 1980s turned attention to the creation of viable electoral systems and formal political institutions such as presidencies and congresses. Political scientists overlooked news media in part because they tended to conceptualize democracy in electoralist terms, or as Lawson stated, to center their inquiry on the ability of free, fair, and inclusive elections to place a procedural floor on elite behavior and guarantee a minimal level of government accountability (Lawson 2002). News media are also conceptually difficult for political scientists because of their location both inside and outside of government. Media organizations formally sit outside government, yet few modern political systems could survive without their services as intermediaries.

The focus on elections and formal governmental institutions led scholars of many disciplines to incomplete explanations of political transitions and democratic consolidation, which failed to predict—or even helped to create—the shallow electoral democracies that cropped up in the 1990s. These democracies produced leaders who were only partially accountable to their societies and excluded portions of their population from real representation (Diamond 1999). A wider analytical net, which includes civil society and mechanisms linking society to government, gives us more tools for understanding why that happened and how democracy might be deepened in the future. As Schmitter points out, democratic consolidation involves institutionalizing activity in multiple "partial regimes" that guide political action simultaneously in many interrelated spheres. To O'Donnell, the "vertical" accountability of elections must be accompanied by the "horizontal accountability" that comes from multiple and overlapping organizations in government and civil society that check abuses of public power (O'Donnell 1998, 112–26; Schmitter 1992). Especially in new democracies, where corporatism, clientelism, and other authoritarian experiences have stunted the representational capacity of political parties and labor unions, news media can play important roles of linking citizens and governors and monitoring government.

News media, however, do not always take on the beneficial roles envisioned in classical democratic theory. In fact, their behavior seems to produce contradictory effects on citizenship and democratic governance. In South America, Waisbord found that assertive news organizations denounced abuses of power as those young democracies consolidated, but those same journalists often ignored the questionable behavior of political allies and equally scandalous social problems. In Eastern Europe, Bennett found that electronic media spread oppositional messages and values unintentionally or from abroad, helping to bring down the walls of fear and isolation atomizing those authoritarian societies. Once their political transitions ended, however, media gave new citizens few informational tools with which to learn to debate and deliberate political messages during the consolidation of democracy (Bennett 1998; Waisbord 2000).

Traditional approaches to international media systems that categorized countries as democratic, authoritarian, socialist, or communist do not reveal much about these contradictory behaviors, unfortunately. The press systems literature does not speak directly to transitional media systems because of the greater fluidity and diversity in these systems compared to the world of the 1950s, 1960s, and 1970s. Greater national variation, and especially variation within the democratic category, is the result of processes of economic and political liberalization in Latin America, Eastern Europe, and Asia after the 1970s, as well as the effects of intensified economic liberalization in the United States and Western Europe (Curran and Park 2000a, 2000b).

In new democracies, journalists' identities are more flexible, political upheaval more likely, and important decisions about media-state relations and ownership regimes have yet to be cemented into place through law, ideology, and practice. Many new democracies suffer from prolonged or repeated economic crises that challenge the ability of media to be financially autonomous. Moreover, journalists and news organizations in new democracies have to contend with a combination of holdover authoritarian traits (such as excessive state control), a culture of journalism subservience, and the possibility of physical repression.[2]

However, the old press systems typologies remain useful as benchmarks for analyzing transitional media systems when, in addition to media's relationship with the political and economic systems, a third axis measuring the nature of journalism norms is added. Most national media systems today define themselves not only by their affinity to political liberalism or authoritarianism, but also to public service or market-driven orientations.

Categorizing media systems according to the type of state, economic system, and journalism norms would additionally serve as a measure of internal variation within "democratic" media systems, which is greater than it was twenty years ago. For example, while the dominant model in U.S. journalism is market-driven, some news organizations and journalists still reflect values and behaviors oriented toward public service. In Mexico, you find civic, authoritarian, and market-driven approaches coexisting and competing for hegemony.

Studies by Hallin (2000a) on tabloid television and Lawson (2002) on media opening are among a handful of deeper analyses that are beginning to fill a gap in comparative media studies. They focus on the transition of more authoritarian television news forms to a popular, tabloid-style television journalism or to a broader style of democratic journalism. Hallin's argument is that commercial television took on tabloid features in Mexico in response to liberalizing political and economic conditions. Lawson's argument prioritizes the rise of competition between top television networks during economic liberalization, but also acknowledges the importance of human agency in the creation of an independent press and more open radio airwaves. Each work sheds light on part of the media transformation process, but neither directly confronts the variation of media responses to liberalization or the origin of the divergent paths of newsroom development that began before liberalization.

In addition to state-centered and media-centered approaches, researchers occasionally propose a society-centered approach to political change and consolidation that locates journalists and artists within the "upsurge" of civil society during political transitions. In this view, gradual liberalization of the macropolitical environment allows oppositional behavior to spread and to pressure elite actors for further opening (O'Donnell and Schmitter 1986, 48–56; Diamond 1992). Society-centered approaches are helpful because they locate portions of the media within a process of civil society emergence (or reemergence) during political transitions. They fall short of complete understanding because they do not specify the organizational basis of civil society, which explains the pattern of diffusion of oppositional values and behavior and the inability of societal groups to better shape the quality of the democracy that eventually stabilizes.

Some researchers who study social movements emphasize how social interaction within organizations is necessary for the "cognitive liberation" of aggrieved individuals. McAdam (1982) demonstrates in a study of the origins of the Black Power movement in the United States that aggrieved individuals discovered the universality of their predicament and begin to interpret events similarly because of interaction within organizations such as churches, self-help associations, and student groups. Broad, societal-level transformations associated with modernization in the United States created a "structural opportunity" for a change in the condition of African Americans, but these societal changes needed social interaction in organizations to materialize as oppositional values and behaviors. Structural opening and cognitive liberation, centered in organizations, explains the rise of social movements, but maintaining momentum for change becomes more difficult once government and elites respond to the status quo.

Communication scholars noted the organizational basis of media behavior a long time ago. Most accounts depict media as separate organizations created to produce a product—news—with optimal economic efficiency within the U.S. capitalist system. These studies focus on organizational interaction with the wider environment (1950s), the routinization of journalists' work (1970s), or the effects of the market and politicians' media management strategies on news production (1980s and 1990s).[3] The tendency to focus on individual organizations and single levels of analysis have led researchers in the United States to underemphasize standardized patterns of behavior and values across media organizations that suggest the presence of widely institutionalized work.

Herbert Gans's research inside the newsrooms of ABC, CBS, *Time,* and *Newsweek* in the early 1970s was the first to explore in detail the impact of journalists' shared values on news production. Gans (1979) finds that a set of unwritten, even subconscious values guided journalists in the United States and appeared in their news texts in that decade. Mostly middle class and Anglo American in origin, these values supported the status quo in politics by presupposing the existence of intrinsic system-regulating features in U.S. democracy and capitalism. More recently, De Uriarte (2003) cites Gans's discovery of U.S. journalists' ethnocentric worldview to explain how attempts to diversify news content by hiring more Hispanics failed in the 1980s and 1990s, because Hispanic journalists were socialized into the mainstream culture of U.S. newsrooms. Likewise, Epstein (1973) notes the homogenizing ideological effect of newsroom socialization in his study of television personnel in the 1970s.

This work on newsroom values, culture, and socialization processes helped identify the clashing cultures of journalism that arose in Mexican newsrooms during the 1980s and 1990s. Moreover, the emergence of a civic-oriented media in Mexico has similarities to the resurgence of civil society described by O'Donnell and Schmitter, as well as McAdam's political process model of social movement development. Additionally, studies portraying media as organizations correctly illuminate the multiple pressures on news content from political, economic, and social power centers in the organizational environment. How do we tie all of these strands of research together into a cohesive approach to media stability and transformation?

An Institutional Lens on the Media

The lens provided by sociological studies of organizations and institutions integrates these separate lines of research into a comprehensive theoretical approach. Institutional analysis answers the question of how news media change by highlighting the impact of ideas on change agents (institutional entrepreneurs) who muster the resources necessary to change newsroom culture, the phenomenon of "selective diffusion" from innovative organizations, and the interaction of individuals and organizations with shifting cues and constraints in a liberalizing macroenvironment (Powell 1991).

What are institutions and how are they transformed? Institutions are widely shared understandings of roles, values, and behaviors that guide social action. Institutionalization implies the internalization of shared cognitive and normative frameworks that endure across time and space. They both create and can be sustained by shared visions and "mental models" of reality. The frameworks can be carried by logics of instrumentality (I act this way because it benefits me), appropriateness (I act this way because I—and those I admire—think it is appropriate), or orthodoxy (I act this way because I always have, everyone else does, and it is natural). Institutions, in this synthetic view, are overdetermined systems: sanctions, values, intrinsic direct reward, pressure to conform, and unchallenged routines and assumptions about the world work together to give a particular meaning system its directive force (Scott 1995, 33–61; Senge 1994).

Institutional theorists focus not only on the effect of coercive rule systems and laws on institutional stability and change, but also on the importance of perceived legitimacy, normative acceptability, and orthodoxy that are socially constructed. Coercive, formal rules might not guide members of a particular institution, but rather unwritten, informal rules about what is appropriate or normal.

Institutions can be regulative structures that impede behavioral change, but can also produce shared visions that empower and enable innovative behavior by conferring rights, responsibilities, and duties. Empowered minorities create visions of normatively appropriate behavior or conceptual correctness that resist domination by a hegemonic group. Slaves or conquered peoples assert the "hidden transcripts" of an identity forged through the common experience of coercion (McAdam 1982; Scott 1995). In an organizational setting, shared visions "create a common identity (and) . . . compel courage," writes business scholar Peter Senge (1994, 208). Senge argues that shared visions are created through the desire to participate in a project of profound importance to participants. Visions "derive their power from a common caring. In fact, we have to come to believe that one of the reasons people seek to build shared visions is their desire to be connected in an important undertaking." For journalists, being a citizen in a democracy conveys a far different vision of their professional rights and responsibilities than does being a subject of an authoritarian state. Journalists who conceive of their role within the framework of citizenship actively resist structures that impede their autonomy and assertiveness, and seek out others in a common enterprise.

Institutions can be maintained through rational readings of incentives in the environment, but can endure past supportive environmental conditions. Management theorists have noted, for example, that institutions created to maximize instrumental cues in the environment outlast their utility if institutionalized identities, values, and behaviors become "frozen" (DiMaggio and Powell 1991b, 65–66; Schein 1985). While institutional frameworks are enduring by definition, they are not static. Changing environmental conditions, new role models, and contact with influential change agents promoting differing frameworks can stimulate the formation of new cultures and cognitive identities. The differing frameworks can coexist or compete in the organization or wider organizational field. Once the new frameworks become widely shared, they can be considered a new or reconstructed institution. One measure of institutional change can be the density of the innovative organizational style within an organizational field. Students of institutional change across time in the largest American corporations, U.S. labor unions, Canadian voluntary organizations, and newspapers in Argentina, California, and Ireland describe a process of restructuration of an institutional field. The change process begins when an innovative organization disrupts the organization field. The innovative form gains legitimacy through replication and may come to dominate the field through dispersion and the "death" of inertial organizations through competition (Hannon and Freeman 1987; Powell 1991; Schein 1985, 279–96; Singh, Tucker, and Meinhard 1991, 400).

In his explanation of institutional change in American industrial firms,

Fligstein noted the importance of empowered change agents guided by alternative visions of the organization's mission, as well as the presence of role model organizations in the organizational field (1991, 334). The firms, as part of an institutionalized field of organizations, changed their behavior in relation to two forces: "First, key actors in those organizations articulated a new view of the firm's strategy and had the power to implement that view. Second, other firms in the organizational field acted as role models so that key actors were able to bring about a change in strategy. Some form of shock in the organization's field was a necessary, although not sufficient, impetus to change."

As different drivers of institutionalized behavior may appear at different times, there are also multiple levels or jurisdictions in which institutions manifest themselves (Scott 1998, 124–48). In the case of media, institutional jurisdictions include: an individual media organization; populations of organizations, such as groups of similarly behaving newspapers; organizational fields, such as all newspapers in a specified media system; and a wider media institution, in which thought and action is shared by journalists in the majority of all media organizations.

Cook (1998) offers a model of news media as an intermediary political institution, like a political party system, in his book *Governing with the News*. Besides sharing an intermediary location between formal governmental institutions and civil society, the similarity between political parties and news media extends to their structure. Both media and party systems are trans-organizational institutions, meaning that they are made up of many organizations and need not behave homogeneously once they no longer share a "trans-organizational agreement" on values, expectations, and norms of behavior.

Extending Cook's argument that a "trans-organizational agreement on news processes and content" demonstrates that U.S. media act as a single institution, it is logical that an institution made up of many organizations can splinter into different populations of organizations once a transformation of core values and behaviors begins. In fact, Powell urges deep, ethnographic studies of the effect of "outlaw entrepreneurs," "partial diffusion" from innovative organizations, "exogenous shocks," and "internal stresses" on the cohesion of fields of organizations such as newsrooms (1991, 198–201). In the case of news organizations in transitional societies, some—but not all—may strive to gather political news in an assertive manner, maintain their autonomy from powerful actors, and produce news representing many viewpoints, just as some political parties may resist authoritarian prohibitions while other parties behave more docilely (Cook 1998, 70, 109, 110).

Except in certain revolutionary settings, institutional transformation implies the simultaneous weakening of one institutional form and the strengthening of another. The process is not necessarily uniform or complete, but can be partial and selective. The creation of new institutional forms in peripheral organizations, or the isolation of some organizations from the larger field, may produce situations in which the diffusion of innovation influences only a portion of the organizational field while another portion may remain isolated from change or incorporate only some elements of the new form. A recombination of innovative elements is especially likely in organizations operating in complex environments (Powell 1991, 197–201). When a cluster of organizations incorporates similar innovations, a branched path of institutional development forms. The result is the division of a unified, transorganizational institution into separate populations of organizations.

Ideas about partial diffusion and branched development paths suggest that institutional transformations should not be thought of as moving linearly along a continuum from authoritarian to democratic types, as some researchers of political transition imply. Authoritarian and democratic traits can coexist in an eroding institution. Moreover, in trans-organizational institutions such as news media, some organizations push innovation, while others resist, and still others create a third developmental path. Hybrid media systems including authoritarian, democratic, and other kinds of organizations are just as likely to emerge from a process of institutional change as new, unified institutions that are either democratic or authoritarian in nature (See Powell 1991, 197–201).

The realization that media institutions can evolve into hybrid systems through the partial diffusion of innovation allows us to more deeply explore what happened to Mexico's media. First, institutional entrepreneurs in Mexico's civic-oriented media changed their newsrooms. As civic innovation gained legitimacy, this new organizational style spread to a wider population of organizations. Beginning in the mid-1990s, after the impact of economic liberalization began to be felt, a second branch of institutional development opened and began to challenge the civic trend. Television newsrooms largely responded to the changing cues in the environment without absorbing the values inherent in a civic approach. They took on market-driven characteristics and changed coverage in ways that distinguished them from both the authoritarian model and the newer, civic-oriented approach. Only when news organizations changed the normative underpinnings of journalism to support the imperative of news promoting citizenship did they become more civic in nature. As one of the early institutional entrepreneurs, *El Norte-Reforma* publisher Alejandro Junco, stated, "Journalism has to do with certain values. A bottle of wine may be well-packaged, but the true product is the wine, is it not?" (Christie 1999). By the late 1990s, a glance at the headlines on crowded Mexican newsstands told readers that newspapers were behaving differently. Widely institutionalized values and behaviors had disappeared and a hybrid news model had taken its place.

While Cook argues that the U.S. media are a trans-organizational political institution such as parties, state legislatures, or bureaucracies, Waisbord (2000) implies that a new type of reporting in South America in the 1990s responded to an unspoken agreement on the appropriate form for journalism in those new democracies. He argues that watchdog journalism, in which media monitor government and publish or broadcast exposés about abuses of power, emerged in certain populations of media outlets in a newly liberalized political and economic setting. Yet, the partisan and commercial interests of media owners, as well as the norms of South American journalists, limited the range of issues South American media addressed. Waisbord's approach is useful because it synthesizes cues from the environment, cultural norms and organizational dynamics such as owners' power to set newsroom policy and direction to explain the emergence of a new type of journalism in South America.

An Integrated Approach

This study integrates the multiple layers and directing logics of institutional analysis in order to explain variation in the timing and direction of newsroom transformation in Mexico. Newsroom change started at the individual and organization level. In the initial stage, normative appropriateness explains the behavior of institutional entrepreneurs, who marshaled organizational resources to create newsrooms fused with civic values even though they risked confrontation with the state. Innovators of the first wave of civic journalism were motivated both by opposition to the continuation of the one-party state, and by knowledge of journalism paradigms from abroad or academia that separated the media from state control. To create civic newsroom cultures these change agents had to overcome instrumental cues from the state-controlled environment and the orthodoxy of internalized scripts and routines embedded in the authoritarian media institution. Early civic innovation was limited to print media, occurring in newsrooms that were more resistant to intervention from the state. Government officials monitored television broadcasts directly from the Interior Secretariat because they were more concerned with those messages that reached massive audiences. Meanwhile, newspapers and magazines, which had smaller, more elite readerships, found somewhat more space for maneuvering (Levy and Székely 1987; Camp 1986).

On the other hand, instrumentality and orthodoxy at the individual level better explain resistance to newsroom change. Once liberalization of the political and economic environment began in the late 1980s, resistance to change was based on cognitive blocks that filtered out information that conflicted with traditional ideas of how journalism, politics, and society functioned in Mexico. Resistance was enforced in top-down fashion by media owners and chief editors, but was also carried in embedded newsgathering routines and unquestioned understandings of relationships with news sources.

In recent years, institutional theorists have called for an integration of approaches to explaining human behavior. In particular, Scott (1998, 33–34) offers an "omnibus definition" of institutions useful in an integrated approach: "Institutions consist of cognitive, normative and regulative structures and activities that provide stability and meaning to social behavior. Institutions are transported by various carriers—cultures, structures and routines—that operate at multiple levels of jurisdiction. In this conceptualization, institutions are multifaceted systems incorporating symbolic systems—cognitive constructions and normative rules—and regulative processes carried out through, and shaping, social behavior."

Scott's definition incorporates instrumentality, appropriateness, and orthodoxy as the directive logics of institutionalization, while also highlighting the "duality" of institutions: Institutions shape behavior, but institutions are reliant upon behavior for maintenance. Thus, institutions have both a reproductive (maintenance) and productive (change-oriented) nature.

Giddens (1984) called the process of institutional maintenance "structuration," or the continuous re-creation of the social structure. For Giddens and others, the basis of institutional stability is cognitive. People in similar social positions share mental pictures of reality that are the result of common experiences. Common experiences produce regularities in thought, goals, interpretations, and strategies. Bourdieu called shared pictures of reality "habitus" and attributed them to the shared experiences of people within particular portions of a social class. Organizational analysts, such as Brint and Karabel, call habitus "mental sets" (1991, 67–68, 223n17), while management theorists, such as Senge, dub them "mental models" (1994, 174–204). Whatever the name, our mental pictures of reality shape what we consider possible or acceptable, what we reject as impossible or not acceptable, and what we do not even identify as a possibility (Powell 1991, 65; Scott 1998, 33, 61).

Mental pictures of reality are based on tacit knowledge, which consists of untested assumptions that become "knowledge" below the level of awareness. Tacit knowledge can be passed through generations; however, it may have formed initially as a response to economic or normative calculations. As Schein (1985) suggests, there could be a process of institutionalization in which economic or normative rationality creates models of the world that later are accepted without challenge, even when the initial conditions creating those models change. Once in place, mental models can be a powerful source of inertia, creating organizations and institutions that outlast economic or normative efficiency. Once tacit knowledge has coalesced as mental models of the world and one's place in it, cognitive scripts may prevent actors from recognizing or assessing new options when societal values and cues from the environment begin to shift, resulting in institutional inertia.

Schein argues that the "founders" of organizations create a group culture of shared values and mental models that resist change as the organization matures and the environment in which it operates transforms. Initially, the organizational culture creates a stable and predictable setting "that provides meaning, identity and a communication system" to members of the organization. Years later, however, "the same group may find that its culture has become so well embedded, so traditional, that it serves only to reinforce the assumptions and values of the older, more conservative elements in the group. It may continue to provide stability, but it may no longer provide meaning and identity to those segments of the group who are more responsive to external changes. . . . In an even more extreme condition, revolution, restructuring and massive replacement of people may occur, and possibly a genuinely new cultural paradigm may be created" (Schein 1985, 271–72).

Inertial news organizations in Mexico, such as *Excélsior* on the eve of the 2000 presidential election or Televisa prior to the ascension of younger management in 1997, exemplify Schein's description of a frozen organization. Most of those who wanted to change *Excélsior* had left, and others were powerless against newsroom leadership. Tacit knowledge based on previous experiences blinded newsroom leaders and their followers to the pending demise of the traditional news model. A similar situation existed at Televisa in 1997, as congressional and mayoral elections in Mexico City approached. However, the network's adherence to traditional notions of journalism and society were disrupted when longtime owner Emilio Azcárraga Milmo died, and a younger generation of managers took over.

While mental models can prompt organizational players to reject conflicting information or filter out competing paradigms, the ability to create adaptive models of the world is possible. Adaptive mental models are the key to creating what Senge (1994) and others call "learning organizations" that can anticipate, survive, and sometimes impel important changes in the macroenvironment, such as changes in government regulation and the appearance of new competition. Civic and market-driven newsrooms in Mexico exemplify adaptive mental models. Civic newsrooms stimulated change in other news organizations in the 1990s and, more recently, successfully lobbied for the country's first access to information law in 2002. Market-driven news organizations in Mexico adapted by reflecting the increasing pluralism in Mexico's electorate.

The concepts of organizational culture, tacit knowledge, and mental models help explain much of what happened in Mexico's media. Mexico's subordinate media system was highly institutionalized for four decades during the reign of the country's hegemonic party system. As Scott (1995, 34) would say, it had become an "over-determined system"—social and material incentives, pressure for conformity, cognitive filters, and normative values all acted together to give the institution directive force.

Most journalists accepted their subordinate roles on a cognitive and normative level during the period of single-party dominance in Mexico because of the political system's legitimacy with the urban middle and working classes. Instrumental incentives, such as advertising contracts or direct payoffs, further cemented the relationship. Mental models became so strongly entrenched that even when the original circumstances that created the Mexican media institution began to change with political and economic liberalization in the 1980s, the majority of journalists and media organizations continued to follow old routines and behavioral norms.

While static mental models created inertial newsrooms, adaptive mental models fostered change. In fact, many new, civic newspapers would only hire inexperienced college graduates or very young journalists who had not been socialized into the traditional view that the correct role of journalism was to support the state or one's own material interests. Creation of a shared vision of a new style of journalism was an obvious strategy in the offices of the Tijuana newspaper *Frontera*. In the newspaper's offices, the company's value-laden mission statement is posted where journalists, visitors, and others view it repeatedly. At Mexico City's *Reforma* newspaper, the formal dress code was designed to increase reporters' status vis-à-vis politicians and create a sense of shared purpose. In my interviews with journalists at civic newspapers, I found that they had similar views of their profession, even if they formally competed for exclusive information.

Change agents as newsroom leaders were centrally important to both the emergence and diffusion of the civic news organization. They created vanguard organizations and made sure a second wave of publications under their leadership followed a civic logic. Vanguard organizations are what Powell calls "multiplier organizations"—in this case, newspapers that created innovations that resonated throughout the wider press and eventually splintered it into distinct populations of publications (1991, 198–99). In his case study of five Latin American newspapers that set new standards for journalism in their countries, Alves (1998) calls such publications "democracy's vanguard newspapers."

The Mexican case suggests that change agents with organizational power were able to transform individuals' mental models and forge new professional identities and group cultures. The change mechanisms they utilized were direct socialization, role modeling, and selective hiring. The civic news models they created then dispersed through a wider organizational field via network expansion, personnel turnover, and mimicking. Legitimacy of the civic style increased with gradual liberalization of the environment.

Institutional analysis also allows us to identify the multiple levels and logics of drivers of media transformations. Environmental cues varied depending on the type of media at issue. National television news producers faced greater governmental supervision, confronted less competition, and needed larger markets for profit than did radio or newspapers. However, within a single media type (television, radio, or print), the environmental stresses were largely uniform at any given time and location. Given that uniformity, the differing developmental paths chosen by news organizations facing similar structural constraints cannot be explained solely by changing external cues. Organizational dynamics and the mental models of organizational leaders were also important factors.

By viewing media through institutional lenses, we see that the transformation of Mexico's media was a process bringing together individual, organizational, trans-organizational, and macroenvironmental drivers in the newsroom. Four jurisdictions of institutionalized thought and action converged and combined in ways that determined the timing and direction of newsroom transformations. Outside ideas, oppositional values, and transformative experiences drove the creation of civic-oriented identities on the individual level, while self-interest drove authoritarian identities and, later, market-driven identities. At the organizational level, the actors that gained control of the newsroom determined the path of newsroom transformations and field-level influences, such as prestige and new types of competition, which pushed change during the later stage of transformation. Finally, at the societal level, political liberalization enabled the diffusion of civic identities and cultures to adaptive newsrooms, and economic liberalization created market-driven identities and cultures. Frozen mental models and leadership stagnation blocked change in inertial newsrooms, despite new cues from society and the wider media. The interaction of each of these jurisdictions produced the variation in the timing and direction of newsroom transformations in Mexico.

The Process of Media Transformation

Figure 2.1 illustrates the institutional model of media transformation and explains the creation of civic media organizations during the restructuring of the authoritarian media institution into separate populations of newsrooms. The orientation of a newsroom is measured by the authoritarian, civic, or market-driven news content it produces. The interacting domains that produce institutional change are the environment (top row), individuals' mental models and identities (bottom row) and an intermediate domain of contention located within organizations and institutions. Individual change leads to organizational change only when the individuals have the ability to shape the dominant values, norms of conduct, and worldviews of the newsroom.

The process of institutional restructuring in Mexico's newspapers started at the individual level with the diffusion of new ideas about the role and practice of journalism across institutional boundaries. Institutional entrepreneurs with organizational resources learned of new paradigms orienting media toward the citizenry (and later the market) via educational experiences abroad, direct knowledge exchange between journalists of different countries, books, and domestic academic training in economics and communications theory. In a similar finding, Camp (2002a) discovers that experiences abroad and international networks aided the formation of the worldviews of Mexico's contemporary elite. Other scholars trace the diffusion of North American economic paradigms to Latin America via educational networks (Centeno and Silva 1997; Domínguez 1997).

In the first stage of civic emergence, new ideas about journalism and the media's relationship to the state converged with personal values that conflicted with the continuation of the hegemonic party system, creating an impetus for action. Sometimes oppositional values came from a Catholic background or a free market orientation, especially in the north. In other cases, oppositional values were the result of leftist political orientations or disagreements over economic policy, especially in Mexico City.

Some journalists who spoke of frustration at media subordination in the 1980s were unable to transform their newsrooms because they were not in positions of power or did not make up large enough numbers to influence newsroom policy. Civic-minded journalists in traditional newsrooms resisted

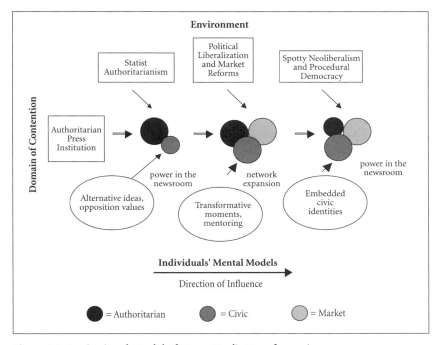

Figure 2.1 Institutional Model of News Media Transformation

authoritarian behavioral patterns in a number of ways, including criticizing the regime in vague terms in the hope their audience could read between the lines, producing news about art and literature in "culture" sections where intellectual critiques were tolerated, placing sensitive information near the end of news stories where editors might miss it or be willing not to censor, or leaving their newspapers altogether when civic newspapers finally formed. "I wasted a year and a half there," lamented reporter Ariadna Bermeo of her time at a traditional news organization, the newspaper *Excélsior.* A few journalists admitted to succumbing to instrumental incentives, such as payment for docile news stories, even while doubting the legitimacy of the practice.

In order to transform their newsrooms, however, change agents required organizational resources. Although some journalists became well-known enough by winning national awards to be given more freedom in their own work, individual reporters could not really transform their work or their publications without obtaining central positions in the organizational setting (Bass and Burkhardt 1992). In the early period, only publishers or managing editors could successfully act as change agents in most cases. However, one early civic innovator *La Jornada,* was formed after almost the entire *Unomá-*

suno staff deserted the newsroom when they believed that newspaper's independence had been compromised. For change agents, newsrooms became their classrooms. Resources included direct socialization through training institutes and workshops, selection of compatible personnel, and especially indirect socialization through role modeling. As institutional entrepreneurs, they marshaled sufficient resources to transform organizational culture and behavior. An editor who started his reporting career at a civic-oriented newspaper in the 1980s commented of his professional orientation, "It came from my bosses at *El Financiero*. Basically, it was a culture there. It was a way of being that I progressively assimilated, by learning and listening."[4]

Political and economic liberalization in the mid-1980s changed the cues coming from the environment and unleashed a second wave of newspaper transformations based on a diffusion of innovation from the civic-oriented core. Opposition party candidates slowly gained ground at the local level beginning in 1985 and won their first state governor post in 1989. By 1993, there were four states under opposition rule and by 1999, the year before the ruling party lost the presidency, eleven states and the Federal District had experienced rule by governors from opposition parties.

Most of these opposition governments changed the norms of media-state relations in favor of more independence, ending traditional practices of direct payments in exchange for positive coverage; the new rhetoric equated media payoffs with corruption. Opposition party electoral victories also signaled that the market for political information had become more diverse.

At the same time, the federal government began a process of economic restructuring that made the demands of consumers more important to news organizations. Beginning in 1986 and accelerating in 1990, the government began to open the economy to international markets, sell off state-owned corporations, and generally deregulate the economy. This process, known as structural adjustment throughout Latin America, accelerated at the end of the 1980s and into the 1990s. The privatization and deregulation of major advertisers, such as banks and telecommunications companies, and the strengthening of foreign firms in both areas, meant that the government controlled fewer economic resources with which to threaten and entice news companies.

Much of the implementation of Mexico's structural adjustment program occurred in the context of economic crises. Monetary devaluations and economic recessions restricted the government's budgetary capabilities, prompting cutbacks in money formerly used to buy advertising and coddle reporters. At the same time, the crises also eroded the public's confidence in government-produced information at a time when the number and prestige of independent and foreign analysts were growing. The new importance of the market, the public's increasing political pluralism, and increasing skepticism of government information prompted a restructuring of the newspaper market in Mexico City in favor of civic newspapers. The government's dependence on international investors made repression of civic news organizations more costly, especially because of civic organizations' growing reputation abroad.

Economic liberalization and political opening led to systemic shocks that shook journalists psychologically, causing them to question traditional mental models and identities. Assassinations within the political elite, guerilla campaigns, high levels of corruption and impunity, and callous government response to suffering delegitimized a media institution that supported the *priísta* status quo. "*Basta ya*" (enough already), one editor said when questioned about the repeated scandals, using a phrase associated with the Zapatista insurgency in the southern state of Chiapas.

Liberalizing trade increased the flow of information from abroad, which, in turn, made more journalists come into contact with information that shook tacit understandings of the world. International organizations of assertive journalists made contacts or direct inroads into Mexico's corps of reporters and editors, and foreign educational institutions trained Mexican journalists. As new ideas about the media's monitoring, agenda setting, and public service functions proliferated, they lent further credibility to the civic style of news and wrested credibility from the authoritarian model of a subservient media. Liberalization also favored civic organizations by making them points of reference abroad. Vanguard civic newspapers became a new standard for young journalists and others who began to question the traditional model.

This new prestige was not lost on traditional organizations open to change and a few, such as *El Universal* in Mexico City and *El Informador* in Guadalajara, began efforts to transform their publications. An *El Universal* editor initially agreed to participate in this study because his competitor at *Reforma* regularly received favorable mentions in writing by U.S. academics. Second-wave organizations that responded to the increasing legitimacy of orientations linking news to citizenship followed a path of development that increased autonomy, pluralism, and assertiveness in the search for the news. They mimicked innovative organizations by placing journalists trained at core civic newspapers in central positions, training new cadres of journalists, and intensely resocializing older journalists using outside consultants.

Creating a strong sense of mission in civic newsrooms was extremely important given latent and sometimes active threats in the environment.

Even after liberalization began in the mid-1980s, the government retained substantial power to coerce compliant behavior. Besides direct pressure on editors, pressure from news sources and peers on the reporting beat could derail civic aspirations in reporters. Publisher Alejandro Junco of *El Norte* and *Reforma* built an armor-like plating of values and alternative identities in his young reporters to fight servility, entreating them to remember that they were the depository of the citizen's "right to information" and to identify with the newspaper's civic project. It worked in many cases. Reporter Maria Idalia Gómez, who helped found *Reforma* in 1993, explained: "I committed myself to the *Reforma* project. I was *Reforma*."[5]

Political and economic liberalization did not change newsrooms that exemplified Schein's frozen or stagnant organizations. The managers of Mexico City's *Excélsior*, for example, blocked contradictory information, limited personnel turnover, and relied on the old system to carry them through. At *Unomásuno*, the owner and publisher colluded to prevent change. *Novedades*'s owners fired several generations of foreign journalists who tried to change newsroom culture.

Finally, while liberalization prompted civic change in some organizations and had little effect on others, other newsrooms changed because their owners saw that greater political pluralism and stronger market incentives had changed the political economy of the news business in Mexico by the late 1990s. These market-based shifts convinced a younger generation of broadcast network executives to change their news coverage. National broadcast network owners made news much more plural, and also more sensational. They based their decisions on commercial calculations. Little or no attempt was made to inculcate civic values inside their companies. A search for profit meant these organizations began to cover opposition parties more in news coverage to attract wider audiences and advertising from all major political parties, but the news companies continued to support the regime when key interests were threatened during the 2000 election. Coverage of confrontational politics and episodic coverage of government corruption after 2000 also helped to increase ratings and, therefore, profit. Approaches that suggested systemic problems and solutions were rarely offered, however.

The market-driven transition of broadcasting newsrooms is also the result of interplay between individual, organizational, trans-organizational, and environmental variables. However, broadcast network owners did not hold oppositional political values. They looked to Wall Street rather than Watergate for inspiration, and had to negotiate the demands of the mass market and the fact that the state retained controls over licenses and future frequency concessions. Like the publishers of several vanguard civic publications, both Emilio Azcárraga Jean of Televisa and Ricardo Salinas Pliego of TV Azteca took business courses at universities in the United States, but their training did not steep them in ideas about the media's role in democratic societies that newspaper publishers Junco of *El Norte* or José Santiago Healy of *El Imparcial* gained from taking journalism courses in the United States and Spain. Moreover, these television moguls came from business families, which reinforced their drive for commercial profits and sales. One of the few times Azcárraga Jean received his father's praise was after his first presentation to Wall Street analysts on a trip to New York City (Fernández 2001). Prior to becoming a media owner, Salinas Pliego was the third generation to own and operate a large retail chain famous for its installment payment plans.

For these men, the logical transformation path after Mexico's elections became more competitive was to make electoral news more balanced and present criticism in new, tabloidized formats. These techniques would please mass TV audiences and garner advertising dollars from local governments, now controlled by former opposition parties with new public financing, while minimizing the chance of a direct confrontation with the state through more assertive news coverage about the central figures of the PRI regime that continued to control the presidency until 2000.

In all of these newsrooms, the hierarchical power structure of news organizations was important. Organizational leaders—usually owners, but also state governors when analyzing government-owned media—made and imposed newsroom orientations. Usually, personnel changes were necessary to overcome inertial values and decisions, but wholesale imposition of new values or personnel replacement was not necessary. The organization changed with its leader. This is apparent at Mexico City's *El Universal*, where a longtime editor led the change toward a civic newsroom model, and also at Televisa, where the country's largest network shifted toward a market-driven model. One executive at Televisa who started as a young journalist in the company in the late 1970s explained that although network journalists observed the shocking events that shook society in 1994, the company's journalistic model and his own ideas about the news did not change until a new, younger owner took over the company in March 1997. "Look, I don't want to give the impression that here, I thought one thing and they didn't let me act," he stated. "Of course not. In other words, this was a change that operated throughout the company. I was a small part of this change. It could not have happened if the company wasn't willing to change. When did we change? At the moment when we realized the company wanted to change."[6]

Market-driven journalism did not flourish in the printed press. Inertial publishers tentatively made coverage of elections and Congress more plural and experimented with color photographs, eye-pleasing graphics, and more streamlined front-page designs in the late 1990s in an effort to draw back defecting readers. But style changes dominated substantive ones, and the stylistic flourishes did little to move the publications beyond the authoritarian model. Moreover, the commitment to pluralism was short-lived, as coverage became openly biased against the top opposition candidate in the 2000 presidential election, eventual winner Vicente Fox. *Novedades*, for example, prohibited the publishing of polls with Fox in the lead as the campaign trail wound down to the final days. As the campaign ended, *Unomásuno*—in the words of its editor—ran an "enthusiastic campaign" on behalf of the PRI candidate, while "slandering" the opposition. When the PRI lost the election, editor Rafael Cardona expressed guilt over his complicity in *Unomásuno*'s actions. His orders apparently had come from above. "We did this together, you and I," Cardona wrote to publisher Manuel Alonso.[7]

Applying an institutional lens to news media behavior ties together ideas from diverse studies of media, politics, and organizations to offer a powerful explanation for the transformation of Mexico's media into a hybrid system. It focuses our attention on the role of change agents, newsroom leadership, and the newsroom itself as a space where multiple institutional jurisdictions combine to direct the behaviors that produce the news. Within Mexican newsrooms, organizational leaders—driven by either static or adaptive mental models of journalism and society—determined whether, in what direction, and at what time newsrooms would be transformed. They created newsroom cultures and assembled newsroom staffs that reflected their mental pictures of journalism and society. The influence of outside cues on newsroom leaders explains the partial diffusion of civic innovation, the rise of market-driven journalism, and the persistence of authoritarianism in an inertial or adaptive form. In Mexico's postauthoritarian society, these clashing concepts of journalism and society continue to struggle for hegemony. They manifest themselves as newsrooms in conflict.

Part II

THE CIVIC MEDIA TRANSFORMATION

3 Authoritarian and Democratic Models of News Production

> As reporters we felt that it was important to represent all of the political currents, that the newspaper reflect pluralism, but in the end the internal interests of the newspaper would win out. They wouldn't change your words, but the strategy was that your story always was accompanied by another story or editorial that tore it to shreds . . . this editorial would burn your story, saying outrageous things about the person you were covering and qualifying their statements, and besides, the space they gave you was very small.
>
> Reporter Ricardo Hernández on political reporting in the late 1980s

When institutions break down, new ways of thinking and behaving arise to challenge the old forms. Differences of thought and action appear not only between individual players in an institution, but across organizations such as community colleges, art museums, and newsrooms (DiMaggio and Powell 1991). Mexico's media institution remained essentially unchallenged for decades. Cracks appeared in the late 1960s, but the wider political and economic environment did not permit the spread or survival of the innovative newsrooms that challenged PRI hegemony. By the 1980s, however, the state's political and cognitive controls on the media had loosened enough for a vanguard of change-oriented journalists to drive a wedge into the authoritarian media institution. How far and in what direction had the fissures spread before the regime-ending presidential campaign of 2000? Did the messages and symbols carried in the news help undermine the definitional power of an autocratic state?

Democratic and Authoritarian Models of News Production

Literature on comparative media systems describes a broader authoritarian news model, which helps to locate Mexican journalism of the 1940s through the 1980s. Since news content is the outcome of ingrained values, concepts, and behaviors of the people who make up the newsroom, newsroom culture manifests in news content and, through that, is measurable. As several authors have stated, news models are ideal types against which to measure media performance. In practice, individual journalists, news organizations, and media systems may lean toward one model or another, but rarely reflect them in all ways (McQuail 1987; Hallin 2000a).

Figure 3.1, below, maps alternative news models found in authoritarian, transitional, and democratic societies. As a normative schematic, it represents both the ideal and the real; a cognitive construct of how the press system is viewed and a construct of the reality of media relations with society and the state. The models are linked to a nation's political system in obvious ways, but also express the variation that exists within democratic and authoritarian political systems. As McQuail notes, virtually none of the national press systems in the world are governed by one "pure" normative model, but exhibit a mix of traits from various models (1987, 109–10). What makes these normative theories important as guides for comparative research is the degree to which any one model explains media behavior in a national system, as well as their use as signposts against which to measure across systems or at different points in a period of systemic transformation.

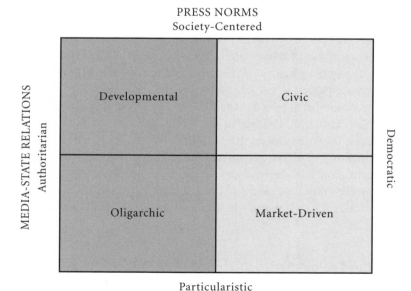

Figure 3.1 Comparative Media Models

The models are based upon comparative press systems research, as well as descriptions of national press models. The horizontal axis depicts the media-state relationship and runs from an "authoritarian" relationship of government control and media support of the state to a "democratic" relationship of media independence from government and potentially conflictive media-state relations. The vertical axis depicts whether the news media play a society-focused role or serve the interests of a particular individual or group. The four outcomes include two authoritarian options, a developmental model and an oligarchic model. Both authoritarian options support a system of minority rule, but in the oligarchic option rulers and private media owners use media to further group or individual interests, while in the developmental model, autocrats attempt to further what they perceive as societal interests. The democratic outcomes are either civic-oriented or market-driven. Both democratic alternatives support political pluralism in society, but to a greater or lesser degree. Market-driven media respond to commercial criteria, treating audiences as a market to sell to advertisers. Market-driven news reflects the degree of political pluralism in media audience segments important to advertisers. In the civic option, the press responds to the broader needs of citizens rather than autocrats or advertisers. The civic media encourage democratic participation and representation by providing citizens with a wide range of political information about elections, policy, and public officials.[1]

The Authoritarian Model

The seminal *Four Theories of the Press* (Siebert, Peterson, and Schramm 1956) has been revised many times, but scholars continue to agree that the unchallenged reproduction of regime messages is a signature trait of an authoritarian news model. However, the role of the media within the authoritarian model may vary. In a developmentalist view of the press, the role of the media is to foster the economic, political, and social development of society. Many postcolonial regimes in Africa and Asia, as well as South American military dictatorships in the 1970s, were influenced by a developmentalist approach to news production. Journalists in these societies were expected to support authority, not challenge it, because media were viewed as a tool for nation building. Information, or truth, became the property of the state. Because of the state's absolute control over news media, developmentalist news systems often devolved into more typical authoritarian systems, where the rationale of nation building was only a façade for the use of the media to further the interests of the state or its allies (Hachten and Hachten 1996, 34–37).

In another variant of an authoritarian news model, an oligarchic media system, news production responds to the particularistic interests of a ruling group or clique. Central American media owners often reflect this model (Rockwell and Janus 2003). Media barons make news production decisions based on their own interests as members of local, regional, or national oligarchies. Media owners overlap with economic elites, political elites, or both. They are willing to use news production to support a shared interest in protecting private property and maintaining the status quo. When their visions have diverged with those of the ruling political elites, some oligarchic media owners have opted to openly break with the government. These breaks are most vividly illustrated in the coup under Salvador Allende in Chile and, more recently, the failed attempt to remove Hugo Chavez from power in Venezuela (Dinges 2005).

Mexico's Authoritarian Model

Mexico's particular political system and culture shaped a unique media institution that remained intact for much of the twentieth century. However, the Mexican media from the 1940s to the 1990s approximated a variant of the authoritarian news model. President Lázaro Cárdenas (1934–1940) created the forerunner to the PRI and organized much of society along hierarchical lines linked to the party. Cárdenas hoped to shape Mexico's postrevolutionary media system with a developmentalist mission in mind, and some of that rhetoric lingered when journalists defended their informal ties to the PRI years later. But by the time that newspapers and radio chains coalesced around elite families in the 1940s, the media's role and structure had become oligarchic. A small number of elite families controlled most of Mexico's mass media and used it to further group interests by supporting the one-party state, with which they were allied and in some cases connected by family ties (Bohmann 1989; Fernández Christlieb 1985; Torres 1997). Journalists, meanwhile, viewed themselves as part of the regime rather than civil society. Their worldview was one in which to support the state was considered normatively appropriate, and, eventually, orthodox.

The worldview underlying Mexican authoritarianism was that journalism should support the benefactor state.[2] To do that, Mexican news media played different roles for elite and mass audiences. Journalists sent messages between elite groups within the government and ruling party to help them interpret the strength of competing factions and promote or obstruct career ascendance. For the masses, journalists reproduced unified messages and symbols reinforcing regime legitimacy in a one-way communication flow moving from rulers to their mass of subjects. The messages and symbols transmitted to mass audiences helped to: legitimize single-party rule; maintain the image of the omnipotent, benevolent president; build a PRI candidate able to cure any ills caused by the outgoing administration; transmit a façade of competitive elections to a nonparticipating public; and label regime critics as traitors and radicals (Adler 1993a, 1993b; Bailey 1988).

Mexican journalists took a passive, noncritical approach to reporting that relied either on the stenographic transferal of speeches and press releases to the news pages, or code-like political columns written for the already initiated. Journalists forged subordinate relationships with sources that would have been considered conflicts of interest if the media had not been in symbiosis with the state. Assertiveness in reporting occurred only to support the regime or a particular benefactor in the PRI or government.

The media's passive relationship with ruling politicians, subordination to the regime, and reproduction of a PRI monologue are reflected in transcripts of presidential press conferences. One reporter's "question" at President Miguel de la Madrid's first press conference in 1982 was: "Today, as you grant us the first press conference of your government, we wish to thank you for granting it to us and offer you testimony of our support for your work. We have been witnesses to your untiring labor and we have tried to inform our readers, listeners, and viewers of your work and of the necessity of supporting it. Do you wish, Mr. President, to direct a message to the people of Mexico . . . and to give us the answer to some question in particular that you would have wished us to ask?"[3]

As Altschull (1984) points out in *Agents of Power: The Role of the News Media in Human Affairs*, journalists' support for authoritarianism does not have to be coerced. Authoritarianism under the right conditions can be as legitimate to journalists as a more democratic model of news production. This was the case in Mexico for most of the last century.

The institutionalization of Mexico's authoritarian media system resulted from the long-term legitimacy of the postrevolutionary political system. Mexico's hegemonic party system, presidentialist governing structure, and state-led economic development model garnered five decades of legitimacy for the PRI regime. Until 1982, the political system's legitimacy generally was premised upon appeals to the ideals of the Mexican revolution, resolution of the problem of presidential succession, corporate and clientelist control of organized groups, targeted co-optation and repression of opposition leaders, and concrete material gains for urban dwellers (Camp 2002b; Lustig 1992). More particularly, the support of Mexican journalists for the state did not stem from fear of prior censorship or overt repression. Most reporters considered themselves part of a valid system, rather than autonomous outsiders, and so affirmatively endorsed the political status quo, sought to legitimize it, and attacked its detractors. Self-censorship was common because of internalized agreements about which subjects should be publicized and which kept from public view.

Media support for the state produced concrete material benefits and prestige for decades, but the relationship endured beyond the ability of the state to bestow such generous incentives; instead, it became a normatively appropriate and cognitively unquestioned worldview (Riva Palacio 1998). As explained by Roberto Rock, editor of *El Universal*, this is the attitude he found when he entered the world of Mexico City newsrooms in the 1970s:

> They were transcribers, let's say, of official information. But that's because the newspapers were that way, too. There wasn't any grave moral conflict. I don't know about other countries, but in this country, the Mexican state was a benefactor state. Let's say an authoritarian state, but that didn't matter to many people because their problems of survival and support were taken care of. . . . It wasn't even an issue of corruption; it was an issue of ideological conviction. And all of the previous generation of journalists entered one of those newspapers, and assumed that the work was done that way. The old journalists assumed that supporting the government and eventually helping out some friends close to the newspaper companies or some business of the newspaper companies was what it was all about. And they felt important because of that. No one would take that away from them. But the issue of being critical, of being independent, the role of being a watchdog of the government, of public service, was very remote because the journalist assumed himself to be part of political life more than the social life of the country. So, he considered himself a companion at the table of the political elite.[4]

Journalists reproduced political speeches, press releases, and press conference statements that were created by government offices. After a night of carousing, a press officer would even write a reporter's story if he had trouble thinking clearly the next day. As former press officer Carlos Ferreira explained, an "entire system" of relationships, understandings, and ingrained behaviors promoted this reportorial passivity:

> When I was the press officer in the Senate, I had to explain to the reporters that the job of the press officer was to be more intelligent than the reporters. So, the reporters would tell me at three in the afternoon, "You haven't let us work. I don't have a story." I told them, "Don't worry. The radio boys are going to do it. They are already bringing in (a transcript of an interview with a politician), and I already sent it off to be photocopied so that you have a story." . . . Unfortunately, we converted journalists into people who sit and spin, into people who look for the most comfortable way of life. In fact, they no longer had to work. It was an entire system.[5]

Given institutionalized passivity, subservience, and support for the regime, information Mexicans needed for democratic debate, deliberation, and accountability was not widely available, despite official rhetoric equating the PRI regime to a democracy that only needed perfection. Mexico's authoritarian media institution deprived Mexicans of the right to information. Without it, they became mere subjects of an authoritarian regime.

Democratic and Adaptive Authoritarian Alternatives

What alternatives might have emerged to challenge the Mexican authoritarian news model once the political and cognitive controls of the PRI regime began to wane? Comparative media system research suggests several possibilities. First, an authoritarian model might continue to exist in an inertial form, resisting change in society and politics, especially where restricted groups continued to control both political and economic power. Alternatively, authoritarianism might adapt to more local conditions in the pockets of the country where democratic competition remained stifled or where elites of many parties found it useful to co-opt or control the media.

In contrast, variants of a democratic press model could arise. The democratic model, in which news media function independently of the state, is the antithesis of the authoritarian model. At least two variants of the democratic model are applicable to societies where transitional political systems move toward representational government and market-based economic systems.

The first derives from a civic-oriented concept of journalism and society.[6] Civic journalists act independently of the state, are assertive in their search for the news, and support a diverse discourse on the regime rather than only reproducing the messages of the state and its allies. This approach considers news and the journalists who produce it as facilitators of citizen participation in politics and, specifically, in holding public officials accountable. In this model, journalists influence government by providing citizens with information in a form that encourages reasoned opinion and political participation that holds government accountable to society.

Through analysis of the comparative media systems literature, I identified the worldview, roles, coverage norms, and implications of a civic journalism model (McQuail 2000; Bennett 2005; Rosen 1994; Dzur 2002; Haas 1999; Hughes 2003). Again, this is the description of an ideal type rarely attained in purest form. Civic journalism as a model is autonomous of political, economic, or cultural power that may inhibit robust debate and deliberation. Civic-oriented news coverage presents diverse views of the political regime and other power centers, and sources include non-elites rather than only official voices. Reporting is assertive and comes from multiple sources of information. Statements are verified or alternative perspectives are offered. Writing is easy to understand, concise, and inviting. Framing of the news is systemic—in other words, context is provided, and causes and consequences are discussed. The implications of civic coverage are that journalism encourages the creation of a vibrant public sphere of debate and deliberation, which in turn helps to activate a participatory citizenship and government accountability.

A second option within a democratic political system is a market-driven news model. This model increasingly drives journalism and news media in democratic countries with private-sector media operating in free-market economies. In the purest form of a market-driven system, the worldview guiding media workers is that news should create a mass market for advertisers. Media workers and owners support a democratic regime as long as it supports commercialization of the news. Civic-oriented professionalism of journalists and market-driven news production criteria may clash, but as Epstein (1973) and Hallin (2000a) found in the United States, the commercial logic dominates through imposition or the socialization of journalists (Curran and Park 2000). Despite uncertainty about the regime, a commercial logic emerging in a transitional political setting can encourage democratization. Since media producers respond to ratings and advertisers rather than government dictates, news includes opposition voices and messages to attract larger audiences. These messages help to undermine autocrats' definitional power by covering a greater diversity of perspectives and issues. However, the ability of market-driven media to create a robust public sphere is limited by calculated diversity and assertiveness that can stop short of critically examining key political, commercial, or cultural actors. Moreover, market-driven journalism sometimes takes the form of sensational, tabloidized news that can heighten conflict, distort the public agenda, and possibly increase alienation from political participation (Ansolobehere, Behr, and Iyengar 1993; Hallin 2000b).

In a market-driven system, the role of the media is to facilitate communication between advertisers and clients. News themes include candidate-centered electoral messages focusing on competition, conflict, and candidates' personal attributes, as well as instances of crime and corruption, which are depicted as disconnected events in sensational formats. Sources are politically diverse to the extent they attract audiences and advertisers; common people are included in stories in a paternalistic way rather than as empowered citizens. Reporting can be assertive or passive depending on audience and advertiser demands. Statements are not always verified or contested when they produce sensational news; alternative perspectives are offered to heighten conflict. Writing is dramatic. Framing is episodic—context is not provided and coverage treats issues as events rather than systemic tendencies.

Each of the alternative press models can be reduced to a set of defining characteristics that can be used to measure media content. Under the authoritarian model, news media repeat only regime messages, are subordinate to the state, and passively transfer messages to the populace. The implication of the model is that the news obstructs the creation of a public sphere. Civic-oriented media present diverse views of power, act autonomously, and report assertively. The implication is that they provide the political information necessary to encourage the creation of a robust public sphere. Market-driven media are autonomous from the state but not from the market, offer diverse political information, and are assertive when audiences and advertisers demand it. Their tendency to focus on personality and conflict and to present systemic problems as disconnected events limits their ability to create a robust sphere of debate and deliberation.

Content Analysis

What models of thought and behavior drove journalism as Mexico approached its first democratic presidential elections since 1911? Did they conflict? Which dominated? To answer these questions, I used a largely qualitative content analysis assessing the frames, themes, and rhetoric in the news, but I also compared simple counts of news items supporting or challenging maintenance of the PRI regime. The results provide a snapshot of news production four months before the PRI fell from power in peaceful elections. The elements of the three models used in the analysis of newspaper content are: the authoritarian model is not autonomous, not assertive, and not diverse; the civic model is autonomous, assertive, and diverse; and the market-driven model is variably autonomous, variably assertive, and variably diverse.

The content analysis measures newspaper coverage using the three signature traits of authoritarian and civic-oriented news coverage—whether news contains politically diverse messages or only those of the regime and its allies; whether news demonstrates autonomy from powerful actors associated with the regime; if news was gathered in an assertive manner. A manual explaining the criteria for coding decisions appears in the appendix. I selected twelve consecutive dates for analysis (March 1–12) because of their largely unremarkable nature and because consecutive dates allowed particular stories to develop over the period under analysis. The March 5 anniversary of PRI's founding allowed for later analysis of coverage of that event between newspapers and over time, but no automatic bias was built into the sample since opposition party members could be called upon to comment on the party's pronouncements. I analyzed only coverage on front pages because journalists evidently placed importance on those issues or actors and because readers are more likely to see front-page news. I identified 297 news items from the forty-eight front pages in the sample. A single item could encompass more than one stand-alone headline, article, photograph, or graphic when those pieces covered the same issue or event on the same day in the same newspaper. This was to make coverage comparable across newspapers since some publications broke up coverage into separate pieces in an attempt to be more appealing to readers, while others put all of the news in a single, longer text. Approximately 15 percent of the 2000 cases were double-coded by a native Mexican Spanish speaker with knowledge of the media system during the political transition. Inter-coder reliability scores (Cohen's Kappa) were 0.856 or higher for all the variables. Simple agreement controlling for chance was 90.6 percent and higher.[7]

I selected four newspapers for analysis to represent the range of general interest newspapers in Mexico City over a twenty-year period. These four newspapers led circulation for general interest newspapers in the 1990s and, in 1999, reached 60 percent of the metropolitan area's 2.3 million readers, according to Gallup de México's MediaMax readership survey. *Excélsior* was, for years, the most-read newspaper in Mexico City. In 2000, journalists and opinion leaders considered *Excélsior* a traditional newspaper that had changed little since 1976, when a government-instigated labor revolt removed top editor Julio Scherer and installed new leadership. *El Universal, Excélsior*'s circulation rival, also was considered a traditional, regime-affiliated newspaper. *El Universal*'s news coverage underwent a transformation in the late 1990s when a new editor hired more critical columnists and young reporters. Observers credited the last two newspapers in the sample, *La Jornada* and *Reforma*, as leaders of a more independent, assertive style of Mexican journalism. *La Jornada*'s staff became identified with the left, while *Reforma*'s owners were identified with the right. Since both the left and right opposed the PRI by the end of the 1990s, their ideological divergence should not make a difference in an analysis of press orientation toward regime change.

To compare newsrooms and make claims across the wider press, I had to ensure that each publication had an equal opportunity to provide content for analysis. I did this by employing a number of safeguards. First, the same dates were coded for each newspaper so that each had the potential to cover the same events in the same way. Second, content was coded into two data sets, depending upon whether the appropriate unit of analysis was an actor mentioned in a news item or the news item itself. This was because some news items mentioned several actors of interest, while others only mentioned one. The "news actors" data set contained 565 cases. The "news items" data set contained 297 cases.

As a third safeguard, I equalized differences in the amount of content to be coded that resulted from differences in the size of the newspapers. Broadsheet publications and newspapers with more stories on the front page would supply more content for analysis than tabloids and other broadsheets whose designs called for placing fewer stories on the cover. Of the four newspapers in the sample, *La Jornada* is the only newspaper that uses a tabloid size in which the article text rarely appears on the front page. To make the quantity of *La Jornada*'s front-page content comparable to the others, I calculated an average number of lines of text on the front pages of the other newspapers. I tested a method in which I coded the same amount of text from *La Jornada* as the average of the other newspapers, but decided the rule should be applied flexibly for high-profile stories. In the end, I was satisfied that this method created a comparable set of coded content from *La Jornada*, *Reforma*, and *El Universal*. *Excélsior* uses broadsheet newsprint like *Reforma* and *El Universal*, but its editors place many more news items on the front page. This meant that there would be an over-sampling of items from *Excélsior*. However, because the appearance of more items on *Excélsior's* front page was due to a decision of *Excélsior's* editors rather than the result of a physically larger format, I included all of the *Excélsior* items rather than exclude some in an attempt to reconstruct a format more similar to *Reforma* and *El Universal*.

Finally, I weighted the sample according to each newspaper's readership, in order to be able to make claims about the press's potential to influence readers. I used data from the 1999 MediaMax readership survey by Gallup de México to get the proportion of total readership each newspaper reached. While advertising specialists consider the annual Gallup studies the most reliable, the studies do not note the frequency of newspaper reading (daily, weekly) nor the number of times a single newspaper was read by different people. Based on internal newspaper circulation figures, I estimate Gallup magnifies circulation by about five times. This is not an unreasonable increase since newspapers are rather expensive in Mexico and tend to be shared by families and friends. In any case, since the Gallup standard was applied uniformly, the proportions used to weight the sample should be correct even if total readership is slightly magnified. The number of readers followed by the proportion of the sample for each of the newspapers is: *El Universal* 651,340 (.4472); *La Jornada* 352,567 (.2583); *Reforma* 218,665 (.1602); *Excélsior* 142,124 (.1041); total readers weighted 1,364,696.

Diversity—How Many Voices?

Diversity in the news ensures that citizens can hear many voices on and interpretations of a variety of political and social issues. It was assessed by asking three questions: (1) Did opposition voices appear as much in the news as much as regime voices? (2) Did news coverage present a single interpretation of an issue, a dominant interpretation, or multiple interpretations? (3) Was coverage limited to elite political circles or did it also include reports about the economic realm, the rule of law, civil society, and social institutions such as the church and family?

To answer whether newspapers presented opposition voices in the news as much as regime voices, I compared the number of news items mentioning the president and actors in the PRI to mentions of opposition politicians in parties and local or state governments. This method somewhat underrepresents regime coverage since it does not include other executive branch members or economic elites in partnership with the regime. However, that is balanced by the fact that opposition figures in civil society and economic elites who contradict the regime also were not included. The direct comparison of the presence of regime politicians to the opposition is more concise, requires less interpretation by the coder, and is equally revealing.

The analysis found that the press as a whole only slightly favored the voices of the president and the PRI to those of the opposition. As shown in table 3.1, regime politicians were mentioned in 17.1 percent of coverage. Opposition politicians were mentioned in 15.6 percent of coverage. Looking at it another way, for each eleven regime politicians who appeared in the news, ten opposition politicians appeared. However, individual newsrooms behaved differently from one another. Journalists at *Reforma* and *El Universal* featured the opposition more than the president and the PRI. Only *Excélsior*'s staff substantially slanted news in favor of regime actors.

A second test for diversity in coverage measures whether underlying perspectives that guide news coverage support or challenge the continuation of authoritarianism. Media analysts note that underlying interpretative logics, or news frames, guide the selection and presentation of sources and information in the news (Altheide 1996). A story about street protests, for example, can be guided by a law and order frame or a social justice frame. Did news frames in our sample offer diverse perspectives on important issues and events? To measure this, I identified whether a news item was guided by

Table 3.1 Diversity in the News

1. Covered Opposition Voices (% of all actors)

	Excélsior	El Universal	Reforma	La Jornada	Press
President or PRI	26.0	14.5	11.9	21.4	17.1
Opposition party candidates or governments	14.4	15.2	13.4	18.2	15.6
PRI/Government-to-opposition	1.8:1	.95:1	.89:1	1.18:1	1.13:1
n=565					

2. Presented Competing Interpretations in the News (%)

	Excélsior	El Universal	Reforma	La Jornada	Press
One frame	74.8	60.3	69.6	63.5	64.1
One frame dominant	24.3	29.4	25.0	28.6	28.5
More than one frame	.9	10.3	5.4	7.9	3.43
n=297					

3. Reported Diverse News Topics (%)

	Excélsior	El Universal	Reforma	La Jornada	Press
Electoral	40.5	29.8	25.2	39.7	32.71
Economic	23.7	22.9	25.2	23.8	23.58
Rule of law	13.3	22.1	16.3	19.0	19.45
Civil society	15.0	14.5	28.1	14.3	16.67

one perspective or underlying logic, two contrasting perspectives with one dominating the other in terms of space and placement, or more than one perspective treated in equal fashion. The analysis found that newspapers presented only one perspective in two out of every three news items, and almost never presented competing frames in a balanced way. Variation in newsroom behavior was again notable. Of the four newspapers in the sample, *El Universal* most-often presented more than one perspective in a news item, while *Excélsior* was most likely to present only one perspective.

Analyzing diversity in news topics reveals what the press placed on the public agenda and left out of the public eye. This occurred at a time when the regime was failing to contain corruption, human rights abuses, and other issues associated with the rule of law; could not establish a system producing economic growth for the majority of Mexicans; and did not foster broader discussion of racism, gender discrimination, or sexuality. To analyze diversity in the news agenda, I separated coverage into five domains—the electoral, the economic, the rule of law, cultural institutions, and civil society. The electoral domain included coverage mentioning political parties and politicians. The economic realm covered both state- and private-sector commercial actors, including economic secretariats and economic policy, business elites, and the private sector, generally. Coverage of the rule of law mentioned drug traffickers, the armed forces, human rights abusers, and corrupt public officials. Although the armed forces in Mexico stayed out of the presidential palace after the 1940s, unlike most other Latin American militaries, they were included in this category because of their links to human rights violations and drug corruption. News about the church, families, and gender roles made up the realm of cultural institutions. The domain of civil society included news about political groups operating outside the state as well as ordinary Mexicans such as respondents to public opinion polls or people in the news who were not celebrities or connected to political organizations.

The analysis found that coverage of politicians and parties dominated the news. Almost one-third of press coverage during the period under analysis was about actors in the electoral domain. This coverage was, no doubt, influenced by the approaching presidential elections, yet the way campaigns were covered indicated an elite focus centering on candidates and parties rather than voters or groups affected by elections and government. Economic news followed electoral coverage, accounting for approximately one-fourth of all coverage. Coverage of corruption, human rights violations, and other issues associated with the rule of law accounted for about one-fifth of all coverage.

The focus on the political elite and the electoral process became clear when it was compared to news about civil society or cultural institutions. Actors in civil society were mentioned in 17 percent of the sample, while political actors constituted almost 33 percent. However, civil society coverage was inflated by reporting on protests at the National Autonomous University of Mexico (UNAM). Protesters involved in the UNAM strike accounted for about half of the civil society coverage. Finally, cultural issues and actors received the least attention. Churches and families (including issues of gender) made up just 7.6 percent of total front-page coverage, less than one-fourth of the amount of attention given to electoral actors. More than half of the cultural issues coverage was about gender due to stories about International Women's Day.

While elite-centered political and economic coverage tended to drive the news agenda, newsrooms behaved differently from one another. *Excélsior* was most inclined toward coverage of the political elite and parties. *Reforma* and *El Universal* covered politicians and parties less proportionally, presenting a more balanced news agenda. *Reforma* stood out by emphasizing civil society even more than coverage of politicians and economic actors. *Reforma* covered "average" Mexicans as respondents to public opinion polls, people affected by government policies, and crime victims. All four publications covered the university protesters, but only *La Jornada* reported on the armed protest movement (the Zapatistas in Chiapas). Nongovernmental organizations were covered on only one occasion, in *Reforma,* and that was because the president mentioned them in a press conference.

Autonomy—Who Decides?

For this analysis, I defined the exercise of autonomy as a critical stance toward the powerful in politics and society. I measured it by asking three questions of the news content: (1) Who were the targets of criticism in the news—powerful actors in politics and society traditionally associated with the PRI regime, or weaker actors traditionally associated with the opposition? (2) Did the press treat elite actors generally (both pro- and anti-regime) in a positive or negative manner? (3) Did the news confer legitimacy on the perspectives of powerful pro-regime actors or weaker, oppositional actors? Table 3.2 presents the results of this analysis.

Was the press able to assert autonomy by publishing criticism of the most powerful beneficiaries of the regime, or did criticism in the news target less powerful and/or oppositional figures? To answer this question, I coded as traditionally powerful actors in Mexican society the president, PRI, business elites, economic elites, state economic secretariat officials, military officers, and conservative elements of the Catholic Church. Less powerful actors and institutions included opposition parties and politicians, independent economic analysts, nongovernmental organizations, independent activists, church members who espouse liberation theology, and women in nontraditional roles. There was no coverage of homosexuals in the sample. Criticism in the press may be somewhat overstated because I considered both direct and indirect criticism of these actors. For example, when the press reported on the arrest of a leading banker on fraud charges (a direct criticism) or that an economic secretariat official had to defend deep cuts in education spending (an indirect criticism), I coded this information as critical of the pro-regime elite.

This measure found that the press criticized powerful actors traditionally associated with the PRI regime almost three times more than less-powerful actors, meaning that the press as a whole was able to act autonomously when it wanted to. But two qualifications must be made. First, the press refrained from publishing criticism in 38 percent of the coverage, almost four in ten cases, so the exercise of autonomy was moderate rather than robust. Second, only certain newspapers published critical information about pro-regime

Table 3.2 Autonomy

1. Targeted Pro-Regime Actors in Criticism (%)

Newspaper	Pro-Regime	Oppositional	Both Sets of Actors	No Criticism	Other/NA
Excélsior	15.7	26.7	5.2	50.6	1.8
El Universal	30.9	11.8	8.8	44.1	4.4*
La Jornada	47.6	9.5	15.9	25.4	1.6*
Reforma	50.0	16.1	0.0	32.1	1.8*
Press	36.8	13.2	8.5	38.3	3.2

n=297

2. Portrayed Societal Elite Critically (%)

Portrayal	Politicians	Economic Elite	Cultural Elite	All Elite	Non-Elite
Positive	40.4	37.8	65.8	40.0	34.7
Negative	21.2	27.4	5.3	18.0	38.6
Balanced	23.3	20.0	10.5	17.9	11.9
Neutral	13.0	14.8	13.2	13.7	13.9
Nonapplicable	2.1	0.0	5.3	2.5	1.0

n=467

3. Conferred Legitimacy on Oppositional Actors (%)

Newspaper	Pro-Regime	Oppositional	Both	Neither	Ratio—Power: Less Power
Excélsior	82.9	10.8	1.8	4.5	7.7:1
El Universal	57.4	30.9	5.9	5.9	1.9:1
Reforma	44.7	37.5	1.8	16.1	1.2:1
La Jornada	36.5	54.0	1.6	8.0	.7:1
Press	52.6	35.8	3.7	7.9	1.5:1

n=297

Note: An asterisk symbol (*) means there were less than five cases to analyze. "Other" is U.S. government or drug traffickers, which are powerful, but may or may not have benefited from regime change.

actors: *Reforma* was most critical of powerful actors, followed by *La Jornada*, and then *Excélsior*, as least critical of autocrats and their allies. *El Universal* took a middle position between the two extremes.

The second measure of autonomy asked whether the press portrayed elite actors generally in a positive or negative manner. To judge positive or negative treatment of an actor, I used a wider measure than the reproduction of praise or criticism. I considered the language used to describe the actor and his or her actions; whether or not the actor's version of events was contradicted or accepted unquestioningly as truth; the position and amount of space the actor received in the news item and the front page as a whole; and whether or not there was an implied criticism in the meaning of the language. Additionally, there were two alternatives to positive or negative treatment. An article that contained a roughly equivalent amount and distribution of positive and negative information about an actor was coded as "balanced." An article presenting neither positive nor negative information was coded as "neutral."

The evidence showed that the press covered elite actors, especially church leaders, much more positively than negatively. The press negatively portrayed non-elite Mexicans slightly more often than positively, but much more negatively than elite actors. Newspapers varied by how much autonomy they demonstrated on this measure. *Excélsior* demonstrated the least autonomy. For example, of eighteen *Excélsior* news items mentioning the president, fourteen were positive (78 percent). On the other hand, of four mentions of the president in *Reforma,* one was positive, one was negative, one was balanced, and one was neutral. Looking at coverage of the economic elite, *La Jornada* published the most negative articles, followed by *El Universal, Reforma,* and then *Excélsior.*

The final test of autonomy asked whether the underlying logic of a news item (news frame) legitimized pro-regime or opposition perspectives. The analysis found that the frames that legitimized the perspectives of powerful pro-regime actors in politics, business, and elsewhere were present in more than half of the coverage (53 percent), while frames that legitimized the perspectives of weaker actors appeared in 36 percent of items. Rarely were both perspectives present.

Again, variation in newspaper behavior was apparent. News frames legitimizing the perspectives of less powerful oppositional actors guided *La Jornada*'s coverage in more than half of the cases—far more than in the other newspapers—due, in part, to its framing of the university student strike as a justified protest. This was followed by *Reforma*'s coverage, which used news frames legitimizing oppositional players in politics and society in 37.5 percent of news items. *Reforma*'s negative framing of the strike and positive framing of a decision to use the military to fight drug-related crimes increased the newspaper's level of pro-regime framing. The news frames in *El Universal* legitimized regime elite in more than half of its coverage (52 percent). Pro-regime framing of economic performance was most pronounced, followed by framing the UNAM strike as a disturbance. *Excélsior* rarely framed news coverage in a way that questioned the perspectives of pro-regime elite.

Assertiveness—How Is News Gathered?

Assertiveness in newsgathering is an important component of civic-oriented news production because it provides citizens with information they need to hold public officials accountable. In assertive news coverage, journalists question, rather than passively accept, government announcements and actively seek information on issues such as corruption, cronyism, and policy failure. Without assertiveness in newsgathering, journalists transfer their democratic agenda-setting function to politicians, the economic elite, and, in Mexico, the church hierarchy. I measured assertiveness with the following questions: (1) Did journalists' reporting style indicate passive reception or an active search for information? (2) Did journalists seek multiple sources of information? (3) Did the newspaper itself or an outside actor provide the interpretation, or frame, of the news event? Findings from these measures are reported in table 3.3.

I defined passively reported news items as those based upon staged events, press conferences, group interviews, press releases, and letters to the editor. A mixed category included breaking news that did not come to light as part of staged interviews, reporting from public documents such as

Table 3.3 Assertiveness

1. Reported in Assertive Style (%)

Newspaper	Passive	Mixed	Assertive
Excélsior	81.6	10.3	8.0
El Universal	25.9	24.1	50.0
Reforma	34.0	24.0	42.0
La Jornada	41.3	28.3	30.4
Press	37.0	23.7	39.3
n=241			

2. Used Multiple Sources (%)

Newspaper	Mean	Std. Dev.	n
Excélsior	.96	.8269	109
El Universal	2.2	2.2411	68
Reforma	1.7	1.7294	56
La Jornada	2.0	2.3277	63
Press	1.9	1.781	297
n=297			

3. Provided the Interpretation (%)

Newspaper	Newspaper Sets	Outside Actor Sets	Ratio
Excélsior	14.4	85.6	1:5.9
El Universal	29.4	70.6	1:2.4
Reforma	42.9	57.1	1:1.3
La Jornada	28.6	71.4	1:2.5
Press	29.7	70.2	1:2.4
n=297			

government budgets or police reports, and articles by newsmakers that were requested by the newspaper on a specific issue. News items that used multiple sources of information as well as polls conducted by newspapers were considered assertive reporting.

I found that journalists were about as likely to accept information passively as they were to seek out information assertively. Journalists assertively reported the news in 39.3 percent of the coverage they produced, while they passively accepted information from sources in 37.0 percent. Journalists sought news in a mixed manner in 23.7 percent of coverage. This test uncovered a striking level of variation in newsroom assertiveness. *Excélsior*'s staff rarely took an initiative to seek out news on its own, reacting to newsmakers in more than eight of ten news reports. Journalists at *La Jornada* also were passive in their approach to news coverage, though not as much as at *Excélsior*. Journalists at *Reforma* and, especially, *El Universal* clearly behaved differently from the other two newspapers. *Reforma* reported assertively in four of every ten cases analyzed, while *El Universal* did so in five of ten cases. The pattern was especially noteworthy in *El Universal*, where editors made a conscious effort to include varying perspectives by sending multiple reporters into the field to gather different perspectives on the same news events and to summarize those varied reports on the front page. *Reforma*, on the other hand, was more likely to be enterprising in its approach by conducting opinion polls and seeking story ideas other than government meetings and daily partisan wrangling.

The second assertiveness measurement asked how many sources of information a newspaper consulted for daily coverage of a news issue or event. Journalists sought an average of 1.9 sources per story, although this is a somewhat conservative figure because photographs were counted as one source and columns with no citations were counted as zero sources. There is certainly room to improve, however, since news that gives voice to all stakeholders in an issue rarely has just two sides to cover. As with other measures, there was variation in newspaper behavior and a gap between *Excélsior* and the other three publications. *Excélsior* cited the fewest sources on its front page, 0.96, while *El Universal* cited the most, 2.2 per item. *La Jornada* and *Reforma* cited 2.0 and 1.8, respectively.

The last test for assertiveness in reporting analyzed whether the newspaper itself or an outside actor decided the interpretation of an event, or the framing, used in an article, graphic, or picture. Newspapers interpreted the event when journalists identified important issues and published information about them, or when they changed the message set by a newsmaker who convoked the media at a press conference or staged event. Similarly, journalists determined the frame by seeking out opposing or alternative perspectives or changing the message offered by the newsmaker. Newspapers let outsiders determine the interpretation of an event when they followed the frame set down by newsmakers or did not take coverage of breaking news beyond the most readily available account. For example, *Excélsior's* editors let the president set the frame when they printed verbatim a speech that called anti-globalization protesters naïve and disingenuous. *La Jornada* provided the news frame when it focused on a presidential candidate's wavering statements about a $65 billion bank bailout instead of his speech of the day. This measure found that the press was assertive in about one case in three. In fact, only *Reforma* determined the news frames of its coverage on its front pages fairly regularly. The newspaper established its own news frames in more than four in ten reports. Given the event-oriented nature of news, this is a strong indication of assertiveness. *La Jornada* and *El Universal* were moderately assertive according to this test, setting their own news agendas in about three in ten news items. *Excélsior* determined the interpretations of news events in less than two in ten reports.

Analysis Results

The content analysis found that newspaper coverage in Mexico at the end of the country's political transition exhibited a mix of civic and authoritarian traits. A core of civic-oriented newspapers published voices and symbols challenging the continuation of autocracy in Mexico months before voters peacefully ended the seventy-one-year-old single-party state, but the civic news model did not go unchallenged even within those newsrooms. A conflict of worldviews, norms, and values was indeed playing out on Mexico's news pages.

Tests for diversity in news coverage found that newspapers focused on the opposition almost as much as the ruling party and president, but rarely provided contrasting points of view within the same coverage. They principally defined news as elite electoral politics rather than issues and actors connected to civil society, the rule of law, or social institutions such as the church and family. Individual newsrooms, however, defined and reported the news in very different ways. The variation in behavior allowed readers to find more politically diverse coverage in *Reforma, La Jornada,* and *El Universal.* Journalists at *Reforma* especially stood out for presenting readers with a diversity of views of the regime. They covered the opposition more than regime politicians, and civil society and business as much as politicians and parties. Journalists at *Excélsior* stood out as the most authoritarian in orientation.

The newspaper highly favored news from the electoral realm, and within the realm, the focus was on the ruling party and the president.

The tests for autonomy uncovered a similar clash between authoritarian and civic news concepts. On all three autonomy measures, about one-third of coverage demonstrated autonomy by including messages and perspectives critical of the regime and its traditional allies. Civic-oriented behavior was most notable in coverage criticizing pro-regime politicians and the PRI, but this criticism occurred infrequently and news frames more often legitimized pro-regime positions than opposition stances. Again, *Reforma*, *La Jornada*, and *El Universal* exhibited civic behavior. Even in these newspapers, however, journalists' autonomy was limited according to the actor in question. Their deference to politicians generally, as well as the church hierarchy, was especially notable.

The three tests for assertiveness found that journalists did not act as assertively as envisioned in the civic model, but also behaved very differently than the authoritarian model embodied in the president's office reporter thirteen years earlier. As a whole, journalists reported news in an assertive manner in about four in ten news reports and set their own agenda in three in ten reports, but only consulted about two sources of information per story. The same newsrooms that demonstrated more autonomy and diversity in coverage also behaved more assertively.

Table 3.4 presents a score of 1.0, 0.5, or 0.0 for each newspaper and for the press generally for each of the nine measures of civic-oriented news production. This creates a civic journalism score, which locates each newspaper and the press on the additive civic journalism index, depicted in figure 3.2. The analysis of press behavior found that a civic model of journalism and news production competed with Mexico's authoritarian media model near the end of the PRI regime. While a newspaper's civic orientation varied depending on the measure used and the actor covered, the analysis clearly demonstrates that *Excélsior* followed an authoritarian model of news production, while *Reforma* and, to a lesser extent, *La Jornada* followed a civic model. *El Universal* fell in a mixed category, but leaned toward civic journalism. The press as a whole fell squarely in a mixed range. The average was calculated considering the size of readership of the four newspapers in the sample.

The analysis provides evidence that the civic press contributed to the weakening of the definitional power of the PRI regime. These newspapers presented the voices and symbols of the political opposition as voters prepared to remove the ruling party from power more than seven decades after it first assumed the presidency and centralized political authority. A cautionary note must be added to this depiction, however. Newspapers demon-

Table 3.4 Civic Journalism Score, 2000
(0–3=Authoritarian Model; 3–6=Mixed; 6–9=Civic Model)

	Reforma	La Jornada	El Universal	Excélsior	Press
DIVERSITY SCORE	2.5	2.0	2.5	0.5	1.5
Covered opposition voices	1.0	0.5	1.0	0.5	0.5
Presented competing interpretations in the news	0.5	0.5	0.5	0.0	0.0
Reported diverse news topics	1.0	1.0	1.0	0.0	1.0
AUTONOMY SCORE	2.5	2.5	1.0	0.0	2.0
Criticized regime actors more than opposition	1.0	1.0	0.5	0.0	1.0
Included criticism of societal elite in coverage	0.5	0.5	0.5	0.0	0.5
Conferred legitimacy on oppositional actors as much as pro-regime actors	1.0	1.0	0.0	0.0	0.5
ASSERTIVENESS SCORE	2.5	1.5	2.0	0.0	1.5
Multiple sources were cited	0.5	0.5	0.5	0.0	0.5
Reporting style was assertive	1.0	0.5	1.0	0.0	0.5
Newspaper interpreted the event	1.0	0.5	0.5	0.0	0.5
CIVIC JOURNALISM SCORE	7.5	6.0	5.5	0.5	4.5

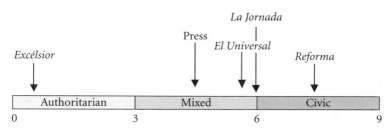

Figure 3.2 Civic Journalism Index, 2000

strated most diversity of voices, autonomy, and assertiveness when covering the electoral sphere. Neither the church nor the military were treated critically, although the sample of mentions of the military was too small to draw firm conclusions. The richest Mexicans were likewise absent from coverage. In effect then, civic norms were strongest when journalists covered the electoral opening. Issues of economic and social justice remained off the media agenda and shielded from public view unless mentioned by the political opposition or international actors.

4 Ending the Monologue

The Rise of Civic Journalism

For many years, our traditional "presidentialism" imposed its monologue.
Today, more than ever before, governing means dialogue; the nation's
strength can no longer come from a single point of view, a single party, or a
single philosophy.

President Vicente Fox on Inauguration Day, December 1, 2000

As Mexicans prepared for their last presidential elections of the twentieth century, the PRI could no longer count on the news media to uniformly reproduce its monologue. In fact, some Mexican newsrooms produced coverage that helped undermine the authoritarian system by reflecting a civic orientation of assertiveness, autonomy, and political diversity. By the 2000 elections, as normative and coercive controls on media subordination declined, civic journalism contested authoritarian and market-driven alternatives for control of Mexican newsrooms. Traditional, authoritarian newsrooms continued to reproduce the PRI monologue, were subordinated to the regime, and were passive in their reporting styles, while oligarchic authoritarian forms followed any master who furthered the owner's personal, partisan, or group ambitions.

How did these conflicting models of journalism, the news, and society develop over time? An evaluation over time of press treatment of the president, the ruling PRI, and opposition parties and figures reveals which authoritarian characteristics the press shed, which civic characteristics it donned, and whether this transformation included all press organizations. Analysis of the news over time also identifies the pattern and timing of newsroom transformations, in this case the emergence and dispersion of a vanguard of civic-oriented innovators that led change from within an authoritarian institution. Finally, an analysis of coverage of actors from outside the electoral realm over the last two decades identifies the limitations to the movement toward civic journalism. Essentially, civic orientations were strongest when covering actors linked to the opening of formal politics or public forums such as congressional debates and campaigns. This was in part because of accentuated commercial pressures, but also because of the particular traits of Mexican political culture.

Methodology

The following analysis measures the direction and timing of change in news content from 1980 to 2000. The period was chosen to allow assessment of news media behavior before and during a phase of profound political and economic transition. Although some analysts place the beginning of Mexico's political transition with the student protests of 1968, the regime was able to reconsolidate its grip on power in the 1970s by increasing repression of non-electoral actors, bringing student protest leaders and the Mexican Communist Party into the electoral system, and distributing fresh resources from an oil boom (Camp 2002b; Levy and Székely 1987). In 1982, however, the boom ended, the peso crashed, and Mexico entered a deep recession with heavy international debts. Inflation soared and purchasing power plummeted. In response, the government slashed social spending and began to liquidate or sell off government-owned enterprises. Poverty increased (Lustig 1992). The 1980s became a "lost decade" for development, and frustration boiled. The regime's eventual response was a gradual electoral opening to the conservative opposition, which shared its neoliberal economic philosophy and the creation of targeted poverty alleviation programs to undercut support for the left-center opposition. Gradual political liberalization was designed so that the regime could hold onto power while building new alliances around an alternative economic model based on market forces and a closer alliance between Mexico and the United States. The strategy prevented violent upheaval until 1994 and forestalled the transfer of federal power to the opposition for six years after that. The bottom-up electoral strategy meant Mexico's municipalities, states, and eventually the federal Congress took on a multiparty hue in the 1990s, even as the executive branch remained solidly *priísta*.[1]

The content analysis traces changes in press coverage in five-year increments during this period of societal transformation from 1980 to 2000, using the same sample of publications presented in chapter 3—*Excélsior, El Universal, La Jornada,* and *Reforma.* The same protocol, which produced controlled agreement (Gamma) of 0.913 and higher, was used to code items in all five points in time. There are two slight differences in the methodology, however.

The first difference is the replacement of *La Jornada* by *Unomásuno* prior to 1985 and *El Norte* for *Reforma* prior to 1995. This was necessary because both *La Jornada* and *Reforma* began publication during the twenty-year period under study. I chose *Unomásuno* and *El Norte* because they are the direct predecessors of *La Jornada* and *Reforma* in terms of newsroom culture and a large part of the personnel. *Unomásuno*'s experiment with civic journalism ended after its publisher accepted a loan from the government to get through difficult times in the early 1980s. Most of the staff that formed *La Jornada* in 1983 departed *Unomásuno* in protest of the publication's loss of autonomy. I chose *El Norte* to represent *Reforma* prior to the latter's opening in 1993 because the family company owning *El Norte* founded the Mexico City publication on the same editorial principles as the earlier paper, and *Reforma* was directed by the same publisher and editors. The second difference in methodology is that articles, photographs, and other news items that treated the same topic on the same day were considered a single unit of analysis in an effort to minimize changes in front-page design over time. The annual sample sizes for the analysis were 154 (1980), 194 (1985), 235 (1990), 231 (1995), and 239 (2000), for a total of 1053 analyzed items.

The Societal Context of Media Transformation

Peruvian author Mario Vargas Llosa dubbed Mexican presidentialism "the perfect dictatorship." Indeed, the political system that emerged from the factionalism of the twentieth century's second and longest social revolution eventually solved the Achilles' heel of authoritarianism—leadership succession—and became the most stable political system in all of Latin America. Mexico's political system evolved into a strong presidential system in the decades following the 1910 Revolution. While considering the opinions of powerful regime allies, such as domestic capitalists and the military, the president largely set his own policy direction. He did so by controlling enormous extra-constitutional powers related to political appointments, state patronage, and the national security apparatus. Co-optation became the preferred method of dealing with real and potential dissent, but the president and his aides were able to apply repressive tactics in a targeted manner because of the legitimacy enjoyed by the system among the general population. Regime legitimacy was based on economic growth for the urban population, political stability as compared to the rest of Latin America, and the manipulation of the ideological symbols of the Revolution in ritual ceremonies and the mass media (Bailey 1988; Cook, Middlebrook, and Molinar 1994; Camp 2002b, 147–48; Levy and Székely 1987, 109). All served the system well until the 1980s.

Response to the prolonged economic crisis in the 1980s could not be controlled as easily as earlier challenges to the regime such as railroad strikes in the 1950s or student protests in 1968, both of which essentially were confined to a single segment of the population. Mexico had become a socially complex, urban, and industrialized society by the 1980s, and the crisis lingered long enough for most of the population to feel its pain. The "lost decade" bolstered the political appeal of the partisan opposition, while slashing the amount of state patronage available to buy off dissent. Pragmatic business leaders became more politicized and many left the PRI or the ranks of the politically agnostic to join more-traditional conservatives in the National Action Party (PAN). Among those was Vicente Fox, a Coca-Cola executive who became one of several opposition candidates robbed of a governor's chair by voter fraud. Fox and other *neopanistas* regenerated the PAN, which had previously garnered only about 15 percent of the vote in national elections and seemed a perpetually loyal opposition force content to be dealt leftovers by the PRI. The party's national presence grew in the 1980s and its organizational capacity strengthened. Unlike traditional conservatives, Fox and other *neopanistas* would not give up on reforming the government. "Sí se puede," or "it can be done," they cried. Fox became governor of Guanajuato in 1995, and president of Mexico in 2000.[2] In the PRI, some left-wing members left the party due to a dispute over market-based economic policy and the decision of President Miguel de la Madrid (1982–1988) to pass over their preferred presidential candidate, Cuauhtémoc Cárdenas, for Budget Secretary Carlos Salinas de Gortari. The defecting *priístas* brought together the historically fractured leftist opposition for the 1988 presidential election and created the country's first large, center-left opposition party, the Democratic Revolution Party (PRD), in 1989. Cárdenas, the coalition's presidential candidate in 1988 (and considered by many to be the legitimate winner of the election), became Mexico City's mayor in 1997.[3]

As electoral fraud and economic pressure persisted in the 1980s, dissatisfaction grew. Voter fraud and the slow pace of electoral reform spurred peaceful protests along the northern border. After the 1988 election, protests spread, and activists around the country began national coalitions of human rights groups that put electoral rights high on their agendas. At the same time, a small group of Mexico City intellectuals marched into the countryside of Chiapas to begin organizing for armed rebellion. In the cities, inept government response to the Mexico City earthquake and state withdrawal from many social and economic activities stimulated a new force in politics made up of nongovernmental organizations such as neighborhood associations, women's groups, taxpayers' associations, and professional organizations of lawyers, economists, and others. With the exception of some of the NGOs, which entered into negotiations for state resources while at the same time affiliating with the PRD, these groups operated outside the reach of both the state and formal political parties.[4]

These events set the organizational groundwork for a swelling of civic participation in the 1990s, after a second economic crisis undid the regime's attempt to reconsolidate as a neopopulist party that could co-opt the organized poor with selective subsidies and the middle class with promises of higher standards of living. After the peso devalued in December 1994, about one million jobs disappeared in ten months. Interest rates spiked so that the middle class lost new homes and cars bought on credit. Perhaps as important, Mexicans lost the dream of first-world economic status promised during the 1994 presidential campaign as the reward for signing the North American Free Trade Agreement (NAFTA).

As Mexicans withstood the pain of a second economic crisis, public corruption seemed to reach new heights. The economic crisis beginning in 1994 coincided with two political assassinations thought to be tied to ruling party power struggles and, soon after, publicized cases of high-level corruption. Swiss police found bank accounts worth more than $100 million under aliases for the brother of outgoing President Carlos Salinas (1988–1994). Raúl Salinas, already jailed on the charge of ordering the murder of the PRI's general secretary, José Francisco Ruiz Massieu, said the money came from investors in a venture capital fund. The investors included some of the families that benefited most from Carlos Salinas's sale of major state-owned corporations, such as the public television network Imevisión, which later became TV Azteca. A $65 billion bank bailout during the administration of President Ernesto Zedillo (1994–2000), meant to help middle-class debtors and prevent the failure of the banking system, became riddled with questionable loans to wealthy business owners, corporations, and politicians. Greedy officials even pilfered a food program for the poor (Hughes 1995).[5]

Outraged, many Mexicans declared the system bankrupt politically, economically, and morally. By 1998, only 30 percent of Mexicans said they were "very" or "somewhat" satisfied with how "democracy" was functioning in their country (Hewlett Foundation 1998, A7). While most preferred continued reform of elections, some increased political activity outside of the PRI system. After the Zapatistas appeared in Chiapas on New Year's Day, 1994, two other armed groups surfaced in Guerrero in 1996 and 1997. Crime spiraled as old social controls came apart. New debtors' associations organized protests of policy decisions and banking scandals and represented the interests of defaulted debtors in negotiations with the state. Human rights organizations created a national, nonpartisan election monitoring program in state elections across the country. These new voting rights activists statistically compared voter rolls and census figures to spot manipulated polling station data. They sent volunteers with video cameras to monitor contentious polling stations. They also began analyzing media coverage of state and national elections beginning in 1993. After its armed rebellion ended, the Zapatista movement brought many of these organizations into a loose national coalition, using a new technology, the Internet, to coordinate meetings and protests.

Faced with fewer resources for co-optation and more dissent than perhaps any of his *priísta* predecessors, President Ernesto Zedillo opted to continue electoral and economic reform rather than increase repression. He negotiated a series of political reforms with opposition party leaders that, in 1996, finally guaranteed the autonomy and financial capacity of the federal elections bureaucracy and improved the overall fairness of federal elections by monitoring television and radio campaign coverage and increasing the amount of public funding available to all political parties. Much of the money went into purchasing television ads. Perhaps most importantly, Zedillo usually kept his political operators away from state-level elections and encouraged his fellow partisans to win fairly rather than through voter fraud. The reforms allowed the opposition to capitalize on public discontent. The PAN and PRD added seven more state governors' posts, including Mexico City, to the four they had earned during the Salinas years. In congressional elections held in 1997, civil society, parties, and the new electoral institute made sure federal elections were both free and fair. The PRI lost its absolute majority in Congress for the first time. Voter support for PRI congressional candidates had declined throughout the 1990s. In 1991, 61.4 percent of voters supported the PRI, 50.3 percent in 1994, 39.1 percent in 1997, and 37 percent in 2000.[6] Congress could now be a legislature, rather than just a rubber stamp and source of political patronage.

When these trends converged in the July 2000 presidential elections, the legacy of Mexican presidential campaigns was one of myth creation and ritualistic participation rather than democratic competition. Presidential succession limited information and competition to the top echelons of the PRI. The central component of system renovation was the *dedazo*, or the outgoing president's ability to personally select his own replacement. Façade campaigns and elections made news, but the real competition for power took place before the campaign in the context of factions and personalities within the PRI that sought the favor of the outgoing president. Rather than offer citizens a choice of parties, personalities, or policy directions, campaigns introduced the public to the next president through rallies and news coverage, polished his image as powerful and benevolent, and absolved him of blame for problems that might have developed during the previous six-year term. The real succession process of behind-the-scenes maneuvering for the presidential nod was conducted in secret and surrounded with code-like terminology. *Dedazo,* for example, meant "the pointing of the finger" and was constructed by connecting the word for "finger" (*dedo*) with a colloquial expression that generally meant "this is big" (*-azo*). The outgoing president, who selected his own successor, was known as the *gran elector,* or the big voter (Adler 1993b; Bailey 1988; Butler and Bustamante 1991; Levy and Székely 1987, 111–12). Thus, the primary function of presidential campaigns was to shift responsibility for past mistakes from the political order to the outgoing president and to create a new, omnipotent presidential figure in the form of the ruling party candidate. While PRI politicians took their messages directly to the people in the early years after the revolution, broadcast and print media still widened the reach of their voices. In the last decade of the single-party state, mass media became the necessary ingredient for the amplification of regime messages and for the introduction of competing visions from the opposition.[7]

News media played an important role in the succession. They transmitted the dominant messages of the regime largely without question or criticism, facilitating systemic renovation every six years and protecting the incumbent's image in the interim. As the veneer of a PRI presidential candidate glowed during the campaign, the current president similarly was shielded from public criticism as much as possible during the *sexenio,* or six-year administration. My analysis of newspaper political coverage found that the blame for problems fell not to the president, but instead to lower-level bureaucrats, bickering politicians, big business, reactionary conservative conspiracies, the United States, or other, murkier foreign interests. As seen through the lens of the media, the incumbent president was a decisive decision maker, final arbiter, or benevolent father figure of the common Mexican. Few competing voices in the mainstream press were given the presence or legitimacy to challenge the hegemonic vision of the president, the PRI, or the passive institutions and practices that supported them. The right-wing opposition was portrayed as extremist and unpatriotic. In some cases, the political right, the clergy, and conservative business organizations were said to be "conspiring" with the United States against Mexico, as embodied by the president. The left, which entered the electoral arena only after the political reforms of 1977, was portrayed as divided, overly intellectual, or prone to violence when it received coverage at all. For example, the president was portrayed as a defender of the peasantry in the headline, "JLP Against the

Deception of the *Campesino:* CNC" (*Excélsior,* March 2, 1980). The right was portrayed as conspiring with the church in the story, "Obscure Electoral Panorama with the PAN-Cleric Alliance" (*Excélsior,* March 6, 1985). Finally, the left was mired in self-criticism in "The Left is Plagued by Cowards, the Weak-Kneed, Dreamers and Conciliators: Falcon" (*El Universal*, March 2, 1985).[8] Yet by the time a new political party took office in Mexico in December 2000, the system's messages were not amplified so strongly, passively, or noncritically as in the decades of the hegemonic party.

Coverage of the President, the PRI, and the Opposition

Content analysis uncovered three trends in the way press coverage of the president changed between 1980 and 2000. The first trend was the increase in assertiveness, autonomy, and diversity of viewpoints found in coverage of the president compared to coverage of members of the PRI and opposition actors. The second trend was that coverage changed in spurts rather than continuously, producing a pattern of peaks and troughs in the data. The third trend was the variation in the amount of coverage change depending upon the newspaper under analysis.

As measured by a decline in exclusive focus, positive treatment, and passivity in reporting, press coverage of the president became substantially more civic in orientation between 1980 and 2000. The declining figure of the president is clearly visible in the trends depicted in figure 4.1, which traces presidential coverage change in five-year-increments for the four newspapers in the sample and the press generally. Press figures were weighted in 1995 and 2000 to reflect broad shifts in readership. As a whole, press coverage devoted to the central figure of Mexican authoritarianism dropped from 62.5 percent of all front-page political coverage in 1980 to 20.5 percent twenty years later. Meanwhile, opposition voices in the press rose from just 5 percent of political coverage in 1980 to 44 percent in 2000. Coverage of the PRI stayed about the same.

Besides being covered less, the presidential figure also lost some of its shine as the press asserted more autonomy. A general trend of declining positive treatment of the president is visible in figure 4.2. Positive press treatment of the president, as opposed to balanced, neutral, or negative treatment, dropped from 69 percent in 1980 to 47 percent in 2000. This assertion of autonomy by the press was conditioned, however. The press was more willing to challenge the president by including opposition voices that criticized him in balanced coverage rather than to present the president in an overwhelmingly negative fashion.

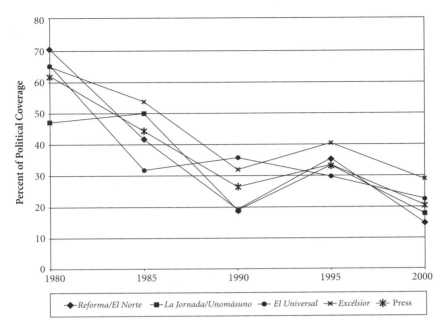

Figure 4.1 Volume of Presidential Coverage

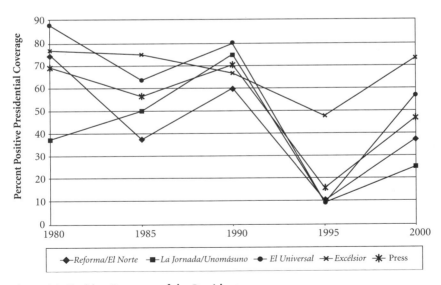

Figure 4.2 Positive Coverage of the President

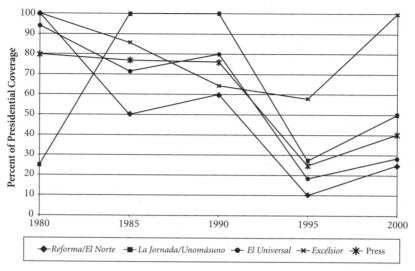

Figure 4.3 Passive Reporting about the President

Finally, the data show a general trend of increased assertiveness in press coverage of the president. Newspapers were more willing to seek out information about the president than rely passively on staged events, press conferences, press releases, and curbside interviews. Passivity in reporting about the president fell from 80 percent in front-page coverage to 40 percent two decades later, as seen in figure 4.3.

By the last year of the PRI regime, the content analysis found strong evidence that the central actor of Mexican authoritarianism had become a contested figure. The president was covered less, competed with more voices, was not always presented in a positive fashion, and had to expect reporters to seek out information rather than passively accept the official line.

A second trend noticeable in the data is that there are peaks and troughs across time in the transformation of media coverage of the president. In other words, as Bennett (1998) noted in media coverage of the "democratic revolutions" in Eastern Europe, there appear to be exaggerated moments or critical junctures where positive treatment of the president plunged. Passive coverage and emphasis on the presidential figure also fell in this way, though in a less dramatic fashion. The greatest challenges to the president's definitional power in the media occurred during the economic crises in 1985 and 1995.

These exaggerated moments of autonomy, assertiveness, and diversity corresponded with systemic shocks in the news environment, which journalists recall in interviews as motivation for questioning their subservience to a decaying political system. These moments also indicate group experiences in which journalists learned they could widen the boundaries of press-state relations. Journalists and newspaper owners learned when increased criticism and pluralism would be tolerated, and when negative consequences might result. For example, because *El Financiero* criticized the government's debt negotiations in the mid-1980s, it lost all government advertising (Riva Palacio 1994). Indeed, as gauged by these three indicators of news diversity, autonomy, and assertiveness, presidential authority over the media after the critical junctures passed was never reestablished at its previously high level. The system's grip on the messages and symbols transmitted in the media eroded over time, as journalists reacted to systemic shocks and accumulated knowledge.

A similar pattern of peaks and troughs in critical coverage was found in a separate analysis of coverage of the Mexican military from 1986 to 1998. Figure 4.4 depicts a straight count of news articles that mention both the Mexican military and human rights in fifteen Mexican newspapers. Because of the relatively scarce coverage of the Mexican armed forces, especially in connection with an issue as controversial as human rights, the sampling technique identified entries in an electronic newspaper archive through a keyword search rather than the analysis of random dates of coverage used in other analyses. Similar findings from the different methodologies and actors would support the generalizability of the ability of shocking events to alter the coverage of powerful actors over time through a process of learning and the resetting of coverage boundaries.

For the analysis of military coverage, stories were identified in a keyword

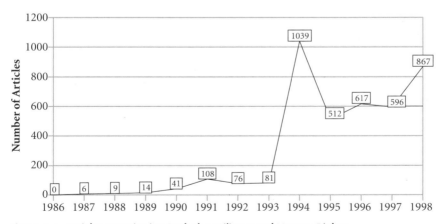

Figure 4.4 Articles Mentioning Both the Military and Human Rights

search for *ejercito* (army), *derechos humanos* (human rights) and *Estados Unidos Mexicanos* (United Mexican States), the last being a phrase attached to all articles about domestic issues in the Infosel, S.A. de C.V. database of newspaper content, a *Reforma* newspaper group company. The database contained articles from *El Norte, Reforma, El Universal, La Jornada, El Financiero, Siglo 21, Excélsior, Unomásuno, El Heraldo de México, El Nacional, El Sol de México, El Economista, El Día, El Porvenir,* and *El Diaro de Monterrey.* The sample of articles cannot be considered either complete or random because it was constructed based on assessments of which stories were important enough to save for the archives of the newspaper chain. However, the number of articles about the military and human rights saved by the country's most significant newspaper group grew dramatically over the decade, along the same trend line established in the analysis of coverage of the president. Partial retreats to complacency occurred after spikes in critical coverage of specific events, such as a shootout between the military and judicial police in 1991, the Zapatista uprising in 1994, and a counterinsurgency campaign in Guerrero in 1996. The previous low level was never reestablished. This suggests a process of learning occurred.

The first decline in media subjection to the president occurred in 1985 when Mexico was in the middle of a six-year economic downturn. The country experienced one of several devaluations, inflation remained high, and private analysts sought out by some members of the press suggested that interest rates were about to shoot even higher. Meanwhile, the conservative opposition was gaining wider support as more moderate, pragmatic business leaders joined the party's ranks—including, eventually, President Vicente Fox. Fox followed the example of his mentor, 1988 PAN presidential candidate Manuel Clouthier. In 1985, Clouthier had appeared in news coverage as a business leader who offered a contrasting voice to that of the government, even though, at times, the media had vilified his business owners' organization as unpatriotic and reactionary.

By 1990, however, a new PRI-affiliated president had taken office. Then-president Carlos Salinas employed a proactive media strategy and activist reform agenda. The press chronicled his announcement of a vast new campaign to improve the conditions of the country's poor, later known as Solidarity. Salinas's rhetoric embraced both foreign investors and the domestic dons of capitalism, who responded in kind. At the same time, the president of the PRI publicly challenged organized labor leaders affiliated with the ruling party, accusing these opponents of Salinas's market-based economic reform of manipulating their membership to promote personal goals.

The only negative news about the regime during the period was about the politically motivated violence that occurred after fraudulent state elections in Guerrero and Michoacán, but that coverage did not mention the president directly. The opposition was portrayed as the cause of the violence in most of the coverage, while the interior secretary appeared in the news as patiently negotiating a peaceful settlement.

The *El Norte* articles, "Guarantees Demanded for Tourists" (March 2, 1990) and "Protesters Dislodged from Town Halls; 20 Die," (March 7, 1990) are interesting exceptions to the purely passive coverage of postelectoral protests in 1990. The coverage illustrates how civic newspapers tentatively expanded the boundaries for critical coverage.[9] In the first article, reporter Ana Vila Freyer reported that police beat eight protestors to the point that they had to be hospitalized. She noted the protesters were, on average, seventy-five years old. However, the newspaper's editors placed the report under a lead paragraph and headline that focused on worries about the tourism trade.

The second article was much more direct. As the newspaper's lead story of the day, it was stripped across the top of the front page. Vila Freyer directly contradicted the official version of events about police officers killed during the forced evacuation of blockaded city halls without ever mentioning the president or government authorities. After describing the events, including the deaths, the fourth paragraph went on: "Officially, there are no deaths, wounded or detained." The reporting was thorough, contrasting official and eyewitness versions of the deaths of police officers who apparently were mistakenly shot by their own comrades. Other newspapers implied that they had been shot by members of the PRD.

Civic-oriented newspapers and journalists criticized the regime by means of indirect, implied, and concealed criticisms. They never went so far as to link the president to the confrontations in the two states, though the president chose the PRI's gubernatorial candidate, and his interior secretary "negotiated" with the opposition. Whether he ordered the dislodging of protesters that lead to the twenty deaths is something only the inner elite would know, but it was a worthwhile question that was too risky to ask.

The second critical juncture in coverage of the president occurred in 1995. At this point, Mexico was in a second economic crisis, which seemed at the time to be more devastating than the crisis of the 1980s. At the same time, journalists gave cases of corruption a higher profile than they had ten years earlier, including stories that directly touched the president's office. President Ernesto Zedillo was confronted not only by a huge devaluation of the peso, rampant inflation, and the prospect of recession, but also by a political situation that raised questions about the depth of corruption within his party. In an open quarrel with former president Salinas, Zedillo attempted to end the conflict by jailing the ex-president's brother, Raúl, for the murder of a PRI colleague and shifting the blame for the economic crisis to the ex-president. Yet Zedillo did not escape unscathed, as critical views of the presidency and the PRI gained ground even against the backdrop of Salinas's disparaged image. The United States government, the Mexican cabinet, political columnists, and, for the first time, multiple public opinion polls blamed Salinas for the country's economic and political woes. However, the economic crisis became too deep, and Zedillo's proposed economic solution was too painful for the majority of Mexicans for the president to escape the period without a tarnished reputation.

The third notable trend in the analysis of coverage of the president is that, while all newspapers became more assertive, autonomous, and diverse, some publications changed more than others. *Reforma* and *La Jornada* tended to lead the coverage changes following 1990. *El Universal* took an intermediate position. *Excélsior*'s resistance to change in relation to the other newspapers was especially notable: it lagged behind other newspapers in transforming the amount, nature, and passive approach to presidential coverage.

The extreme positions in presidential coverage in 1980 belonged to *Unomásuno* (forerunner of *La Jornada*) and *El Norte* (founder of *Reforma*), a gap that could be explained by ideological or geographic differences. *Unomásuno*'s left-oriented staff was much more critical of the president than *El Norte* in 1980, devoted less time to him, and was more assertive in its search for information. This changed in 1985, however, as much of the staff left to form *La Jornada*, which, at the outset, was a weaker and more tentative publication vis-à-vis the president. By 1990, when its circulation had increased, *La Jornada* began to assume a leadership role in producing more plural, autonomous, and assertive coverage of the president.

In 1980, *El Norte* remained weakened from confrontations with President Luis Echeverría (1970–1976) over coverage of his economic policy and the investigation of the kidnap-murder of prominent Monterrey businessman Eugenio Garza Sada. Additionally, Echeverría's openly populist rhetoric conflicted with the free-market business orientation of Monterrey. Echeverría cut *El Norte*'s newsprint supply 83 percent in response to critical coverage, which the publication eventually replaced with imported newsprint (Fromson 1996). However, *El Norte*'s editors were unable or unwilling to criticize Echeverría's successor, José López Portillo (1976–1982). At the beginning of his term, López Portillo was a much more palatable president in the conservative north than Echeverría had been; economic growth soared in 1980 thanks to temporarily high oil export earnings. However, López Portillo would lose his popularity after a peso devaluation and his surprise nationalization of the banking system in 1982.

El Norte began to demonstrate more civic news tendencies in 1985, during the presidency of Miguel de la Madrid (1982–1988). By then, Mexico's banks had been nationalized in a futile attempt to stop capital flight, which antagonized the business community and northern Mexico generally. The country was suffering through a prolonged economic crisis, and political polarization surfaced in sharp relief. By the time *Reforma* opened in Mexico City in 1993, the environment it inherited from *El Norte* was much more conducive to autonomy, assertiveness, and diversity in news production than it had been thirteen years earlier in Monterrey. The newspaper immediately became a change leader and analysts cite its opening as a watershed event in Mexico City journalism.

After years of strong support for the presidential figure, *El Universal's* approach to presidential coverage became much more balanced in the second half of the 1990s. While the president's point of view still received dominant placement in most coverage, negative voices and messages made their way into 90 percent of the publication's front-page news in 1995. One year later, in 1996, *El Universal* entered an open confrontation with President Zedillo over coverage of the assassination of former PRI presidential candidate Luis Donaldo Colosio and the hiring of critical political columnists from *La Jornada* and *El Financiero*. Newspaper executives believe this led to the arrest of *El Universal's* owner, Juan Francisco Ealy Ortiz, on tax evasion charges.[10] Although the president's image in *El Universal* improved in 2000, it was not as gleaming or as prominent as in previous years.

Excélsior, meanwhile, was the victim of government intervention in 1976, after which its editor and many members of its staff left to form *Unomásuno* and the critical newsmagazine *Proceso*. *Excélsior* never regained its leading position as an independent or assertive publication in relation to other Mexican newspapers. It demonstrated more allegiance to the traditional political system's central figures than the other publications in the 1990s, even though the level of its support also dropped over the two decades. Coverage of the president in 2000 remained completely passive.

Limitations to Civic Journalism

Was civic change in the news media limited outside of the coverage of electoral actors, politicians, and government, as the analysis in chapter 3 suggests? The data from the longitudinal analysis offers additional evidence that press treatment of other realms of society did not change as much as coverage of the electoral-governmental realm.

For this analysis, four social actors were chosen to represent spheres of news coverage beyond the electoral sphere. An "average Mexican" category (people who were not celebrities and were not related to organized groups associated with the state or political parties) represented an aspect of civil society. The business elite represented an actor in the commercial sphere. The military, because its increased roles in drug interdiction and anti-guerilla campaigns brought about charges of corruption and human rights abuse, represented an actor associated with the rule of law. Finally, the church represented the realm of cultural institutions.

Along with the president, the church and the military were considered "untouchable" in the Mexican press. However, after 1968, the military took on missions that increasingly brought it into contact with civilians, which sometimes resulted in human rights violations (Wager and Schulz 1995). Although no high-ranking army officer has yet been brought to trial publicly as a result of those allegations, numerous stories of abuse appeared in the civic press during the armed phase of the Zapatista conflict in 1994 and during confrontations between guerilla organizations and civilians in Guerrero beginning in 1996 (Gutiérrez 1998). Questions about military involvement in drug trafficking, including cases involving high-level commanders, sometimes occurred, though not often enough to appear in my random sample of coverage. In the 1980s and 1990s, the church became more controversial when priests decided they should speak out publicly on behalf of their congregations, be they marginalized indigenous communities in the south or northern urban communities where electoral fraud had kept the PRI in power during the 1980s.

Besides these two traditionally untouchable figures, new untouchables appear to have formed. One, the business elite, became increasingly powerful as wealth concentration grew during the Salinas years and after the signing of NAFTA. Salinas's privatization of state-owned enterprises favored family-based commercial groups, while the new export-oriented growth model favored these same large enterprises over smaller businesses and domestically focused companies. As the groups and their owners became more powerful, private sector advertising became more important to newspapers' financial survival. Journalists were keenly aware of this shift. In a focus group discussion with Mexico City editors in July 1999, the only time group members asked for the tape recorder to be turned off was when they discussed the editorial impact of advertising by the telephone company owned by Latin America's richest man, Mexico's Carlos Slim.[11]

The evidence suggests that these actors were only partially protected from press scrutiny, however. Like the president, the military and the business elite lost much of their luster over time. Purely positive coverage of the military dropped from a high of 70 percent in 1985 to 33.3 percent in 2000.[12] Positive treatment of the military began to decline after the armed forces were used to back up police quelling postelectoral violence in Guerrero and Michoacán in 1990, and against the Zapatista rebels and their civilian communities in Chiapas in 1995. In the 2000 sample, the army's image included questions about its role in Chiapas, drug interdiction, and a political corruption case.

Purely positive treatment of the business elite dropped from a high of 75 percent in 1990 to 33.3 percent in 2000. The business elite was heavily criticized in the press in 1980 and 1985 for sympathizing with the conservative opposition and playing a role in the economic downturn of the 1980s. Press treatment of business leaders became much more positive in 1990 in response to Salinas administration rhetoric promoting the private sector. As a new economic crisis emerged in 1995, however, the press viewed the business elite with a more critical eye. Business leaders, especially bankers, were criticized during the 2000 presidential campaign for their part in a flawed $65 billion bank bailout that scandalized the country.

Increased questioning of the military and the business elite in the 1990s was not because of increased press assertiveness, but because of the greater willingness to cover a diversity of voices outside of the PRI. The decline in positive coverage of the military was the result of critiques from the opposition or actors in civil society who were included in news accounts, rather than newspapers asserting their own coverage agenda. In 2000, the press passively received information regarding the military in 80 percent of news items and passively accepted information about business leaders in 55 percent of coverage. The critique of the military and the business elite was a response to unfolding events.

The press became more assertive in its search for information about the church than it did with the military and business elite. The church inserted itself into the electoral arena, and so may have legitimized more assertive press scrutiny of this traditionally unquestionable actor. The new attitude toward coverage of the church was less dramatic than changes in coverage of the military or business elite, however. While coverage of the church was less passive in 2000 than in 1980, it was still largely positive.

Criticism of the church increased in 1985 as murky political figures supposedly linked the clergy to an "alliance" with the PAN and the United States against the president. In 1990, some journalists questioned the wisdom of the

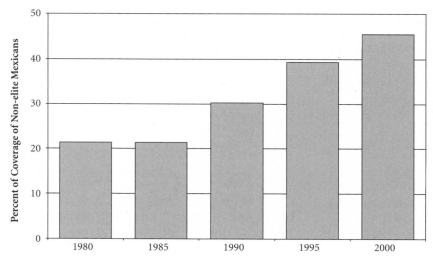

Figure 4.5 Average Mexicans Presented as Empowered (vs. Passive)

Salinas administration's decision to reopen formal diplomatic ties with the Vatican. However, by 1995, even given criticism of Chiapas Bishop Samuel Ruiz's role in negotiations with the Zapatista rebels, almost 60 percent of the coverage of the church remained purely positive. By 2000, more than 65 percent of news coverage presented the church in a positive fashion.

While the analysis of press treatment of the military, church, and business leaders revealed moderately more civic behavior, press coverage of average Mexicans changed dramatically. Figure 4.5 illustrates the change. Over twenty years, the press turned the average Mexican from someone who was spoken for by politicians—a victim of natural disasters or a victim of crime—into someone who took an active role in shaping her or his life in 48 percent of coverage in 2000. Average Mexicans had been treated as empowered in only 22 percent of cases in 1980.

Empowerment of the average Mexican in the press took several forms, from coverage of a protest over fraud at a savings institution to a poll on the Mexico City mayor's approval rating. Empowerment was not always equivalent to "positive" treatment, however, as shown by a story about a mob's attempt to lynch a criminal suspect during the period sampled.

This analysis of press coverage of political figures and societal actors during the last two decades of the PRI regime uncovered three trends in Mexican news production as the country underwent profound societal change. First, the press became much more assertive, autonomous, and diverse in its coverage of the president and other major political actors between 1980 and 2000. Second, while all newspapers moved in the same direction, some newsrooms led change and others followed. A vanguard of civic-oriented newspapers represented by *Reforma* and *La Jornada* emerged in the 1980s and their number expanded in the 1990s with the inclusion of transitional newspapers such as *El Universal*. Third, there were limitations to the adoption of a civic model of journalism. News about actors in the electoral realm and civil society changed most notably. Critical news about the business elite, the church, and the military appeared when the press recorded opposition voices raised in public forums.

5 The Limits to Civic Journalism

Carlos Slim reached the *Forbes* magazine list of billionaires in 1991 after making an important purchase. The owner of a relatively modest stock brokerage, he joined foreign investors as the lead partner in a group that bought the Mexican government's billion-dollar national telephone system, Telmex. As part of the purchase agreement, the presidential administration of Carlos Salinas granted Telmex a seven-year monopoly—free from competition in local service or long-distance calling—so investors could recoup the money they would spend updating the system's infrastructure. It was a good deal for Telmex, as it was for Slim. *Fortune* magazine named Telmex the second-most profitable company in the world in 1995. In the deluge of deregulation and privatization that followed the Telmex sale, Slim acquired important retail chains, one of the world's largest Internet providers, wireless operations, railroads, Mexico City's tallest skyscraper, and forty-five buildings in the capital's historic downtown, where he and a popular leftist mayor, Andrés Manuel López Obrador, sponsored a $2 billion renovation project. Slim's fortune reached $8 billion by the end of the decade (Medina 1995a, 1995b).

Slim became the richest man in Mexico and Latin America in the 1990s. As the century opened, his financial power reverberated through the domestic media. Each public move made by a Slim company received ample coverage. Radio programs broadcast his press conferences live. When he opposed President Fox's economic policy in 2003, his statements dominated front pages. His participation in downtown renovation that year received similar treatment. Aside from Slim's ability to generate news coverage, the billionaire's advertising power cast a long shadow in the newsroom.

A top newspaper editor in Mexico City speaking in 2003 (three years after the PRI lost its hold on the presidency), explained the influence of Slim's holding company, Grupo Carso: "There has been a shift from the government to the corporations in the capacity to influence the media. And the media listen with greater attention to the new groups of companies that pressure them. Now the media don't listen attentively when the government is worried, but they do listen to Grupo Carso, for example. Grupo Carso is a group of businessmen who have about 120 businesses. Carso is a group that is more important for newspapers than the government."[1]

Editors at all of Mexico's largest newspapers made similar comments in interviews in 2003. For example, since *El Universal* took on a more critical edge in the late 1990s, the newspaper has resisted sometimes serious pressure from advertisers in government and the private sector, including big banks. *El Universal* is uniquely secure in Mexico because it carries thirty to forty pages of paid classified advertising daily and is the country's largest-circulation daily newspaper, according to independent studies. When the newspaper entered a direct confrontation with the Zedillo government in 1996, its classified ad base gave managers confidence they could weather a four-month boycott by major government agencies. Similarly, *Reforma* is a financially strong publication that diversifies its advertising base with a goal that no one company or government entity should supply more than about 5 percent of its ads. *Reforma* has suffered "mini boycotts" from advertisers who become angry at the newspaper's coverage. At *La Jornada*, critical coverage of a program called Fobaproa, in which the government took over failed loans to help bail out private banks, caused an ad boycott.

Reporters in these publications and less financially secure newspapers have the impression they must tread lightly when it comes to powerful business owners such as Slim. According to ratings service IBOPE's radio and television survey for 2002, advertising just from Telmex and its cellular phone spinoff Telcel means Slim controls the country's second-largest advertising account (Casteñeda 2003).

Why, and to what degree, did billionaires and a handful of other powerful figures in Mexican society gradually replace the president and top political figures as "untouchable" in the Mexican press? In order to answer these questions, I assess whether the word "untouchable"—traditionally used to describe taboo figures for the media—is still completely accurate. In the pages of the largest circulation, most assertive newspapers in Mexico, the protection once afforded to the untouchables has not disappeared, but is gradually eroding.

This exploration of coverage of the most powerful figures in Mexican society reveals a lot about the reach of the civic transformation of Mexican journalism and, ultimately, what journalism may contribute to the deepening of democratic participation, representation, and accountability in the country. Although civic-oriented newspapers made important changes in journalistic practices during the 1990s, the practices of civic journalism weakened as reporters moved beyond critical and assertive coverage of electoral actors and government into other realms. Billionaires, drug dealers, and especially the Catholic hierarchy seemed more immune from assertive reporting. When criticism of these actors occurred, it was presented through the statements of government officials and candidates rather than reporters' own investigations. In this sense, the critical and pluralistic coverage that existed outside of elections and government was a spillover from greater electoral competition and the opening of political coverage. Ultimately, these barriers to civic-oriented journalism limit the possibility that journalism can promote a deeper democratization of the country.

Did the limited reach of civic newsroom change result from journalists' *un-civic* conceptualizations of legitimate reporting practices, restrictions placed on journalists from within their own news organizations, or pressures on newsrooms emanating from the outside environment? My analysis finds that environmental conditions and internal newsroom restrictions are more important factors. Civic-oriented changes in journalists' views of their roles in politics and society outpaced what media owners or the wider news environment would support in actual practice. In particular, economic vulnerability held back aggressive reporting on new economic elites such as Slim. Physical threats hampered assertive coverage of drug traffickers, and owners' support of the Catholic Church tamed religious coverage.

Why is it important that civic journalism in Mexico and elsewhere reach beyond the coverage of elections and formal political actors in government? Just as liberal democracy requires more than free, fair, and regular elections, the fulfillment of the promise of civic journalism to enhance governmental accountability, political representation, and citizen activism in social and political life requires more than just balanced and assertive reporting about elections and government. Liberal democracy requires the universal application of the rule of law, a degree of equality in political representation and economic opportunity, and the means to hold political representatives accountable for systematic impunity and gross inequality (Diamond 1999; Foweraker and Krznaric 2002; Mainwaring 1999; Vilas 1997).

In much of the world, however, journalists do not contribute as they might to making democracy more accountable, representative, and citizen-based by covering the range of actors and issues important to society. To paraphrase Robert Entman (1989), today's world has a growing number of democracies without full citizens. Journalists' contribution to this situation may stem from adverse physical environments, conflicting organizational imperatives, or alternative worldviews that constrict the boundaries of what is considered legitimate journalism. In other words, twenty-five years after a wave of democracy began to sweep the globe, journalists rarely have the physical, organizational, *and* cognitive liberty to pursue a civic mission.[2]

Three questions about the reach of civic journalism in Mexico arise from this discussion: Is coverage of powerful figures assertive and critical? How does coverage of new and old "untouchables" compare? Why does this pattern of coverage occur, or more specifically, how might environmental, organizational, and cognitive factors, separately or in unison, explain coverage patterns?

The New Untouchables?

Table 5.1 compares front-page treatment of powerful figures in three newspapers known for producing more civic-oriented news in the late 1990s: *Reforma, La Jornada,* and *El Universal.* It presents the results of a content analysis assessing whether the newspapers treated these figures positively, negatively, neutrally, or in a balanced manner. The analysis compares treatment of electoral and governmental actors from the PRI and the opposition, figures traditionally known as the untouchables of the press (the Catholic Church, the armed forces, and the president), and two new candidates for untouchable status (business elites and drug traffickers, or *narcos*).[3] I included business elites and *narcos* in the list because their power grew to new heights during the 1980s and 1990s as market-based economic reforms and changes in drug transportation routes created great fortunes and eroded state enforcement capacity. The analyzed coverage appeared on a random series of twelve sequential dates in 2000. Coding of positive and negative treatment considered the language used to describe the actor; whether the actor's version of events was contradicted or accepted without question; the position and space the actor received in the story; and whether there was an implied criticism in the choice of language. Balanced treatment presented both positive and negative information. Treatment was considered neutral when neither positive nor negative information was given.

Table 5.1 Press Treatment of Powerful Figures

	Positive (%)	Negative (%)	Balanced (%)	Neutral (%)	Total Sample(%)
Church	57	14	14	14	5
Military	50	50	0	0	5
President	47	12	29	12	13
Opposition party	38	12	31	19	20
Business elites	33	20	33	13	11
Opposition government	29	13	37	21	16
PRI	16	32	32	19	23
Drug traffickers	0	100	0	0	7
Average	34	31	22	12	
n = 132					

Sources: Data taken from *Reforma, La Jornada,* and *El Universal*

The results show that critical coverage varied in intensity depending on the actor in question. The church essentially retained its untouchable status. Church coverage was positive or neutral 71 percent of the time. The presidential figure was challenged within coverage that was balanced or negative in 41 percent of stories, but was positive or neutral in 59 percent. The newspapers criticized the military more often: 50 percent of military coverage was openly negative, while 50 percent was positive. The norm was censorship by omission, however, especially when compared to political parties and government. With the exception of the president, who, by 2000, was immersed in the strident debates of electoral politics, the traditionally untouchable church and military rarely received front-page press coverage at all.

Coverage of drug traffickers and the business elite was more negative. All of the coverage about drug traffickers was negative, while 20 percent of coverage of business elites was openly negative and 33 percent contained negative elements within a balanced presentation. Like the traditional untouchables, newspapers reported much less frequently on these actors as compared to electoral actors.

Does press assertiveness or growing criticism in society explain the unfavorable coverage of drug traffickers, the military, and to a lesser degree, business elites? A closer look at the reporting that produced the coverage shows the press was reflecting wider society rather than assertively seeking out critical information about these powerful actors. Table 5.2 presents the results of an analysis of whether newspapers or outside actors set the agenda for their front-page news coverage. Newspapers were considered to have set the agenda when they sought out an interview on a critical subject and chose

Table 5.2 Press Agenda Setting

News Target	Outside Actor (%)	Newspaper (%)
Drug traffickers	89	11
Church	86	14
Military	83	17
Opposition party	73	24
Business elites	73	27
PRI	65	29
President	58	35
Opposition governments	48	52
Average	72	27
n= 132		

Sources: Data taken from *Reforma, La Jornada,* and *El Universal*

the subject; when they changed the frame of an event organized by an outside actor by adding additional perspectives; and when they followed an orchestrated event but included a conflicting perspective.

The results found that passivity remained extreme. The most civic-oriented newspapers in Mexico set the agenda in only 27 percent of coverage of powerful political and social actors. They were most assertive when writing about governments headed by members of opposition parties and the president, but they were very passive when reporting about drug traffickers, the church, and the military. Newspapers were twice as likely to set the agenda in news about political figures (35 percent) than in news about societal actors (17 percent).[4] Only coverage of opposition political parties, which reporters essentially followed on the campaign trail, appeared to be a partial exception to the trend of relative reportorial assertiveness. When the press was assertive, which was relatively rare, it was responding to greater debate in the country's increasingly pluralistic political setting rather than leading societal change. Meanwhile, assertiveness in coverage of electoral actors did not spill over into coverage of other powerful figures.

The reporting techniques for articles that presented business owners, drug traffickers, the military, and the church negatively support the notion that journalists were reflecting criticism and debate in other public spaces, rather than taking the initiative. All of the critical depictions of business elites were based on presidential candidates' condemnations of bankers that were made in public campaign forums.[5] This answers the question of why, if advertisers are considered powerful, criticism of them appears in the news pages. Four of the nine negative stories about drug dealers also resulted from the establishment of competitive politics in Mexico. Three articles came from presidential campaign events and one from an interview with an opposition government official. The remainder of the negative coverage came from law enforcement press conferences and releases, a U.S. congressman, and two breaking news events. For example, David Aponte and José Gil's story in *La Jornada* on March 1, 2000, "Fox: Drug Traffickers are in the PRI; Labastida Demands Proof," was an exchange of charges between the PAN and PRI presidential candidates on the campaign trail. Rene Gardner's story in *Reforma* on March 9, 2000, following the assassination of Tijuana's police chief, "They are Hiring Assassins to Destabilize," came from a press conference.[6] However, the newspapers gave ample space to the coverage, especially of the assassination in Tijuana, even if they did not investigate drug trafficking themselves.

The press was more assertive in its criticism of the military because of individual initiatives of reporters. *La Jornada* was known for its extensive and sympathetic coverage of the Zapatista rebellion in Chiapas. Its correspondent, Hermann Bellinghausen, wrote two articles that reported the rebels' unanswered criticisms of the military. Justino Miranda of *El Universal* reported the accusations of an opposition party legislator.[7]

Like critical coverage of the military, criticism of the church seemed to respond to ideological and organizational imperatives. In the only item that presented the church in a negative fashion, the censure was delivered as a barb rather than a direct criticism. A caption accompanying a photo of a topless Río de Janeiro carnival dancer in *La Jornada* noted that the Brazilian church was monitoring carnival activities to make sure no religious symbols were used in the debauchery. This dig probably responds to *La Jornada*'s liberal stance on issues of sexuality and religion. In a more balanced article, *El Universal* praised a new papal nuncio, but also reported that church leaders argued behind the scenes over his appointment. In this article, one of the newspaper's top political reporters shared a byline with the religion reporter and probably contributed to its process-oriented approach.[8]

The Power of the Peso

While it is true that advertisers needed Mexico's elite newspapers to target upper-income consumers, a handful of wealthy families and corporations had the power to place enormous pressure on the Mexican media through their control of large chunks of private sector ad spending. During the last twenty years, Mexico's economic model shifted from state-led capitalism to a more market-based approach. This included the sale of more than one thousand state-owned corporations and the deregulation of banking and telecommunications, among other industries. As a result, family-owned companies and multinational corporations replaced the government as the principal advertisers in the media. Private sector advertisers provided 88 percent of total media advertising in Mexico between 1999 and 2002, the first period for which government figures were made public.[9]

Mexican economic reform was implemented in a way that created advertising powerhouses rather than dispersing advertising control widely through the private sector. Market-based reforms sprouted a bumper crop of billionaires through the 1990s. Thirty-four Mexican individuals and families appeared for the first time on the *Forbes* list of the world's billionaires between 1987 and 2000. Twelve of those companies accounted for one-third of all private sector advertising on Mexican radio and television. Print advertising was similarly concentrated.[10] Most voting stock in Mexican companies is controlled by individuals or families, even though non-voting stock or stock with limited voting power is traded publicly. This gives chairmen of the board substantial control of company operations, including ad purchases.

Table 5.3 lists Mexico's top ten advertising moguls for 2002. Together they controlled $1.23 billion of a $3.69 billion advertising market, considering the country's top fifty broadcasting advertisers. Print advertising figures are not compiled publicly, but newspaper executives consulted privately say the list is essentially the same. The leading advertiser in Mexico is billionaire Eugenio Garza Laguera, the patriarch of a powerful Monterrey industrial family and chairman of the board of the company controlling Latin America's largest Coca-Cola distributor. If all of Slim's holdings were considered in the IBOPE list, Grupo Carso—which includes among its many holdings 60 percent of Sears Roebuck de México, 90 percent of General Tire de México, and 51 percent of the Sanborns chain of pharmacies and restaurants—would probably surpass Garza's holdings. On this list, Slim is the country's second-largest advertiser. The third-largest advertiser is Lorenzo Servitje, the billionaire owner of the country's largest bread maker, Bimbo, and a supporter of the conservative National Action Party (PAN). In addition to these companies, Mexican editors report that banks are big advertisers that have used their combined financial power to pressure newspapers.[11]

While most newspapers cannot survive on circulation alone, Mexican newspaper circulation is low by international standards, making these publications even more dependent on advertising revenue. During the recession of the mid-1990s, circulation dropped about 20 percent and, compared to 1994, popular tabloids either didn't exist or didn't bring in enough readers or advertisers to matter much until after 2000. In the early 2000s, Mexico City's largest dailies each sold about 100,000 copies daily. Including popular tab-

Table 5.3 Broadcast Advertising Giants

Name	Wealth (billions of U.S.$, latest year)	Year Entered Forbes List	Economic Sector of Holdings	Advertiser Controlled	Advertising Rank[a] and Expenditure (millions of U.S.$)
Eugenio Garza Laguera	$2.0 (2000)	1993	Soft drinks, beer, banking	Coca-Cola Femsa, Cervecería Cuauhtémoc, Grupo Financiero BBVA Bancomer	1 / $287
Carlos Slim Domit	$7.9 (2000)	1991	Telecommunications, television, retail, other	Telmex, Radiomovil Dipsa / Telcel and 50% Phillip Morris de México	2 / $258
Lorenzo Servitje and family	$1.2 (1994)	1993	Baked goods	Grupo Bimbo	3 / $194
Angel Losada Gómez	$1.4 (1994)	1993	Retail	Grupo Gigante	4 / $117
Enrique Molina Sobrino and family	$1.4 (1994)	1993	Soft drinks	Pepsi-Gemexa[b]	5 / $115
Pablo Aramburuzabala Ocaranza/ María Asunción Aramburuzabala	$1.4 (1996)/ $1 (2000)	1993	Beer, television	Grupo Modelo	6 / $67
Ricardo Salinas Pliego	$3.2 (1998)	1994	Appliance store chain, TV network	Grupo Elektra	7 / $55
Roberto González Barrera	$1.7 (1997)	1994	Food, baking	Grupo Financiero Banorte	8 / $50
Alberto Bailleres	$1.98 (1996)	1993	Mining, banking, ranching, department store	Palacio de Hierro Department Store	11 / $41
Bernardo Garza Sada and family and Eugenio Garza Laguera	$2 (1993)	1987	Insurance company, beer, beverages, industrial conglomerate	Sigma Alimentos	13 / $37
Jerónimo y Placido Arrango	$1 (1992)	1992	Retail	Wal-Mart	15 / $35
Carlos Peralta and family	$2.5 (1996)	1994	Telecommunications, manufacturing	Iusacell	16 / $30

Notes: a Advertising Rank excludes multinational corporations.

b Pepsi Bottling Company bought control of Molina's Pepsi-Gemex in 2002. See Aguilar (2002).

Sources: Forbes magazine billionaires lists 1990–2000; IBOPE advertising rankings for radio and television in 2002; and company information posted online or at the Mexican Stock Market Web page www.bmv.com.mx. The *Forbes* list is reproduced in Casteñeda (2003). Rankings for press advertisers are not compiled, but the order should be similar to television. Advertisers spend more than ten dollars in the broadcast media for every dollar they spend in newspapers, according to the Mexican Association of Advertising Agencies (AMAP) (see www.cirt.com.mx/inversionpublicitaria.html).

Table 5.4 Distribution of Household Monetary Income (% of GDP)

	1984	1994	% Change (Relative)	% Change (Absolute)
Poorest 10%	1.3	1.0	-22.3	-23.2
Second 10%	2.7	2.3	-15.3	-15.9
Third 10%	3.8	3.3	-13.0	-11.9
Fourth 10%	4.9	4.3	-13.4	-14.4
Fifth 10%	6.2	5.4	-13.7	-14.7
Sixth 10%	7.8	6.7	-14.9	-15.9
Seventh 10%	9.8	8.4	-14.1	-15.0
Eighth 10%	12.8	11.2	-12.3	-13.3
Ninth 10%	17.0	16.3	-3.9	-5.0
Richest 10%	33.8	41.2	22.3	20.8
Gini index	.4535	.5137		

Sources: Instituto Nacional de Estadística Geográfia e Informática (INEGI), Encuesta Nacional de Ingresos y Gastos de los Hogares [National survey of income and household expenses]; cited in Russell (1997, 30).

loids, *Reforma* sold about 200,000 daily and *El Universal* sold about 300,0000 daily in either period, Mexico City newspaper circulation was a fraction of the circulation of the biggest newspapers in the world's other largest cities.

Even though Mexico's government support of marginal newspapers shrunk throughout the 1990s, the number of newspapers competing for scarce readers remained large. The opening of new papers financed by businessmen, rather than politicians, outpaced the closure of insolvent newspapers. Meanwhile, the pool of potential readers remained stagnant. As privatization of state enterprises created new billionaires, the rest of the Mexican population earned less and less in absolute terms. Between 1984 and 1994, the absolute income of the wealthiest 10 percent of the population increased by 20.8 percent, while income declined for Mexicans at every other economic level. Table 5.4 presents changes in household income based on Mexican government studies in 1984 and 1994 (Russell 1997). Other studies, through 2000, report similar results (Camp 2002b). As concentration of wealth increased, poverty persisted. Ten years after entering the North American Free Trade Agreement, the government reported that 62 percent of the population was living beneath the poverty line in Mexico City. When a newspaper costs one-sixth of the minimum daily salary, and about the same as a liter of milk, poverty is an obvious drag on circulation growth.[12]

In interviews from 1999 to 2003, Mexican journalists reported acute awareness of the economic structure of their society. Executive editors stated that advertisers do not have great influence on publications—despite occasional pressures—but a substantial percentage of reporters in my survey of independent publications in 1999 believes otherwise. Whether reporters' impressions were accurate or overly guarded, the end result was the same: cautious coverage. Reporters and editors said in interviews that they had learned to tread carefully with important advertisers.

By the end of the 1990s, newspapers still tended to report negative stories about Mexico's billionaires only when the information came to light in public places, such as the congressional and partisan debates over the bank bailout program Fobaproa. For instance, Slim received critical coverage only when a Citibank vice president testified in a U.S. Senate hearing in November 1999 that the brother of Mexico's president Carlos Salinas invested heavily in the telephone company privatized by the president. Slim was the majority shareholder of the newly privatized company, implying an under-the-table deal during the bidding process. The Mexican press reported the testimony, but no investigative reports followed.[13] The other type of story that contained critical information about Slim reported competitors' complaints about unfair competition from Telmex. Typically, coverage of Slim neutrally traced his companies' financial movements, announced his latest purchases, positively reported his philanthropic efforts, and, in 2003, publicized his criticisms of the government's lackluster economic policy.[14]

My survey of 126 journalists found 29 occasions during which they perceived their stories had been withheld because of internal censorship. Stories about business owners (7) and government figures (7) were most often withheld. Following that, stories about the president (4), the army (2), the church (1), a religious charity (1), drug traffickers (1), the political opposition (1), sexuality (1), police (1), a public university (1), "people at the newspaper" (1), and the newspaper owner (1) were withheld, in the eyes of reporters.

How journalists learned to treat business figures more cautiously was evidenced in a variety of ways. The editor of a political magazine published by a major Mexican newspaper recounted the first.[15] The magazine editor stated he brought the proposed cover to the newspaper's editor-in-chief for approval, per the usual procedure. The editor had placed seven Mexicans featured in *Forbes* magazine's 1998 list of billionaires in cartooned turbans and headlined the story, "The Sultans Want More." The newspaper's editor left the text untouched, but changed the drawing and headlines and changed the cover to reflect a story about the presidential succession in the ruling PRI. The magazine editor said he learned the lesson: "Careful with things about Slim and (television magnate Ricardo) Salinas Pliego. . . . The parameters in which we can write include less control over the texts, but there is still control over headlines, leads, and the subheadlines because this is what people see."

A young reporter at a financial newspaper reached similar conclusions when a cement company threatened to sue the publication because of a story quoting analysts criticizing the company's financial health.[16] The newspaper failed to support him, and although the facts in the story were correct, the paper ran a correction. The reporter said the incident changed the way he approached his work: "I realized that in newspapers, or at least where I worked, big business governs the reporting manual and one should be more cautious."

Other reporters remember being instructed not to cover billionaire Lorenzo Sambrano, politically connected businessman Carlos Hank Rhon, politically connected construction company Gutsa, and others identified only as "businessmen who buy advertising."

Executive editors, while downplaying the actual influence of advertisers on coverage, still felt pressured. Banks banded together in 2003 to pressure *El Universal, Reforma,* and *La Jornada* to tone down critical and assertive coverage of Fobaproa. This program involved the takeover of government loans made in the 1990s to wealthy individuals and companies as part of the government's $12.5 billion bank bailout.[17] The scandals associated with these loans, which played out before the public in Congress and in partisan debates, was thoroughly covered and sometimes aggressively investigated by civic-oriented newspapers. *El Universal*'s editor stated that despite the threats to cut off advertising in his newspaper, individual banks ultimately decided not to go along with the proposed boycott: "They said *El Universal* brings me clients. *El Universal* brings me accounts."[18] Leading editors at *Reforma* and *La Jornada* reported similar pressures from the banks over their coverage of Fobaproa. One *La Jornada* editor stated, "We latched onto the issue from the beginning and never let go. This ripped the cover off the involvement of a series of very important companies and banking institutions. A lot withdrew their ads . . . (Banamex) got very angry with *La Jornada* and never returned. But we have to bear this burden because in the end the duty of the news media is to inform."[19]

While journalists are keenly aware of the billionaires' financial power, they reject the notion that press subservience is either an appropriate or natural relationship with business elites. In other words, the cautious coverage of Mexico's wealthiest seems to stem from a lack of ability to report critically about these powerful societal actors rather than a lack of will. In my survey of newspaper journalists, 81 percent thought journalists' relationships with businessmen should be "independent," "impartial," or "critical." Only 19 percent believed the relationship should be "cautious," "respectful," or "considerate." When probed about the latter responses, the journalists said that they had learned through experiences, such as those noted above, to take this approach. Responding to a separate question, only 50 percent of respondents stated that they believed the media lived up to their responsibility in reporting about business owners.

The Pen and the Cross

The Catholic Church holds a special place in Mexican history. Along with physical subjugation by the conquistadors, Mexico's ample indigenous population faced cultural conquest at the hands of the friars, who arrived holding an exclusive contract for evangelization with the Spanish crown. Many of the oldest churches in Mexico stand atop pre-Hispanic temples, a brick-and-mortar manifestation of the cultural component of the Spanish conquest. From colonization on, the names of Catholic saints have peppered the maps and the festival calendars of the country. The political influence of the Catholic Church was as strong as its cultural impact. The chief advisor to the viceroy of New Spain was almost always the archbishop. While the struggle for independence in the United States was led by landowners, priests led Mexico's independence armies in the early 1800s. With this political and cultural power came economic wealth in the form of vast land holdings. Despite reforms in the mid-1800s, the church continued to run many of the country's schools and to control huge land tracts until the 1910 Revolution. The postrevolutionary regime then slashed the political and economic power of the church, but not its cultural influence. The regime denied priests the vote until 1992, and the Mexican Constitution prohibits priests from using the pulpit in favor of a political candidate (a prohibition that was not always observed after elections became competitive in the mid-1980s). Yet most Mexicans identify themselves as Catholic, and much of the population rejects the Revolution's distrust of the church. Conservative Party presidential candidate Vicente Fox's embrace of a standard of the Virgin of Guadalupe during a campaign rally in 2000 created an uproar in some circles, but a similar standard appeared in the PRI campaign of 1994, and its use by Fox appealed to much of his constituency.[20]

Catholicism's cultural triumph in Mexico remains apparent among an important slice of the electorate. Mexican pollster Alejandro Moreno found that 73 percent of Mexicans identify themselves as Catholic, although a much smaller percent actually go to church regularly. Only 19 percent of Mexicans tell pollsters they belong to no religion. Religious fervor is an influence on voters, the most religious of whom tend to vote for the conservative PAN or the PRI (Moreno 2003, 59). Journalists at Mexico's more independent

Table 5.5 Perception of Freedom to Report Critically

Actor	Very Free	Somewhat or Not at All Free
Church	46.4	53.6
Military	48.1	51.9
Drug traffickers	53.7	46.3
President	54.9	45.1
Bankers who loaned money to the newspaper	58.4	41.6
Politicians who bought ads with the newspaper	73.7	26.3
Government	79.3	20.7
n=122		

newspapers tend to identify less with the church than other Mexicans, but 59 percent of those I surveyed reported practicing a religion. As with Mexicans generally, journalists in the north of the country are most likely to be religious.

The Catholic Church was the actor that journalists felt most restricted in reporting about, even more so than billionaires, drug traffickers, or any other social actor. Only the military came close. With the exception of the president, journalists identified electoral actors as those they felt most free to criticize. Table 5.5 reports these perceptions.

Even though they might not feel able to cover the church freely, most journalists believe the church should be covered assertively. Two-thirds of journalists in my survey believed that journalists should be "critical," "impartial," or "independent" when reporting on church matters. The percentage of respondents who said the media should be "cautious," "respectful," or "considerate" with the church was higher than with other powerful social actors, suggesting an ideological explanation for the tentativeness in coverage of the church. Yet this was not the explanation offered by the 41 percent of journalists who believed the media did not live up to their responsibility in covering the church. Journalists thought that the media treated the church gingerly because journalists report passively in general and follow conservative owners' dictates regarding religious coverage. The latter explanation makes more sense, because the general tendency toward passive reporting does not explain why the church would be treated more gingerly than other powerful figures. Moreover, two editors with the authority to make story assignments at *El Universal* and *Reforma* stated confidentially that owners' religious preferences explained caution when covering the church. "The church is a big issue," said one. "I think it's a sensitive issue, because of readers and the owner, but I feel satisfied with what we have done." Ideology could have played a role in taming coverage of the Catholic Church for a minority of journalists, but restrictions from owners seemed to be a more powerful explanation.[21]

The Perils of Drug Reporting

Tijuana newspaper publisher Francisco Ortiz Franco had just picked up his children from school when a gunman stepped up to his car, emptied four rounds into his head, neck, and chest, and claimed his life in just five seconds on June 22, 2004. Ortiz was three hundred meters from a police station when he died. This was the second leader of the assertive newsweekly *Zeta* to be gunned down in the publication's relatively short history. Editor Héctor Félix Miranda was shot and killed by drug dealers in 1988. Executive editor Jesús Blancornelas narrowly escaped a street ambush in 1997; his bodyguard died. Following Ortiz's murder, the newspaper quickly pointed the finger at either the Gulf Coast Drug Cartel or local racetrack owner Jorge Hank Rhon, who was PRI candidate for mayor at the time of Ortiz's death. Ortiz had met with a committee of international newspaper editors and government prosecutors two months earlier to reopen the investigation into Miranda's murder, and had written articles pointing to Hank Rhon as the mastermind of the killing. On the other hand, his investigative articles often targeted the cartel (Blancornelas 2004; Inter-American Press Association 2004). Blancornelas doubted authorities would solve the murder of his colleague, despite their quick offer of a million-peso reward for information. "A million pesos won't safeguard anyone from the vengeance of drug traffickers," Blancornelas said. He added, "the complicity of police and criminals" would prevent the guilty from being punished (Gómez and Martínez 2004).

The murder of a journalist is an extreme example of the climate of violence in which drug reporting is conducted in Mexico, but the impunity and connection to politicians are typical of the pressures faced by reporters who cover crime, corruption, and trafficking. They constitute a third barrier to the practice of an assertive, pluralistic, and independent form of journalism in Mexico.

Drug trafficking in Mexico began in a serious way when gangsters took over the U.S. government-sponsored cultivation of poppies for morphine production during World War II. A heroin trade developed after the war ended, but three decades later was eclipsed. In the 1970s, marijuana production expanded in rural Mexico and Mexican traffickers became powerful in many regions of the country, carving out territories that at times remain outside the reach of security forces. Presidential candidates kept their traveling campaigns outside of some areas of the state of Guerrero, for example, where drug traffickers were known to control passage. The wealth and corruptive power of these same drug barons swelled even more in the 1980s, when Mexican marijuana smugglers took on a new product: cocaine. As increased U.S. drug enforcement in the Caribbean pushed cocaine-laden airplanes westward, Mexico became the principal trans-shipment point of U.S.-bound cocaine. Despite heightened enforcement, 65 percent of the cocaine reaching the United States still passes through Mexico (Levy and Bruhn 2002; Bureau for International Narcotics and Law Enforcement Affairs 2003).

Drug revenues in Mexico reached astronomical heights and, as elsewhere, a percentage of the profits bought protection. Politicians, police commanders, and army generals have been offered a choice—*plata o plomo*, silver or lead. Both corruption and violence have ensued. Examples of those who chose *plata* abounded—in 2002 alone, Mexican military courts convicted two army generals of drug corruption; the military arrested an entire battalion of forty soldiers for allegedly protecting drug crops; federal agents arrested twenty-five midlevel personnel from police agencies and the military for suspicion of passing information to drug traffickers (Bureau for International Narcotics and Law Enforcement Affairs 2003). As for *plomo,* the U.S. Drug Enforcement Agency reported that drug traffickers murdered four federal officials in 2002; in the same year, the U.S. Consulate in Nuevo Laredo reported that eighteen active and former police officers were murdered, kidnapped, or wounded in drug-related shootings. Another spate of violence occurred in early 2004, when officials found eleven cadavers in a common grave, all executed during a drug gang war along the border. Officials attributed the assassination of two federal agents in Mexico City a few days earlier to the same turf war. The U.S. Drug Enforcement Agency has reported on the particularly public and brutal nature of the violence in Mexico:

> Many narco-assassinations in Mexico take place using assault weapons, such as AK-47s and AR-15s. These weapons are often used during high-profile drive-by shootings and other executions. Victims are sometimes kidnapped and then murdered, and their remains dumped along roadsides or in isolated desert areas. In addition, many drug-related murders are characterized by heinous acts of torture, including severe beatings, burnings, the severing of body parts, and other gruesome tortures. Drug-related violence is prevalent in the states of Baja California, Nuevo Leon, Tamaulipas, and Sinaloa due to ongoing struggles between groups rivaling for control of these strategic drug producing and transit regions. For example, the Mexican press reported that Tijuana, Baja California, saw 249 violent deaths among the general public in 2002, of which at least 70 percent of those deaths were drug related. The Mexican press also reported that 25

executions occurred in the state of Nuevo Leon during 2002 (U.S. Drug Enforcement Agency 2003).

The same silver-or-lead dilemma applies to journalists who report too much about drug trafficking. Rumors swirled in 1993 after newspapers reported that Mexican attorney general Jorge Carpizo supposedly had a list of *narcoperiodistas*, or narcojournalists who aid drug traffickers, but no list was ever made public. On the other hand, traffickers certainly have used lead to silence journalists. Except for Colombia, Mexico was the most dangerous place in Latin America to practice journalism in the 1990s. Reporters wore bulletproof vests to work along the northern border, the scene of numerous trafficker turf wars. The drug beat reporter at *El Universal*, along with reporters from Colombia and elsewhere, received training in 2003 usually reserved for combat reporters.

It is difficult to obtain precise numbers of threats against journalists directly related to drug trafficking. In 1998, 30 percent of the 202 threats against journalists reported by the Mexican Network for the Protection of Journalists were made in connection with crime reporting (Martínez, Pineda, and Martínez 1999). Yet it is often difficult to disentangle threatening drug dealers from corrupt police forces and politicians. Several cases of violence committed against journalists attest to this. The Inter-American Press Association has suggested that border journalist Víctor Manuel Oropeza was killed in 1991 because of his columns alleging connections between local police and drug traffickers.[22] There is little doubt that drug traffickers murdered *La Prensa* reporter Benjamín Flores González in 1997 on the steps of his newspaper offices in San Luís Río Colorado, a town on the Sonoran border with Arizona. Among other articles, Flores had published stories about a half-ton of cocaine that had "disappeared" from Federal Judicial Police offices in his hometown.[23]

Pressure on journalists from drug traffickers is not always so lethal, but can still cause an effective pall over assertive reporting. The publisher of an otherwise assertive daily newspaper in central Mexico stopped covering drug trafficking beyond reporting from police press statements after gunmen rifled his newsroom following a series of stories on a mysterious plane crash in his state. In Mexico City, a reporter at a major daily asked for his beat to be changed when drug dealers summoned him to a meeting in one of the many Denny's-like "VIPS" restaurants dotting the city. A crime reporter for another major newspaper in the capital commented: "I am worried about how much the media here in Mexico are prepared to confront issues related to drug trafficking . . . I think the media owners and the editors really don't know what to do."[24]

The influence that drug traffickers have wielded on newspaper content is evident in journalists' responses to questions in my survey about whether they were ever threatened on the job. One-quarter of the 126 journalists reported that they had been threatened at some time in their careers. Stories about drug trafficking and crime produced half of the thirty-two threats, while political corruption and politics produced most of the others.

Analysis of press coverage and journalistic beliefs suggests that the limited reach of civic journalism in Mexico is a response to pressures on journalists rather than their normative concepts of proper behavior. The power of advertisers in the newsroom (real or perceived), internal pressures from conservative media owners, and external threats of drug-related violence prevent the full expression of civic journalism. In other words, the evidence presented thus far suggests that journalists have more will than means to cover powerful figures outside of the electoral and governmental arenas in a critical, plural, and assertive fashion.

An exploration of journalists' commitment to professional autonomy provides more support for that argument. I asked journalists whether they would accept a job that, at least in appearance, would compromise their autonomy as a journalist. Specifically, I asked if they would accept a temporary job working for a politician and then return to journalism.[25] A majority, 52 percent, said they would never work for a politician even if they formally, temporarily separated from their job in journalism (n=114). However, 24 percent said they would do it for financial reasons and another 24 percent said it was correct behavior and they would do it without question. When asked whether they would work for a candidate, without mentioning a return to journalism, 63 percent said they would never do it, 30 percent said they could do it, and 7 percent said they had done it.

Half of journalists, then, would reject accepting a job, even temporarily, that might reflect adversely on their professional autonomy. About one-fourth viewed temporary outside work as normatively correct. Low salaries, rather than normative acceptance explain the conditional acceptance of the remaining quarter of journalists. Those who said they could work for a campaign or a candidate for financial reasons were the worst-paid among the reporters and editors in my sample. They made 10–13 percent less, on average, than those who said they would never work for a campaign or candidate. Moreover, there may be long-term financial incentives for gaining experience in politics and returning to journalism. Journalists who had worked on campaigns at some point in their careers made 13 percent more than those who said they could work in a political campaign at some time in the future.

An oft-repeated hypothesis among Mexican journalists is that younger generations brought new norms to reporting in the 1990s. While this might be true, financial pressures could overwhelm value commitments to autonomy among the young. Refusal to compromise journalistic autonomy by working in politics actually increased, not decreased, with age. Journalists over forty were less likely to support working for a campaign.[26] This could be because older journalists in the survey earned more and did not feel financial pressure to work outside of journalism, or because older journalists who would work in politics had already left the profession and were not captured in the sample. On the other hand, neither the strength nor the direction of ideological preferences predicted a willingness to work even temporarily in a job that might compromise professional autonomy as a journalist.

Convictions are strongly held among journalists who reject work that might compromise their professional autonomy. An important number of groundbreaking journalists have faced great financial risk to act in coherence with values privileging professional autonomy. In several cases—*Excélsior* in Mexico City (1976), *ABC* in Tijuana (1979), *Unomásuno* in Mexico City (1983–1984), and *Siglo 21* in Guadalajara (1997)—entire staffs walked out the door when newspaper owners or the government compromised a publication's independence.

My survey also found that such strong commitment to professional autonomy was common. Respondents were asked in an open-ended question why they had left each of their previous jobs. More than one-quarter, 27 percent, left a previous publication because they felt their autonomy had been compromised in some way. This is a conservative measure, since some reporters and editors who quit their jobs could not, or would not, continue in journalism and so were not captured in the sample. By comparison, only 7 percent reported leaving a job to obtain a higher salary.

The journalists left previous jobs when faced with (in order of frequency):
- government intervention in the publication and changes in the editorial line in favor of the government;
- internal newsroom practices viewed as corrupt;
- internal censorship of information about the president;
- internal censorship of information about the military and the Zapatista guerillas;
- use of paid information on the news pages;
- pressure over negative coverage of a cement company;
- pressure over coverage of a politically sensitive criminal case;

- pressure over coverage of a strike; and
- an editor's attempt to use a reporter's work to hurt a political enemy.

These journalists voiced an uncompromising commitment to professional autonomy and were willing to go to great lengths to protect their independence, including leaving their jobs during economically insecure times. Sometimes they found other outlets in which to express their version of journalism and society. We cannot know how many left journalism for good.

The evidence suggests that journalists' desire to become more critical and assertive in coverage of political and societal actors drove civic change, but was not always enough to overcome barriers to the full civic transformation of the press. In other words, the creation of new civic-oriented professional identities drove journalistic change where the environment and organizational dynamics were at least permissive. However, the editorial dictates of media owners and the incentives and pressures of broader economic and social conditions limited the reach of civic change to the increasingly competitive spheres of electoral politics and government.

6 How Institutional Entrepreneurs Created Civic Newsrooms

The establishment of a new style of journalism in Mexico was based on a civic orientation that encouraged citizen knowledge and participation in politics. Oppositional values and alternative ideas about journalism changed the professional identities of a cadre of newsroom change agents. In a few cases, change agents were able to take control of their newsrooms prior to political and economic liberalization in the 1990s and remake them in a conscious effort to rework the publications' organization cultures. Once liberalization began, the new civic style diffused to organizations that either were founded in the image of the civic vanguard or implemented comprehensive programs of cultural retooling. The diffusion stage responded to the new environment of news production as well as the work of change agents and the creation of new professional identities among a larger group of journalists. Successful civic newspapers opened new affiliates or, in a few cases, transitional newspapers mimicked the example set by civic-oriented pioneers that had gained financial ascendancy, legitimacy, and prestige in the liberalizing setting. The leadership of newsroom change agents was key to media transformations during both civic emergence and diffusion. These publishers, editors, and groups of reporters responded to oppositional political values and alternative visions of the role of journalists in society.

The creation of Mexico's civic-oriented press was a process of institutional transformation occurring in two stages: emergence in an unfriendly societal environment and diffusion in a progressively more supportive macrosetting.

Civic Newspaper Emergence

During the period of civic newspaper emergence in the 1970s and 1980s, economic and political conditions were restrictive-to-hostile toward civic journalism.[1] While the wary eye of the federal government paid less attention to newspapers outside Mexico City, local politicians sometimes attacked newspapers that published critical news in the provinces.[2] Economic conditions made newspapers' financial independence difficult all over the country. Despite the harsh environment, table 6.1 shows that young publishers, editors, and groups of reporters created early civic newspapers by transforming their newsrooms. Less frequently, they founded newspapers based on civic tenets. In the diffusion stage, civic newspapers were more often founded as direct extensions of the civic pioneers. The table is based on interviews with members of each newspaper, press analysts, and the author's reading of the publications (Lara Klahr 2005; Riva Palacio 1991, 1994; Torres 1997).

The government was a major player in the economy in the 1970s and 1980s. Newspapers relied on advertising from government agencies and state-owned companies, which reached up to 80 percent, according to newspaper owner Juan Franciso Ealy Ortiz in a 2004 interview. As a private industry that was protected and promoted by the state, publications also received subsidies for newsprint and other imported inputs. The federal government also looked the other way at times when newspapers missed payments on taxes or workers' healthcare plans (Riva Palacio 1991, 1994).

If the government was a key player in the economy, it was the only player in politics. The ruling PRI and its ancillary organizations dominated political activity at the federal, state, and local levels. Opposition voices were considered "radical" and "anti-Mexico" (Bailey 1988). The personality cult of the president in office remained powerful, and his use of "meta-constitutional" powers for policymaking, cooptation, and repression was contested only in narrow spheres (Cornelius 1996). As Mexican magazine publisher Héctor Aguilar Camín stated in 1991, "In this republic, you don't say no to the president . . . presidentialism is like a habit of our soul" (Dresser 1994, 160).

Secretive, competing networks called *camarillas* permeated the PRI system and extended informally to high-powered journalists. A politician leading a *camarilla* distributed and collected favors based on patron-client ties emphasizing loyalty and reciprocity. The "friendship" that clique membership produced was based on career ascendance and material rewards. The president headed the network of cliques, but other top politicians led overlapping, competing groups at multiple levels (Camp 1986, 18–19, 178–79).

Journalists fit nicely into this organizational scheme. *Camarillas* turned

Table 6.1 Change Processes in Civic Newspapers

First Wave: Emergence

Newspaper	Date of Substantial Change	Created from Transformation or Founding	Mechanisms
El Norte	1971	Transformation	· Young publisher takes over · International exposure · Hiring nonjournalists · Extensive training · Ethics code
A.M.	1980	Transformation	· Young publisher takes over · International exposure · Training · Ethics code · Influenced by El Norte
Zeta	1980	Founding	· International exposure · Personnel network links with defunct independent newspaper (ABC)
El Financiero	1981	Founding	· Hiring nonjournalists · Personnel network links to defunct civic newspapers (Unomásuno, Excélsior)
El Diario de Yucatán		Transformation	· Catholic, conservative ownership always had oppositional stance · Professional links to the Dallas Morning News and other first wave newspapers, such as El Imparcial
La Jornada	1984	Founding	· Personnel network links to defunct civic newspapers (Unomásuno and Excélsior) · Diversified ownership · Foreign influence
El Imparcial	1986	Transformation	· Young publisher takes over · International exposure · Ethics code · Network links to El Norte · Training

information about politics and government into prized political weaponry. Information "leaked" to the press was used to further personal careers and those of friends who operated in cliques, as well as to attack opponents. Journalists, especially those who wrote political columns, were often used to harm the public image of rival political cliques. This competition was particularly strong during the secretive campaign to win the president's favor and become his self-appointed successor. The presidential succession was a lucrative time for columnists and others who sold their services to praise or prejudice clique leaders with information that was leaked or even invented.

Table 6.1 Change Processes in Civic Newspapers *(continued)*

Second Wave: Diffusion

Newspaper	Date of Substantial Change	Created from Transformation or Founding	Mechanisms
El Sur	1992	Founding	· Network links to *La Jornada* · Diversified ownership
Reforma	1993	Founding	· Ownership and network links to *El Norte* · Hiring non-journalists · Training
El Diario de Juárez	1996	Transformation	· Young publisher · Personnel replacement · International exposure
Público	1997	Founding	· Hiring nonjournalists · Foreign training
El Universal	1996, 1999	Transformation	· Foreign training · Ethics code · Personnel network links to *El Financiero*, *Reforma*, and *La Jornada*
Palabra	1997	Founding	· Ownership and personnel network links to *El Norte* and *Reforma* · Hiring nonjournalists · Training
Mural	1998	Founding	· Ownership and personnel network links to *El Norte* and *Reforma* · Hiring nonjournalists · Training
Frontera	1999	Founding	· Ownership and network links to *El Imparcial* · Training
Milenio Diario	2000	Founding	· Personnel network links to *El Financiero*, *Reforma*, *Público*, *Milenio* magazine, and *Proceso*

n=16

The Mexican legal framework, in effect until 2003, encouraged journalists to enter into compromising relationships in order to receive government information. While a right to information was included in the Mexican Constitution of 1978, the enacting legislation never made it through Congress until after the PRI lost presidential power in 2000. The result was that even independent journalists cultivated friendships with politicians to obtain "leaked" documents. The alternative was to seek information in interminable interviews, where circular responses and detailed histories could lull even the most tenacious reporter into a stupor. I experienced these interviews first-hand during three years of work as a reporter in Mexico. Veteran Mexican journalist Vicente Leñero (1978, 82) and Roderic Camp (1986), a longtime interviewer of Mexican politicians, describe similar experiences.[3]

Press models emphasizing autonomy from government and assertiveness in seeking out news, such as those from the United States, Europe, and other parts of Latin America, were less known in Mexico during the 1970s than they were by the end of the century.[4] While there were always one or two "oppositional" newspapers in the 1960s and 1970s, usually of the left and staffed by Mexicans and Latin American exiles whose lives depended on the PRI's benevolence, these newspapers operated with the blessing of the state. The lack of wider references for autonomous press behavior helped keep journalists docile. Likewise, state ideology and patriotic rhetoric prompted journalists to interpret the ideals of the Mexican Revolution as support of the single-party system (Bailey 1988; Camp 1986, 2002b). Finally, the closed economic model also reinforced an internal, pro-system intellectual orientation by making the importation of cultural material more expensive.

State promotion and protection of news companies, a weak private sector, the hegemony of the PRI-government, and the lack of alternative press models were important restrictions on the parameters in which journalists operated. But if those conditions did not force journalists into a supportive role, additional inducements usually did. The president's office, ruling party, and most government agencies made direct, routine payments to supportive reporters, columnists, and newspaper owners. Moreover, reporters received percentages of the revenue from advertisements they sold to their sources.[5]

Rather than repression or direct censorship, docile news coverage in most of the Mexican press can be explained by internalized agreements on which issues and actors would be covered (Riva Palacio 1991, 5; 1994). The traditional Mexican press institution was successful in turning autonomy and assertiveness in news coverage—virtues of the civic press institution—into deviant conduct. When the government decided to crack down on a civic newspaper, other publications sometimes joined the lynch mob and roundly criticized their civic-minded colleagues.[6] As recently as 1993, traditionally oriented journalists ostracized or ridiculed those who did not accept payments from sources. This happened even in some newspapers that generally produced independent coverage, as journalists driven by civic and traditional orientations clashed within the same newsroom. An editor laughed at Claudia Fernández, then a young reporter at *El Financiero*, when she did not accept a VCR that was given to her as a Christmas present by a source (Fernández 1998).

To survive in the hostile environment, journalists in first-wave civic publications learned quickly that they needed to be able to operate without financial support from the state.[7] Those that survived intact, such as *El Norte* in Monterrey, came to prize financial autonomy. Other newspapers, such as *Excélsior* in 1976 and *ABC* in 1979, could not survive without government support. *ABC* closed outright, while *Excélsior* lost its civic orientation. Their legacy, cadres of civic journalists, lived on to influence other publications, however. The *Excélsior* and *ABC* heritage is found in two first-wave civic newspapers, *La Jornada* and *Zeta*.

The answer to why a civic newspaper style emerged in such an unfriendly environment lies in the changing self-perceptions and purposeful actions of journalists who became committed, first, to changing their publications and, later, to influencing their wider profession. Change agents such as publishers, editors, and groups of reporters, responded to a value orientation that opposed the continuation of one-party rule or the policies it produced, and were influenced by ideas in foreign press models that offered an alternative paradigm separating the press from the state.

Civic-oriented journalists used several methods to transform their newsrooms, including direct retraining, cross-fertilization with established civic newspapers and publications, formal and informal associations where common values and concerns were discussed, and the implementation of regulations guiding journalists' relationships with sources and advertisers. There were three routes of transformation during the emergence phase. Owners pushed change from above, new cohorts of journalists pushed from below, or change moved horizontally as staffs deserted publications when faced with dilemmas brought on by a clash of values or government intervention.

A split in the staff of the newspaper *Unomásuno*, which had been heir to *Excélsior*'s civic style and some of its personnel, led to the creation of *La Jornada*. The publication's journalists—which included former historians, sociologists, and academics, as well as reporters following a leftist political orientation—cited *Unomásuno*'s "moral, financial and political" crisis as the reason for their departure (Rodríguez Castañeda 1993, 236). The staff of *Zeta*, a left-leaning publication in Tijuana, was made up of journalists who left *ABC* in protest of an "illegal" strike fostered by the Baja California state government, which could not tolerate the newspaper's criticism.[8] By the late 1980s, *El Financiero*, an example of "bottom-up" change with a moderately rightist orientation, brought in economists, academics, and financial experts with new ideas and practices, creating what one editor called a virtual classroom in civic-oriented journalism.[9]

Young publishers also transformed their publications in top-down fashion. In the north, publishers at *El Imparcial* in Hermosillo, Sonora, and *El Norte* in Monterrey, Nuevo León, experimented with ways to instill their staffs with new values and skills. U.S. journalism models and conservative values propelled these efforts. *El Imparcial* publisher José Santiago Healy studied journalism at the Jesuit Universidad Iberoamericana in Mexico City, the Navarra University in Spain, and Northwestern University in Chicago. His Catholic and free-market values, which were at odds with the regime, made him question Mexico's brand of subordinate journalism. Healy reported that civic-minded publishers such as Julio Scherer of *Excélsior* and *Proceso* magazine and Alejandro Junco of *El Norte* influenced him greatly. *A.M.* publisher Enrique Gómez of León, Guanajuato, reported being "very dissatisfied" with Mexican democracy. Gómez also credited Junco's example in his decision to make his newspaper more independent and assertive. Gómez was a civil engineer by training and had been exposed to foreign ideas about the press. He was a member of the American Newspaper Publishers Association and took journalism seminars at the Poynter Institute in St. Petersburg, Florida.[10] Junco, who quickly became the most influential newspaper publisher in northern Mexico, appeared to have been influenced by his University of Texas education in journalism, the free-market environment in industrial Monterrey, and the time he spent living and reading newspapers in south Texas. As a young publisher, Junco set up a summer training camp for his reporters, based on U.S. practices, with a professor he had studied with in Austin. The program sought to change journalists' value orientations and identity, as well as heighten their skills. He explained:

> In July 1970, we started a summer institute with Professor Mary A. Gardner of Michigan State University. It was a summer school in *El Norte*. At that time, *El Norte* had a lot of shortcomings, but it was known for being outspoken. We had more maneuvering room in the provinces. A lot of people came because it was one of the few newspapers that told things as they were. People came and said they wanted to work there to exercise their freedom of expression. We told them that "Rather than work for a newspaper so you can exercise your freedom of expression, we're going to teach you something more important. You are going to be a depository of the reader's right to know and that is a right superior to your personal freedom of expression." We started to shift the paradigm of what freedom of expression is and is used for.[11]

La Jornada's experience was different. Some of its founders were influenced by the ideals of *El País* of Madrid, which began publication within months of the death of General Francisco Franco in November 1975 and took up the mantle of Spanish democratization during the critical early years of democratic consolidation on the peninsula. *La Jornada* was created by journalists and nonjournalists, including artists, academics, and some political figures who openly resisted the authoritarian regime.[12] They identified with the Mexican left and were not afraid to show it, according to newspaper editor Carmen Lira. While Junco referred to the public as "readers," Lira referred directly to citizens: "*La Jornada* is produced daily by citizens who are worried about their country, about their newspaper, about their time, and about their surroundings . . . *La Jornada* has believed—and has never stopped believing—in the possibility of a just and more civic country, in the right-responsibility of the citizens to reclaim it and to initiate it, and, because of that, in the possibility of change for our country" (Lira 1999).

While *La Jornada* published more articles about the leftist opposition, northern newspapers have been viewed as more supportive of the Catholic Church and more sympathetic toward the conservative PAN. Likewise, civic newspapers varied in their degree of autonomy and assertiveness. *El Norte*, *El Imparcial,* and *A.M.*, for example, have long prohibited the sale of ads disguised as news items, called *gacetillas*, while *La Jornada* and *El Financiero* publish them with only a discrete identifier. Within *El Financiero*, some journalists were more committed to a civic style than others, producing the friction Fernández described above.

Despite these differences, the general tendency was that all of these first-wave civic newspapers became known for critical and assertive reporting compared to other Mexican media. They were the vanguard, setting the standard and pushing the boundaries for others.

Diffusion of Civic Journalism

As first-wave civic newspapers trained their own staffs and survived in harsh conditions, economic and political liberalization began to transform environmental incentives in favor of practicing their innovative brand of journalism. Environmental changes after 1985 supported the expansion of networks of civic-minded journalists and increased the financial success and prestige of civic-oriented newspapers, leading to the dispersion of the civic model in a second wave of civic newspaper formation.

Beginning in earnest in 1986, and deepening after 1988, the government sold off hundreds of companies and deregulated other industries, such as telecommunications and banking. Revenues from private sector advertising soared, weakening an important source of state patronage and control. At *El Financiero*, for example, the privatization of banks ended the government advertising boycott. Privately owned banks wanted to advertise in the nation's leading financial daily.

Meanwhile, repeated economic crises forced cuts in communications

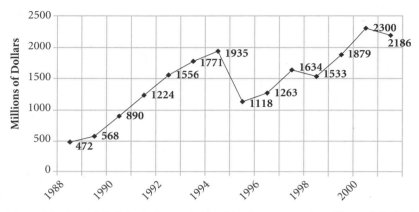

Figure 6.1 Growth in Private Sector Advertising Investment (in millions of dollars)

Source: Data come from the Mexican Association of Advertising Agencies (AMAP). Data prior to 2000 come from a computer printout of AMAP internal data provided by AMAP director Sergio López, Mexico City, November 1999. Later data found online at the Mexican Radio and Television Industry Chamber Web site, www.cirt.com.mx. AMAP figures are based on reports by AMAP members.

areas and created an atmosphere in which government information was considered untrustworthy. The lack of credibility on economic issues and the increasing availability of information from the private sector and foreign sources drove some reporters to diversify their sources of information. This weakened the government's monopoly on information. Figure 6.1, constructed from data from the Mexican Advertising Agency Association, shows the explosion of private sector advertising.

At the same time, government advertising plummeted, losing some of its persuasive power in the newsroom. By 1999, government advertising made up just 6 percent of the total ad lineage in a study of seven Mexico City newspapers, but its importance varied by publication—from a high of 12.7 percent for the low-circulation *El Sol de México* and 12 percent for the financial newspaper *El Financiero*, to 6.7 percent for circulation leader *El Universal* and 5.5 percent for *Reforma*.[13]

As the state withdrew from the economy and suffered repeated crises, the political opposition gained on the ruling PRI at the state and local level. In 1989, the government acknowledged the PRI's first loss of a governor's post to the conservative PAN in Baja California. Candidates emanating from both the PAN and center-left PRD whittled the PRI's domain to twenty-one of thirty-two state governors' chairs, the mayor's post in the Federal District, a majority block in Congress, and dozens of important city governments by the 2000 presidential election.

The alternation of parties in local and state government, as well as in the lower house of Congress, meant reporters covering those beats had to turn to opposition parties and their candidates for information. In the process, these journalists offered more plural news coverage. The arrival of the opposition to power also broadened and accelerated a shift in the federal government's financial secretariats. Those agencies had moved toward using the quality of information to push government messages, rather than relying on payoffs, advertising, or perks for reporters. First-time opposition governments and the now plural Chamber of Deputies accelerated the change, although they still tried to cultivate friendship ties. Some perks continued, but then went underground because of changes in public standards, if not outright prohibition.

As electoral politics liberalized, citizens became more demanding. During the important events of the 1980s and 1990s, readers were attracted to independent coverage in civic newspapers, which contrasted sharply with the traditional press. The history of *La Jornada*'s circulation increases is suggestive of how civic coverage acted as a foil to authoritarian-style news and attracted readers who were increasingly alienated from the authoritarian system. The newspaper's coverage of student protests in 1986, as well as the campaign that almost carried opposition candidate Cuauhtémoc Cárdenas to the presidency in 1988, stood out from traditional coverage, which, according to *La Jornada*'s first editor-in-chief, Carlos Payán, ignored Cárdenas completely and labeled the student protests the work of "lesbians, homosexuals and seamstresses." Circulation of *La Jornada* increased 25 percent to 40,000 during the protests in 1986 and then doubled again, reaching almost 100,000 in the 1988 campaign year. *La Jornada*'s extensive coverage of the Zapatista uprising in January 1994 and a special edition on March 23 of the same year, the day on which PRI presidential candidate Luis Donaldo Colosio was assassinated, took the newspaper to a one-day circulation high of 240,000 before the 1995 economic crisis hit (Payán 1999).

Something similar happened in Guadalajara, Mexico's second-largest city. The newspaper *Siglo 21*'s small starting circulation of 4,000 copies went to 30,000—the most its printing press could handle—in April 1992, within ten days of the deadly gas explosion that ripped through eight kilometers of Guadalajara, the details of which are recounted in chapter 1. In the days after the explosion, while *Siglo 21* carried fifteen to twenty pages of coverage, other newspapers downplayed the event. One local publisher wrote a front-page editorial about the new post-Soviet states. *Siglo 21*, which became *Público* following a staff dispute with *Siglo 21*'s owner, eventually became Guadalajara's third-largest newspaper, trailing only *El Informador* and a sports tabloid, *Esto*.[14]

By 1997, the majority of Mexico City readers turned to one of three newspapers known for a civic style of journalism—*Reforma, La Jornada,* and *El Financiero.* Another publication, market leader *El Universal,* sought to implement a civic style to hold its number one position. *El Universal*'s large classified section sustained it as the newspaper implemented a wide-ranging project of transformation.

Vanguard publications producing critical news coverage gained the upper hand in an environment of freer competition and more political pluralism. Table 6.2 shows the change in newspaper readership in the 1990s, based on independent surveys assessing newspaper readership. Since data prior to 1996 are not methodologically compatible with later studies, only the readership ranking is given. Rankings for *El Financiero* and *Ovaciones* in 1994 were estimated based on 1993 and 1995 positions.[15]

A similar process occurred in Guadalajara, as *Público* and *Mural* competed against *El Informador,* and in Tijuana, where *El Imparcial* opened a sister newspaper, *Frontera.* By 2000, *Frontera* trailed only *El Mexicano* in circulation.[16]

The circulation shift in favor of civic publications was not lost on private sector advertisers, who began to rationalize their purchases on market-based criteria in the late 1990s. *Reforma, El Universal, El Financiero,* and *La Jornada* were the beneficiaries.[17] By 1997, internal *El Universal* studies showed that *Reforma* trailed only *El Universal* in total advertising lineage, making it a new and powerful competitor. *Excélsior* was a distant third. Figure 6.2 shows how many lines of type were devoted to advertising in seven broadsheet Mexico City newspapers in 1999. *La Jornada* was not included in the analysis, which was compiled for *El Universal*'s management.

Table 6.2 Change in Newspaper Readership Rankings for Greater Mexico City

	1991	1992	1993	1994	1995	1997	1999	2000
El Universal	1	1	1	1	1	1	1	1
La Jornada	5	5	5	2	2	2	2	2
Reforma	—	—	—	5	4	3	3	3
El Financiero	8	8	6	6	7	4	5	5
Ovaciones	3	3	3	6	5	5	4	4
Excelsiór	2	2	2	3	3	6	7	7
Novedades	4	4	4	4	5	7	6	6

Notes: The crime and sports tabloids *La Prensa* and *Esto* were not included in these rankings. Reliable data for 1996 and 1998 were not available.

Sources: For source data, please see note 15 to this chapter.

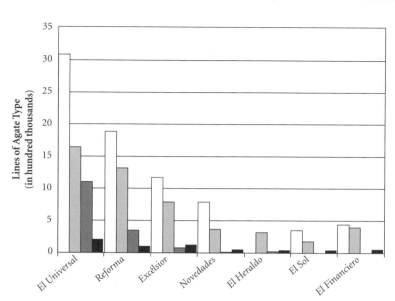

Figure 6.2 Advertising Breakdown for Seven Mexico City Newspapers, 1999

Source: Data come from two internal market research publications at *El Universal:* "Lineaje de enero a junio de 1999 de 7 periódicos" [Lineage from January to June 1999 in 7 newspapers], mimeograph; and Gallup de México, "El Universal," January 2001, pamphlet.

As liberalization changed the environment in which newspapers operated, the growing prestige and financial success of the first wave of civic publications increased. Not only did they gain circulation, but their national and international prestige also impressed other journalists, and the generations of civic journalists they helped create spread out to other newspapers. In the later cases, widening networks of civic journalists, influence from abroad, and living through systemic crises explain the transformation of journalists' orientations.

Dispersion from the vanguard of civic publications to a wider number of newspapers occurred primarily because civic newspapers became profitable enough in the new environment to open sister publications in other cities under the same civic frameworks, as observed in table 6.1. In the case of *Siglo 21* (later *Público*), nonjournalists who looked for guidance from *El País* in Spain sought to fill a gap in the coverage of traditional newspapers in Guadalajara.[18] The "contagion" of civic journalism, once it became politically prestigious and economically successful, is evident only in the transformation of *El Uni-*

versal. However, other traditionally oriented newspapers, such as *El Informador* in Guadalajara, *Vanguardia* in Saltillo, and *Zócolo* in Piedras Negras, have expressed interest in transforming their newspapers.[19]

Civic journalism dispersed beyond founding newspapers through several mechanisms. Newsrooms themselves were the principal paths through which journalists were trained in civic journalism. These newsrooms then exported their product—a new generation—to other newspapers. This occurred either because first- and second-wave civic newspapers were corporately linked, or because the journalists were hired away by other newspapers trying to initiate the civic style.

El Norte's training school not only influenced that newspaper's journalists, but others who later went on to work at *El Imparcial* and elsewhere. Although the school no longer functions, new journalists received the same type of training when Junco founded *Reforma* in 1993, *Palabra* in Saltillo in 1997, and *Mural* in Guadalajara in 1998. Junco said of the school: "The significance of the experiment is that it formed a number of Mexican journalists. Over the years, we brought people to our model of journalism." Of all the newspapers in this study, *El Norte* founded the most influential civic network. By 1999, *El Norte*'s journalists or those who had been trained by them worked in eleven of the sixteen civic newspapers identified in Mexico.

While *La Jornada* never set up formal training schools like *El Norte*, former *La Jornada* reporters and editors have said that their experience in the newsroom influenced them. Those journalists could later be found in key positions at several second-wave civic newspapers, including *Reforma, El Universal,* and *El Sur* in Acapulco.

At *El Financiero*, change was initially introduced by economists and financial experts who came from academic backgrounds, such as Enrique Quintana and Clemente Ruíz Durán. As the economists became journalists, they brought different values and standards to their work and trained a new cadre of reporters to be more thorough, questioning, and independent.

El Financiero's newsroom became another school for civic journalists. A financial editor in Mexico City who requested anonymity said of his professional orientation: "It came from my bosses at *El Financiero*. Basically, it was a culture there. It was a way of being that I progressively assimilated, by learning and listening." The newspaper also sent its legacy of civic journalists to newer civic newspapers, including *Reforma, El Universal,* and *Milenio.*

Today's civic journalists developed as they worked under civic-minded bosses and journalists who taught in universities, or they were influenced by the prestige of now-famous civic pioneers. According to the survey data shown in table 6.3, Julio Scherer, the editor of *Excélsior* until 1976 and, later,

Table 6.3 Journalists' Role Models

Name	%	Name	%
Julio Scherer	17.7	Carlos Menéndez	3.2
Gabriel Garcia Marquéz	9.8	Ricardo Rocha	3.2
Jesus Blancornelas	6.5	Raymundo Riva Palacio	3.2
Manuel Buendía	4.8	Others, national	1.6
Alejandro Junco	3.2	Others, international	1.6
Miguel Angel Granados Chapa	3.2	n=62	

Note: This data was collected in response to an optional survey question: "Who Do You Admire Professionally?"

editor of the critical newsmagazine *Proceso*, was, by far, the most influential role model. Gabriel García Marquez, the Colombian novelist and journalist who now coordinates his own journalism training institute, was second. Junco of *El Norte* influenced other publishers, while Jesús Blancornelas of *Zeta* was mentioned by several of his staff members. Others included *Diario de Yucatán* owner Carlos Menéndes, television and radio journalist Ricardo Rocha, and editor and columnist Raymundo Riva Palacio, all known for their independent, critical styles.

As networks widened, the traditional, supportive orientation of Mexican journalism lost legitimacy. Repeated systemic shocks signaled the decay, if not destruction, of the old regime. Mexico's restrictive political system suffered through a series of political and economic crises in the 1980s and 1990s as its old institutions weakened. Journalists had front-row seats for the government's slow response to the Mexico City earthquake in 1985, electoral fraud beginning in 1986, the indigenous uprising in January 1994, the assassination of Luis Donaldo Colosio two months later, the 1995 recession, and the $65 billion bank bailout in 1999.

Journalists' direct exposure to the widening cracks in the one-party regime caused them to question their role in maintaining the system. In my survey of journalists from eight civic-leaning newspapers in 1999, forty-eight of the fifty-six people who answered an optional survey question said an experience on the job changed their professional orientations. The experiences that most influenced reporters were covering the Zapatista uprising and the Colosio assassination. In interviews that accompanied the survey, journalists explained the impact of covering the shocks that signaled the decay of the PRI regime in the 1990s.

> Chiapas was important. I was 24 years old. It was a lesson that we have forgotten a little about poverty, about the indigenous people's suffering, about their abandonment and the selfishness of the majority of society. The move-

Table 6.4 Transformative Experiences

Experience	%	Experience	%
Covering jarring events	41	Perceived censorship at newspaper	5
Exposure to foreign press models	13	Being a journalist	4
Newspaper training, mentors	11	Covering Central American wars	4
Covering presidential campaign	7	Working for government	4
Covering opposition wins or fraud in elections	7	Other	4
		n=56	

Note: Some respondents listed more than one experience.

ment woke up a great part of society, including journalists. The slap at my conscious was very important. I think that is the reason I am more critical now.[20]

For what I do, the multiple economic crises in this country, as well as the Colosio assassination, have had a much greater impact because they are frequent, constant, jarring, transcendent. And they keep happening. The Fobaproa bank bailout, for example, has tripled the internal debt and is a huge scandal. It is a huge call to us to do our jobs well. Enough already.[21]

Table 6.4 categorizes the experiences journalists identified as transformative. The most important were jarring events such as the Zapatista uprising.

"Chiapas Changed Everything"

A closer look at one journalist's experiences while covering the Zapatista rebellion shows how that event changed mental models of journalism and Mexican society, and in the process made the Mexican press less passive in the face of the government. Ismael García was 31 years old in 1994 when he covered the indigenous uprising in Chiapas for a Mexico City magazine that stayed alive through what he called "a complex network of interests" tying it to politicians, business owners and intellectuals.[22] García described the culture of the magazine as one where a reporter "just knew" the editorial line and didn't cross it. In return for supportive coverage, the magazine's publisher and editors received advertising contracts and exclusive information. Reporters got scoops and gifts "for Christmas, on your birthday and on Freedom of the Press Day. The least they would give you is a computer."

Trained professionally in an authoritarian media institution, García accepted the internal censorship and gifts without question until he went to cover the Zapatista uprising of indigenous farmers in Chiapas. On January 1, 1994, in protest of neoliberal economic policies that threatened their ancestral way of life, authoritarian politics that precluded legal contestation of grievances, and five hundred years of discrimination against native peoples, thousands of Mayan Indians and a few urban intellectuals took up arms against the Mexican army in the southernmost state of Chiapas. Dozens died in the ten days of open warfare before the government declared a ceasefire. Millions of people across the country sympathized with the Indians, who took their name from the popular hero of the 1910 Mexican Revolution, *campesino* leader Emiliano Zapata. The Mexican and international media rushed to San Cristobal de las Casas and the surrounding highlands to cover the largest guerrilla uprising in Mexico since the Revolution.

Mexican reporters in Chiapas quickly developed their own sympathies, or as García put it, they soon decided "who were the repressed, and who were the repressors." After editors back in Mexico City cancelled several of his stories from Chiapas, García quit his job and changed his ideas about how the press should interact with the government. Since the uprising, he has refused to accept more than a birthday card. He eventually joined a civic-oriented newspaper, where he covers the military. Below are excerpts from his interview. The content was reordered slightly to improve readability.

AUTHOR: Journalists in the mid-1990s received gifts from the government every year?

JOURNALIST: Until Chiapas happened. Chiapas changed everything. When Chiapas arrived, the press became uncontrollable.

AUTHOR: You said reporters became angry when air force pilots shot at a caravan of press vehicles in Chiapas? That's when the backlash began?

JOURNALIST: That day the press room in San Cristobal exploded. I'm not exaggerating. We were 450 reporters from all over the world. Imagine. Almost 500 reporters. They shot at Univisión reporter Bruno López, a *compañero* from Agence-France Press, someone from Telemundo, and someone from the magazine *Macrópolis*. They shot at them. We watched the tape. It shook us up because we could see the cameraman stop in the middle of the highway and face the airplane head-on, and you see how the earth jumped when the shots hit it.

AUTHOR: The pilots could see from the plane that they were shooting at press cars?

JOURNALIST: Yes, all the vans were painted "press."

AUTHOR: Soldiers shot at reporters near a road block as well.

JOURNALIST: They hit Ismael Romero from *La Jornada*, now with *El Universal*. They hit him in the arm. He was in a red Volkswagen with Frida Hartz from *La Jornada* and other photographers.

AUTHOR: And the other reporters became angry?

JOURNALIST: Yes. At that time the president's spokesman had been the spokesman for just one day. That day everyone was all over him. . . . He called a press conference to give the official explanation of why they had attacked the press. They put up the Mexican flag, an official microphone, a podium, the presidential shield, the seal with an eagle. They set up an entire theater set. And this guy arrives with his printout to read a press statement, and he lasted two minutes. He started to sweat. He got nervous with everyone attacking him, everyone yelling "assassins."

AUTHOR: The reporters yelled "assassins"?

JOURNALIST: Yes, because of the repression, because the government was aware we journalists needed to be protected from the shooting. That same day they said, "we are going to send you special jackets so you are easily identified." We said, "yes, but jackets won't stop a bullet, pardon me, thin orange press jackets that look like Mexico City subway workers' jackets won't stop bullets." Everyone got really mad and he had to leave.

And the next day there was no government information being fed to the press. We all went out in five or ten cars to look for news. "I'm going to Motozintla." "I'm going to Ocosingo." "Well, I'm going here." Everyone went out on his own to look for news and then we came back to see what everyone had found. We were uncontrollable . . .

AUTHOR: That was a watershed? Mexican reporters had been shot and suddenly there was solidarity? Is that right?

JOURNALIST: Yes, because you were conscious of what side the truth was on, or at least in that moment the truth of what we were living, the war in Chiapas. We knew who were the oppressed and who were the oppressors.

While repeated crises made journalists question their supportive role in maintaining the system, alternative paradigms gave them ideas about what their new role should become. Journalists also reported the importance of studying or reporting abroad on forging their professional orientations. The U.S. and Canadian governments, as well as private foundations, sponsored exchanges between Mexican, Canadian, and U.S. newsrooms. Foreign journalism education took on prestige for younger journalists able to pursue master's degrees or professional certificates in journalism at the University of Madrid (sponsored by *El País*) and the University of Southern California run by former U.S. journalist Murray Fromson. For editors, Harvard's Neiman Fellowships became prestigious.

Trade opening also increased the influence and proximity of foreign media styles, especially those from the United States, Spain, and Canada. Twenty-four percent of the journalists in this survey had lived out of the country and 75 percent had worked or studied alongside foreign journalists.

Of those, 79 percent said they were influenced somewhat or a great deal by those contacts. Journalists aged thirty to forty-nine in 1999 were most likely to have had contact with foreign reporters, precisely those who would have held important reporting or editing positions in the 1990s.

The proposal of a free-trade agreement with the United States and Canada brought more U.S. and Canadian journalists to Mexico, where they worked alongside Mexican colleagues and sometimes within their newsrooms. Latin American journalists from Argentina and Chile also made their way to Mexico, influencing the reporters they directed.

Foreign journalists such as Uruguayan Ricardo Trotti and Warren Watson of the United States at *El Universal* and Argentine Tomás Eloy Martínez at *Siglo 21*, trained journalists in newsrooms where management promoted change. Mexican journalism groups forged ties to foreign associations, such as the Investigative Reporters and Editors branch in Mexico, Periodistas de Investigación, which opened in 1997 and has about 150 members. The Partners in the Americas fostered educational exchanges between about fifteen Mexican newspapers and the *Dallas Morning News* from 1996 to 2000. The Asociación de Periodistas, with ties to the New York-based Committee to Protect Journalists, formed in response to a series of killings and attacks on journalists in 1997 and 1998. The U.S. National Association of Hispanic Journalists held its western regional meetings in Mexico City in 2000 and San Diego/Tijuana in 2002; Hispanic journalists mixed with Mexican colleagues.

Transforming a Titan

The experience of *El Universal* illustrates the multiple pressures on Mexican newspapers in the 1990s and the steps necessary to change the course of a publication. They include almost all of the tactics used by change agents to transform the organizational cultures of their newsrooms. However, this case is different because few authoritarian newspapers could successfully implement a civic program—the mental models and professional identities of newsroom leaders were too deeply entrenched. It took a purposeful and sustained program of cultural retooling for the newspaper to make the change.

As the first edition of the "new" *El Universal* rolled off the presses in September 1999, editors of Mexico City's independent newspapers doubted that the eighty-three-year-old publication could ever change its lapdog approach. Even *El Universal*'s editor-in-chief, Roberto Rock, admitted in private that the paper had been raised in a "culture of submission."[23] Yet the change in the content of the newspaper, above and beyond the addition of color photographs, was immediately noticeable. From a publication that focused on stories and columns devoted to insider gossip for the political elite, *El Universal*, as of early 2000, produced regular investigative reports on topics such as drug trafficking, insurance fraud, and the peddling of used clothes to the poor. It explained difficult issues to readers in simple boxes and graphics, beefed up its metropolitan coverage, and carried a weekly column on personal finance directed at the middle-class city dweller. The quality varied from day to day, but the change in focus toward serving a wider public was notable.

The transformation of *El Universal* did not come about by chance. Purposeful steps were taken to transform the newspaper in an environment of increasing competition and political crisis. Management began direct retraining to teach longtime *El Universal* staff not only new writing and reporting skills, but also to think differently about who they wrote for and what kind of information was credible. At the same time, editors took advantage of widening networks of civic journalists by hiring new columnists, editors, and reporters.

After Rock took over in 1996, the newspaper retrained current staff and began hiring top journalists from competitors who had long practiced more independent journalism. Rock hired columnists Carlos Ramírez of *El Financiero* and Ricardo Alemán from *La Jornada*, and added reporters Claudia Fernández and Miguel Badillo from *El Financiero* to the investigations team headed by former *El Financiero* editor Raúl Hinojosa. Ismael Romero, then a political reporter at *La Jornada*, became the new national editor.

The process accelerated in 1999 with the hiring of editors from established civic newspapers. All of the managing editors for "hard" news—investigations, news, and production—now had experience in previously established civic newspapers, as did the finance and front page editors. Also in 1999, *El Universal* published its first ethics code regulating journalists' relationships with their sources to foster more autonomy. By then, however, most journalists viewed accepting payoffs or "gifts" from sources as aberrant behavior.

As part of the change project, critical Mexican and foreign journalists instructed *El Universal* journalists in reporting and editing workshops. The message was to write more clearly and with context so that a wider audience would understand the information, be more aggressive when interviewing politicians and business leaders, and go beyond official government sources of information. One of the challenges workshop leaders faced was to teach reporters that they were equals of the political sources they interviewed. They also hoped to change reporters' careers aspirations from political gossip columnist to investigative reporter. With cultural retooling, *El Universal* entered the ranks of publications following a civic notion of journalism that is the basis for independent, plural, and often critical coverage of powerful societal actors.

Many doubted that *El Universal* owner Juan Francisco Ealy would carry the change to its ultimate conclusions. While *El Universal* had opened its editorial pages to more diverse columnists before most Mexico City newspapers, Ealy became a media owner during the height of PRI rule and prospered as a result of that system. He broke formally with the traditional system in 1996 when he confronted President Ernesto Zedillo over coverage of the assassination of Luis Donaldo Colosio, who had been Ealy's close friend. The dispute led to ninety-nine tax audits and Ealy's eventual arrest on tax evasion charges. All but one charge was eventually thrown out of court, but federal officials briefly jailed and interrogated Ealy, surrounded *El Universal* newspaper with armed federal agents, and boycotted the newspaper for four months. Making things more complicated, the confrontation came during a major recession, and *Reforma* simultaneously became the biggest commercial competitor *El Universal* had ever faced.

Ealy, by then fifty-six years old, decided stylistic changes would not suffice. He empowered Rock to take over the renovation of his newspaper. Ealy backed Rock's decision to change the newspaper's organizational culture at a key moment when all other newspaper managers opposed anything more than a graphic design makeover. Ealy even sold his sports tabloid to finance a $2 million renovation of the newsroom, the team of foreign consultants, and new journalists hired at higher salaries.

The transformation of *El Universal* followed a universal process in Mexico's civic press formation. Alternative paradigms of journalism and society gave change agents who opposed the regime an idea of what a new style of journalism might be like. When they acquired power in their newsrooms, they created new incentives, hired similarly minded colleagues, and showed other journalists how to make the switch. By the 1990s, expanding networks of civic journalists, the financial success and legitimacy of first-wave civic newspapers, and the changing cues in the macroenvironment all pointed in the same direction, toward adopting a more assertive, autonomous brand of journalism. The mechanisms identified in the institutional transformation process are listed below.

Stage One: Emergence
- Civic founders hold values in opposition to the continuation of the one-party state.

- Founders learn of other journalism models separating the press from the state.
- Founders train new cohorts of journalists (recent university graduates or journalists originally trained in other professions, such as economics).

Stage Two: Diffusion
- Systemic shocks delegitimize maintenance of one-party state for greater number of journalists.
- Economic liberalization increases need to respond to wider market, decreases role of state in supporting media financially, and introduces more journalists to foreign news paradigms.
- Financial, political, and international success of civic newspapers increases their legitimacy.
- Networks of civic journalists expand beyond original civic newspapers.

An institutional analysis of civic transformation in the Mexican press clearly demonstrated the importance of oppositional values, new ideas, and organizational power in creating successful newsroom change agents, while the diffusion of the civic style responded to changing environmental cues, systemic shocks, expanding civic journalist networks, the financial success and prestige of founding civic newsrooms, and the formation of a second wave of civic change agents. A civic news model enabling citizen participation and government accountability appeared inside a core of newspapers that had supported an authoritarian system even prior to economic liberalization and democratization. Once liberalization began, the innovative civic style percolated to a wider number of Mexican news organizations. As Mexico began its period of democratic consolidation, civic newspapers dominated the market in most of Mexico's major cities. For the politically active, they had become obligatory points of reference.[24]

Part III

ALTERNATIVE TRANSFORMATION PATHS

7 Alternatives to the Civic Newsroom

Inertial and Adaptive Authoritarianism

As civic-oriented newspapers became more autonomous, more assertive, and especially more plural over the last twenty-five years, other news organizations followed different transformation paths. The journalism they practiced resisted change, adapted authoritarian norms to a weakening national political system, or responded to stronger market cues in the liberalizing economy. Four models of journalism came to coexist and compete for financial success and prestige in the late 1990s, eroding the once-consolidated Mexican media institution and creating the hybrid media system that exists today in Mexico. In addition to civic journalism, the models guiding Mexican journalism now include inertial and adaptive forms of authoritarianism, as well as a new commercial form—the market-driven newsroom. As people watch television and read newspapers in postauthoritarian Mexico, the headlines and storylines of a young democracy collide and converge.

To discern the origins and practices of the alternatives to the civic newsroom—authoritarian and market-driven newsrooms—I analyzed a set of inertial newspapers in Mexico City, adaptive authoritarianism in several local television stations around the country, and the market-driven transformation of national television news. As with the civic model, the authoritarian and market-driven models are ideal types used for analytical purposes. These models help disaggregate the causes and potential effects of the varying logics driving news production. What we see, in most cases, is that news organizations display a mix of traits that nevertheless incline toward one model more than another.

Inertial newspapers such as Mexico City's *Excélsior, Novedades,* and *Unomásuno* maintained passive, subordinate, and monochromatic pro-regime approaches to journalism throughout the societal transformation of the 1990s. Some local media, such as television stations in the states of Tabasco, Guanajuato, and Tlaxcala, adapted to strengthened local politics as the centralized regime weakened. They subordinated news production to political elites from the local party in power in exchange for job security, advertising, and other perks.

The national commercial television networks Televisa and TV Azteca initially resisted societal change, much like inertial newsrooms. When a new generation of managers took over in the second half of the 1990s, the networks forged a market-driven form of journalism to respond to cues emanating from the liberalizing economy. Market-driven news held contradictory implications for democratization. Commercial television pushed democratization by presenting a greater diversity of political voices during electoral campaigns and moderating the image of the powerful president. As the model became more developed, however, market-driven journalism increasingly equated politics with spectacle. By the time I conducted a detailed content analysis in 2003, coverage of crime, tragedy, and political confrontation had largely driven electoral coverage and issue-based politics from the news. Political information migrated to quiz shows, human interest interview shows, and videotaped acts of corruption presented in an entertainment context.

The Mexican media system, once an institutionalized system of values, conceptions, and norms of behavior, fragmented throughout the 1980s and 1990s. Figure 7.1 offers a graphic depiction of the gradual disintegration of the authoritarian media institution. It contrasts electoral pluralism in society, measured by the percentage of vote for the PRI in presidential elections between 1982 and 2000, with pluralism in press coverage, measured by percentage of coverage of the PRI in different types of media.[1] The graph reveals several characteristics of journalistic change in Mexico: (1) all news organizations moved toward greater pluralism in electoral coverage as society became more plural; (2) the decision to reflect electoral pluralism occurred at different times depending on the type of media, that is, different media began their transitions at different times; (3) assuming that news media can influence political change, then the data depicted in the chart mean that only civic newspapers anticipated greater pluralism in society and could have accelerated the country's democratization from the beginning. Authoritarian newspapers, to the degree that they had credibility and readers late in the societal transition, would have acted as a drag on democratization. Network

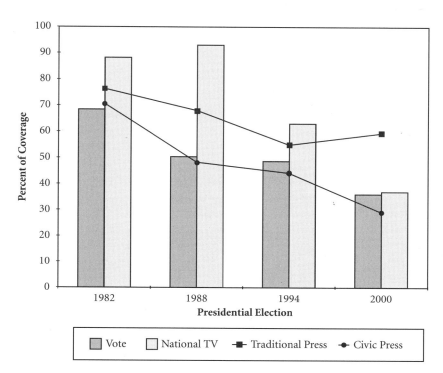

Figure 7.1 PRI Presidential Vote (%) Compared to Political Coverage of PRI (%)

Source: For source information, please see note 1 to this chapter.

television—with its larger numbers and greater degree of credibility—probably slowed democratization until its electoral coverage diversified between the 1994 and 2000 presidential elections. At that point, more balanced political coverage on network television would have positively influenced voter decisions for the opposition.[2]

The same general variables that drove civic newsroom transformations—organizational leadership and culture inside news organizations, partial diffusion across the newspaper field, and democratization and economic liberalization that changed the political economy outside news organizations—also explain how inertial and adaptive authoritarianism emerged as alternatives to civic-oriented journalism. Importantly, the comparison of these change paths also identifies differences in the strength of these causal variables. The principal difference was that the arrival of alternative norms among rank-and-file journalists had more impact in civic newspapers. Hierarchical power structures and the lack of professional autonomy of most journalists in authoritarian newsrooms prevented normative change in lower ranks from influencing newsroom behavior.

This chapter first discusses the trajectory of a number of newspapers in Mexico City that resisted change in society and journalism throughout Mexico's transition to democracy. While civic newspapers including *Reforma* and *La Jornada* in Mexico City embraced assertiveness, autonomy, and diversity in the presentation of political voices, owners and editors of inertial newspapers such as *Excélsior*, *Novedades*, and *Unomásuno* resisted change. The chapter then compares these newspapers, especially *Excélsior*, with a newspaper that successfully changed journalistic models late in the societal transition, *El Universal*. Since all of these newspapers come from Mexico City, all had similar opportunities to anticipate or react to changes in society and the political economy of news production. In other words, the case selection controls for potential differences in what was happening in the environment outside of the newsroom, allowing an exploration of the effects of what was happening inside news organizations and whether that made a difference in the timing and direction of newsroom transformations. Moreover, by specifically comparing *El Universal* and *Excélsior*, I also control for financial strength, since both publications had similar levels of circulation and advertising at the beginning of the transformation period. The least-similar design—similar cases yielding different outcomes—further pinpoints the mechanisms for newsroom transformations.

The chapter argues that decision makers inside inertial newspapers, as products of the system satisfied with its results, believed in the path they had chosen and resisted changes in society and from within the newspaper field. They bet on the ruling party and its associated form of journalism out of habit or conviction, even when a rational reading of the political economy would have told them that such behavior no longer guaranteed financial success or prestige. Their decisions continued to rule the newsrooms because the hierarchical structures of Mexican news organizations limited the potential for alternative voices to influence decision-making. When the seventy-one-year PRI regime ended with the presidential election of 2000, reality finally crashed through the cognitive barriers erected around the men controlling these news organizations. But even then, leaders in inertial newspapers believed they had chosen the wrong side, not misjudged the role of journalism in a democratizing society. Of the three cases examined, all prominent newspapers under the PRI regime, two quietly folded by 2003 and *Excélsior*'s news pages wandered without readers and amid rumors of impending sale, which finally occurred in early 2006.

The local television stations in which adaptive authoritarian news-rooms developed vary according to the party in office at the state level, the strength of the private-sector advertising market, and the ownership regime of the station. Four stations produced highly biased news coverage in favor of the state-level ruling party during the presidential elections of 2000. As the centralized PRI regime weakened, these local media organizations re-sponded by serving ascendant regional elites (when owned by the state) or private sector allies (when privately held). In places where the federal-level opposition gained power, local media owners sometimes chose to favor the new local leaders rather than create more autonomous civic or even mar-ket-oriented newsrooms. What mattered for newsroom decision makers was that the new political power holders controlled state advertising and other patronage for private sector media and, in the case of state-owned news out-lets, controlled personnel decisions.

The mechanisms for the development of adaptive authoritarian news-rooms were similar to those explaining inertial authoritarianism—leaders with top-down control of the newsroom decided to use the news for partisan or personal gain. As with inertial newsrooms, civic norms did not penetrate their mental models of journalism and society. Contrasting the adaptive au-thoritarian stations to the privately held station in Mexicali, where coverage was essentially not biased, shows the importance of normative conceptions and journalistic agency, and that adaptive authoritarianism was not the only potential transition path for local television news.

Inertial Authoritarianism

During the 2000 presidential elections, the director of *Excélsior*, Regino Díaz Redondo, decided his newspaper would continue to act as the standard-bearer for the PRI regime, even though *Excélsior*'s circulation had eroded steadily since 1994 and the weakening ruling party was in no position to help very much. In his memoirs, Díaz Redondo made it clear that he consciously decided to support the PRI under any circumstances because he believed that was the correct and appropriate way to run the newspaper—not because of payments from the party or government, which had been in decline, or be-cause of a calculation of the future costs and benefits of such obvious sup-port. Moreover, he states, the decision was his alone to make (Diáz Redondo 2002, chap. 10).

As other newspapers gave equal or more space to the front-running PAN, Díaz Redondo's pro-PRI leanings reached the pinnacle of expression on June 19 when the newspaper dedicated all of the Mexican news on its front page, and three pages inside, to the campaign of PRI presidential candidate Francisco Labastida. The newspaper also attacked Labastida's chief opponent, eventual winner Vicente Fox, on several occasions. One involved the publication of a "list of contributors" to the Fox campaign. Along with a number of well-known Mexican millionaires and politicians, the *Excélsior* list of Fox contributors included the church of the Reverend Sun Myung Moon, the Legionnaires of Christ, Ross Perot, the U.S. Republican Party, Microsoft, the *Miami Herald,* and *Reforma*.[3] The article also cited a "psychological profile" of Fox that called him "a megalomaniac" (Rojas Cruz 2000).

Even though *Excélsior* was formally organized as a cooperative, its administration was vertically structured. Díaz Redondo stood on the pinnacle of that structure for twenty-four years, since 1976, when he was installed after a government-orchestrated revolt of cooperative members that ousted editor Julio Scherer. Díaz Redondo explained the newspaper's support of Labastida in his memoirs: "It was stated that I supported (PRI candidate) Francisco Labastida for president of the republic. To clarify my position I met with the three administrative areas of the newspaper and separately with the cooperative members who asked for information. I told them that, indeed, the director of a newspaper has the obligation and the right to mark the editorial line of the newspaper under his charge and that I considered Labastida the most appropriate man to be president" (Diáz Redondo 2002, 144).

Such unabashed support for the PRI proved to be a bad business decision. The paper foundered financially after the PRI lost, and the majority of *Excélsior*'s staff voted Díaz Redondo out of office shortly after the election for trying to sell the cooperative to a tycoon linked to previous PRI administrations. Still, the staff said the ouster was because of misuse of cooperative funds, or corruption, rather than a mistaken editorial policy (Ortega Pizarro 2001; Díaz Redondo 2002; González 2000).

However, Diaz Redondo had not acted so differently than the leaders of other inertial newspapers. At *Novedades,* midlevel editors in the sometimes rebellious English-language edition were instructed to downplay coverage of Fox after the April 25 candidates' debate in which Fox distinguished himself. Two weeks before the July 2 election, the newspapers' editors said that no stories about Fox were to be published at all.[4] At *Unomásuno,* in the words of its editor-in-chief, Rafael Cardona, the newspaper also unleashed an "enthusiastic campaign" on behalf of Labastida and published a barrage of "slander" against Fox in the final days of the contest. Again, the decision was made at the top of the hierarchically organized newsroom. "We did this together, you and I," *Unomásuno* Cardona wrote to owner Manuel Alonso in an emotional mea culpa the day after the election.[5]

Unlike the cases of civic newspaper transformation, publishers and editors in inertial publications were late to perceive the need to change, and limited in their actions. Visual adjustments were considered sufficient "to adjust the image of our newspaper to today's needs," as a *Novedades* administrator said three years before the newspaper closed (Ayala 1999). In his memoirs, Díaz Redondo wrote that he found a new benefactor too late to redesign *Excélsior*'s presentation (2002, 132–34). None of these newsroom leaders contemplated cutting off ties to the PRI.

What explains this unyielding support? Reliance on future benefits is not the answer. By 2000, the state had lost its monopoly on financial and political support for the press as the privatization of state companies grew and opposition parties took local and state posts from the PRI. In the early 1970s, the federal government had controlled 80 percent of the advertising in a typical Mexico City newspaper; by 2000, it controlled just 5 percent.[6] Economic crises had diminished the federal government's ability to provide other subsidies as well.[7] Furthermore, by 2000 the capital city government and its advertising budget were controlled by the PRD, all major parties had access to millions of dollars in publicly provided campaign funding, and there was a real chance the PRI could lose the presidency. A "rational" cost-benefit analysis favored one of three options: (1) finding another political benefactor as did adaptive authoritarian newsrooms; (2) adhering to new standards of autonomy, pluralism, and assertiveness like the growing number of civic newspapers around the country; or (3) following a more market-driven approach to journalism, combining greater pluralism for readers and advertisers with colorful designs and more sensationalist articles.

A rational reading of the costs and benefits of a pro-regime strategy cannot be the answer for inertial authoritarianism. Residual financial dependence on the federal government partially explains the maintenance of press subordination to the regime, but is not a complete answer. *Excélsior* reportedly owed millions of dollars to federal government development banks for successive bailouts during the economic crises of the 1980s. However, the newspaper stopped paying the debt in the late 1980s and, in 1996, the Zedillo government set the newspaper completely adrift when it slashed government advertising spending in lower-circulation newspapers, including, by then, *Excélsior*. A bitter Díaz Redondo wrote later that the publication's financial health spiraled downward over the next four years. Yet even when *Excélsior*'s business manager told the editor in 1998 that the newspaper had only enough revenues to cover salaries for two weeks, Díaz Redondo held the course. He did not worry about remaking the newspaper's lapdog approach to journalism, but was concerned that he did not have the money to improve its design or retain the best columnists (Díaz Redondo 2002, 119, 127, 128; Scherer 1995). Likewise, *Novedades* was losing money in the late 1990s, but its survival did not depend on government bailouts. *Novedades* was part of a national chain with a millionaire owner who supported the publication with revenue injections from elsewhere in his expansive business empire.[8]

The PRI regime's inability to guarantee economic resources, political favors, or prestige suggested that inertial newspapers should change their approach. The longitudinal content analysis presented in figure 7.1 found that even inertial newspapers had gradually included more opposition voices in their coverage in the 1990s, but during the 2000 presidential campaign, they again allocated all their resources to the PRI. Why? The answer has to do with what management theorists Edgar H. Schein (1985) and Peter M. Senge (1994) have called static mental models and frozen organizational cultures.

By the late 1990s, cues in the news production environment had changed in support of civic or market-driven journalism, but the unchallenged leaders of inertial newspapers either did not read them correctly or did not care. They had formed professionally and benefited immensely from their close ties to the PRI regime. Like Díaz Redondo, who had gained authority over *Excélsior* through government intervention, tycoon Rómulo O'Farrill Jr. and his family bought *Novedades* with presidential backing in the 1950s. Their connections to the PRI had always served them well. At *Unomásuno*, owner Manuel Alonso was a former presidential spokesman who owed his purchase of the newspaper to a shady deal brokered by the Salinas administration in 1989 (Albarrán de Alba 2001; Bohmann 1989; Fernández Christlieb 1985; Martínez and Ortega Pizarro 2000; Riva Palacio 1996).

These men guided their newspapers in a culturally sealed environment. Each ran their newsroom with the help of an unchanging and compact group of subordinates, and there was little or no infusion of new voices in middle levels of newsroom management. My review of the 1999 directory of Periodistas de Investigación, a groundbreaking Mexican professional organization dedicated to training for investigative reporting, found only one journalist from the three inertial newspapers in a membership list of two hundred. This leads to the conclusion that the cadres of civic-oriented journalists, academics, and economists who helped push organizational change in civic publications did not enter inertial publications, adapted to old standards once they arrived, or soon left. Examples from my interviews of those who left these newspapers included *Reforma* reporter Ariadna Bermeo. Her first job in journalism was writing copy for a well-known *Excélsior* political columnist who sold favorable mentions in her column to regime figures; she subsequently left the paper as quickly as she could.[9] A former *Unomásuno* reporter who requested anonymity described how his columns on President Zedillo were censored in the late 1990s. After one year, he left for *El Universal*. At the *Novedades* group, U.S.-trained editors and reporters resigned over censorship or disagreements over news ethics in 1988, 1991, 1992, and 2000.[10]

Years of success within the bounds of authoritarian Mexican journalism prevented inertial newsroom leaders from accurately perceiving new incentives in politics, the economy, and journalism that pushed change in other media organizations. Within these newsrooms, few new ideas filtered into top management and no one with alternative ideas about journalism was able to muster sufficient organizational power to lead change.

El Universal: From Lap Dog to Watchdog

Only one of Mexico City's twenty-one regime-oriented newspapers attempted a civic-oriented transformation from the 1970s through the 1990s. That was Mexico's largest newspaper, *El Universal*, which was founded just months before the outbreak of the 1917 Revolution.[11] Like other civic news organizations, the newspaper changed most in the realm of government and electoral coverage, and the decision to profoundly transform *El Universal* was the owner's to make. How he reached the decision is more complex, requiring a transformation of his mental model of Mexican journalism, politics, and society.

Juan Francisco Ealy Ortiz spent his entire professional career at *El Universal*, arriving in 1967 at age twenty-three and becoming publisher two years later. Ealy distinguished his newspaper by gently testing the system's limits early in the paper's history. *El Universal* published politically diverse opinion columns, including a column from the jailed leader of the outlawed Mexican Communist Party, among other dissident voices. Ealy was proud of this exhibition of political pluralism, highlighting it throughout his career in speeches and in-house publications. Yet the media owner and his newspaper also thrived under the subordinate PRI media system. Ealy was one of several newspaper owners to receive monthly payments from the president's office in the late 1970s, according to journalist Julio Scherer (1990). Another critic, journalist Rafael Rodríguez Castañeda (1993), stated that Ealy's reporters covering the president's office were among the most passive in the country. The president and cabinet members were Ealy's guests at family and newspaper functions, photos of which lined the walls of his buildings. He met privately with politicians and joined their informal friendship networks. And outside of the editorial section, *El Universal*'s news pages were as subordinate, passive, and nondiverse as any publication of the era.

Ricardo Pascoe, a youthful Trotskyite and later a Mexico City official for the PRD, described the contradictions he found at *El Universal* in the 1980s when he contributed a regular guest column:

> I wrote at *El Universal* for many years and it was a newspaper that seemed to me to be absolutely ironic. From the first page to about the fifth was something, if you will excuse the expression, that made you want to vomit. And suddenly you get to the editorial page, and there were opinions from all sorts of people. There was Helio Flores and Naranjo with their biting cartoons. And then you would turn the next page and return once again to the world of the sickening. In other words, it was really contradictory. Now, that was before. Today it is more, I believe, newspapers are much more open.[12]

Echoing Pascoe, the content analysis of front-page coverage presented in chapters 3 and 4 found that *El Universal* moved from a passive, subordinate, monologue type of journalism in 1980 to a more pluralistic and assertive approach by 2000.

Yet the path of *El Universal*, or any other Mexican newspaper, was not predetermined from some mechanistic response to societal opening and greater commercial competition. Several newspapers in the capital city and around the country had asserted greater autonomy before *El Universal*. Several other publications never did. Why did *El Universal*'s owner decide to profoundly transform his newspaper in the 1990s when *Excélsior*'s Díaz Redondo did nothing? Two factors contribute to the process of answering this question: (1) what ended the newspaper owner's faith in the authoritarian press institution in which he formed professionally and thrived for decades; and (2) why the owner chose a civic-oriented transformation rather than adopt a market-driven strategy or simply switch political benefactors as PRI fortunes waned.

My explanation of the decision to transform *El Universal* formed through an in-depth interview with Ealy, in-house histories of the newspaper that depicted Ealy's vision of *El Universal* over the last two decades, news articles and books mentioning the media baron, and dozens of interviews and informal discussions with his subordinates.[13] My analysis was sharpened by a direct comparison of *El Universal* and *Excélsior*. The following narrative develops the argument, but the short answer is this: Ealy broke openly with the regime because he was personally affected by its degradation. He turned his newspaper toward a more civic approach to journalism rather than other models because of the prestige this earned abroad and because of his interactions with a reformist editor he empowered to remake the newsroom. It is also true, as several Mexican journalists point out, that Ealy's decision to transform the newspaper was made as *El Universal* faced a new style of competition from the civic-oriented *Reforma*. While this was an important influence, probably even a necessary one, it is not a sufficient explanation for the decision to change *El Universal* from a passive, subordinate publication to a much more plural and assertive one. *Excélsior, Unomásuno,* and *Novedades* all faced the same competition and did not change their coverage. The answer for *El Universal*'s civic transformation is more complex. It involves each of the multiple layers of institutional change: societal, institutional, organizational, and psychological. The diffusion of the civic style from one newspaper to another required the transformation of the mental models of those with the organizational power to lead the newsroom.

When Juan Francisco Ealy Ortiz became the publisher of *El Universal* in 1969, he was twenty-five years old and still studying in the economics department of Mexico's National Autonomous University. He had quickly climbed through the administrative ranks of a family enterprise paralyzed by debt and union-controlled management. Thanks to a loan from a favorite uncle who had once been the country's secretary of agriculture, Ealy purchased 41 percent of a newspaper that was on the verge of bankruptcy. He brought an entrepreneurial vision to the publisher's office that he quickly applied to the newspaper. His two goals, he said, were to make the newspaper solvent and to obtain the majority of the newspaper's stock. Working, eating, and sleeping at the newspaper, he accomplished both objectives. By the 1980s, he possessed majority ownership and had wrested power from employee unions that controlled positions such as comptroller and editor-in-chief so that he could solely direct *El Universal*. Three decades later, Ealy recalled that he tackled these administrative tasks with "great passion." In an interview, he appeared to be an intense man in general, but when he spoke of the era in which he took over ownership of the paper, his voice rose and quickened even more. Those days were a formative part of his life.

Ealy's passion for his newspaper accompanied a business acumen. Aside from making *El Universal* a useful vehicle for government advertising—he estimates the government provided 80 percent of all press advertising in the 1970s—his strategy was to build the largest classified advertising section in the country. He was successful. Critical foreign journalists who had little other use for Ealy's newspaper advised newcomers to Mexico City in the early 1990s to look in *El Universal*'s classified section for an apartment. *El Universal*'s classified ads also became a surrogate marketplace where Mexicans gauged the barter value of their possessions. By 1999, even in the face of strong competition, *El Universal*'s confidential internal studies reported that the newspaper carried seven times more classified ad linage than *Reforma* and almost seventeen times more than *Excélsior*. The newspaper also became the first in Mexico City to hire an outside circulation auditor. Under Ealy's leadership, *El Universal* went from the basement of Mexico City newspaper circulation and ad revenues in the late 1960s to the number one position in the early 1990s.

While some in Mexican journalism have viewed Ealy as a typically collusive Mexican newspaper owner—a supporter and beneficiary of the PRI system—the newspaper magnate had always shown tentative signs of autonomy that could be perceived as real or empty rhetoric, depending on the interpreter's point of view. His own view is that he opened up the newspaper's editorial pages in 1969–one year after the government massacred protesting students —in anticipation of the democratic country Mexico would one day become. He said he bought out the government's final share of the newspaper by the 1980s because he thought even partial government ownership of a newspaper was wrong. Ealy said that he did all of this because he was thinking about a future with a pluralistic press and a consolidated democracy. For *El Universal* and Mexico, this was a future that took thirty years to arrive.

While the newspaper's editorial page diversity distinguished it in the early 1970s, *El Universal* lost its groundbreaking edge as civic-oriented newspapers opened in the late 1970s and 1980s. The need to change the news pages became palpable in the 1990s for several reasons. First, a new, assertive style of Mexico City newspaper competitor began to prosper. The civic newspapers *La Jornada*, *El Financiero,* and *Reforma* came to control the number two, three, and four positions in Mexico City circulation as readers turned to more credible newspapers to help them make sense of political and economic shocks rocking the country. Ealy's entrepreneurial sense had always made him aware of competitors in the Mexican press. He likened this sensitivity to a car manufacturer's awareness of competing models of automobiles. Prior to the 1990s, he faced many rival companies but only one model of journalism. New competition came from other PRI-supporting newspapers such as *El Heraldo de México* in the 1970s. The 1990s were different. Ealy ordered a market study that found that *El Universal*'s readers were aging, while *Reforma* appealed to younger, more affluent Mexicans who were frustrated with the government.

As circulation shifts occurred, Mexicans generally and Ealy in particular suffered through a series of systemic shocks that delegitimized the political system, including the assassination of PRI presidential candidate Luis Donaldo Colosio. Ealy's relationship with Colosio went back at least to 1990, when Colosio was stepping down as president of the PRI to become economic development secretary under President Carlos Salinas. Ealy told investigators that he began to meet monthly with Colosio and other business and political leaders in 1990, according to the special prosecutor's report on the candidate's assassination. The "Grupo de los Diez," or Group of Ten, met over lunch at one another's homes, sometimes serenaded by mariachis. These informal gatherings produced the sort of bonds so important to creating trust in Latin American societies, where contracts are solidified as much by personal ties and loyalties than legally actionable contracts. In addition to the newspaper publisher, the group of friends of the late candidate included the governor of Sonora, where Ealy bought a state-owned newspaper in 1994 at Colosio's suggestion.[14]

Ealy acknowledged an especially close relationship with the assassinated politician during an interview in 2004.

> EALY: I was, in effect, a friend of Mr. Colosio. He even said that I was not his friend, but his brother. Our friendship was that close, but I believe that one thing is friendship and another is politics . . .
>
> AUTHOR: Did Mr. Colosio's death make you think the single-party system had to change?
>
> EALY: No, I think that sooner or later the country had to mature, the country had to change.

At the time of the investigation, *El Universal*'s reaction to the assassination suggested that the killing meant more to Ealy and his staff than just another sign of a decaying regime. Though formal charges were never laid, Colosio's public rupture with outgoing President Salinas produced suspicion about Salinas's involvement in the Kennedy-style assassination, officially attributed to a lone gunman. State investigators briefly pursued a conspiracy theory when they formally interviewed Ealy about concerns raised by Colosio's closest collaborators, who never believed their patron died at the hands of a single lunatic. Ealy learned in a particularly moving way that Colosio's family also doubted the official explanation. As the publisher paid his condolences to Colosio's widow following the assassination, her words to him were "they used and deceived us." Days later, President Carlos Salinas called Ealy to Los Pinos and told him to stop reporting on the possibility of a plot to kill the candidate (Jáquez 2000).

After Salinas had left office, *El Universal*'s reporters resumed their investigatation, eventually zeroing in on Salinas himself as the mastermind of the killing. The arrest of Salinas's brother Raúl on charges of ordering the murder of another top PRI politician five months after Colosio's death only added fuel to the fire of suspicion. (After a decade in prison, the charges against Raúl Salinas were dropped in 2005.) President Ernesto Zedillo, Colosio's replacement as PRI candidate, also ordered the newspaper to stop investigating the murder. The newspaper's hiring of two especially critical political columnists—Zedillo's wife previously had likened one, Ricardo Alemán, to a biting dog—also angered Zedillo. According to Ealy and his top associates, in separate interviews, Zedillo's interior secretary used an old line of communication with media owners to tell Ealy to change his ways. He sent a message through the newspaper's older political columnists: *El Universal* and the government were like "two locomotives racing toward a wreck, and that the government would come out unscathed."[15]

When the newspaper did not change its tone, Finance Secretariat officials charged Ealy with tax evasion. Police swarmed into the newspaper to arrest Ealy, but he was home at the time. Tipped off by the newsroom, the publisher escaped to the house of a nearby diplomat and appealed to journalist groups around the world as a victim of state repression. He turned himself in the next morning and was briefly detained before being released pending court action. Although the tax authorities performed ninety-nine audits of the newspaper, filed three charges, and said Ealy owed more than $3.5 million, the courts threw out all but one charge and ordered Ealy to pay a $2,400 administrative fine. The zealousness of the prosecution and its meager results raised Ealy's international stature among publishers, even if questions from his detractors at home were never fully quieted.

Ealy said later that the prosecution reinforced his decision to transform the newspaper: "We reinforced things. I suffered a persecution for almost a year. There is the newspaper, there are the facts. We didn't change a period or a comma. All of the ideas that we had and all of the plans that we had moved forward. This gave me a new push. It was as if they injected me with vitamins to keep struggling and keep saying the truth although now, yes, it really did hurt them."[16]

The decision to change *El Universal* was made, but how to change the newspaper was still to be decided. Foreign press associations and Ealy's loyal young editor influenced the decision.

Foreign journalists and press associations such as the Committee to Protect Journalists and the Inter-American Press Association protested the government's prosecution. While Ealy had participated for years in the Inter-American Press Association, he had never been the center of an international outcry. The new prestige influenced him. He recalled: "I received a lot of support from the foreign press, from foreign associations, a great amount of support. This made me see the situation as one in which I had to keep going forward because they were committing an injustice against a person whose only crime was to say the truth."

When Ealy was arrested, he had just promoted the states section editor, Roberto Rock, to editor-in-chief. Rock was forty years old and had been the newspaper's top editor for four weeks and six days. Along with the break with the PRI, a new style of competition, and attention from abroad, the fourth driver of organizational change at *El Universal* was Ealy's relationship with this reformist editor. Rock pushed for a more expansive transformation of the news pages than initially planned and administered the changes within the newsroom. Ealy's decision to grant wide authority to Rock over the advice of older business managers meant the newspaper would attempt to change newsroom culture along with its outdated design and advertising sales department. A key juncture in the development of the transformation project occurred when Ealy overturned the vote of senior managers with decades of experience who wanted to limit change. The publisher sided with Rock. Democracy was fine for the country, Ealy said when overruling his lifelong associates, but his vote was the only one that counted in that boardroom. This anecdote, repeated by several sources in interviews, shows the importance of owner decision making in media organizations and of trust placed in the top newsroom managers.

Changing *El Universal* required transforming a newsroom of more than 150 employees that had been raised in "a culture of submission," as Rock himself described it. Outside consultants remarked that changing ingrained worldviews and behaviors at the publication was like turning an aircraft carrier around: it needed constant attention and a wide swath in which to maneuver. Rock was the owner's change agent in the newsroom and oversaw the transition at every step.[17]

Son of an *El Universal* linotypist and a lifelong reporter at the newspaper, Rock did not have the typical profile of an acquiescent *El Universal* journalist. His father was a fairly militant unionist, his university training came from the politicized social science department of the National Autonomous University of Mexico, and he formed some of his ideas about media and politics from discussions with reporters at the Washington DC office of the *Baltimore Sun*, where he worked on a six-month exchange supported by the Ford Foundation. Even prior to assuming a leadership role at the newspaper, Rock discussed his views on the necessity of the press acting as a counterweight to political authority with his colleagues.[18]

Brought up within a traditional Mexican newspaper, Rock also learned organizational savvy. He knew how to present options to Ealy and how far to push the owner and his business managers when they resisted change. He tried to subtly introduce Ealy to new ideas about journalism by inviting foreign correspondents in Mexico to meet with the aging publisher. Later, he arranged for Ealy to meet Katherine Graham of the *Washington Post* and the *New York Times* publisher Arthur O. Sulzberger Jr. One reporter Rock hired away from a civic newspaper explained, "I see Roberto Rock as a man wearing a hard helmet, who turns around and tries another way when he runs up against a brick wall."[19]

Under President Vicente Fox, Ealy's sponsorship was instrumental to the formation of the coalition of newspapers, academics, and NGOs known as the Oaxaca Group, which pushed through a groundbreaking access-to-information law in 2002 and a so-far stalled legislative initiative to allow reporters to protect confidential sources. Ealy and his newspaper promoted proposals to prompt federal investigations against crimes against journalists, finally adopted in February 2006, and helped form a task force of reporters to investigate the murder of journalists. There were some things Ealy would not do, however. According to several published reports, he cancelled a magazine story that questioned how a close personal friend had received concessions from the government to run lucrative gambling parlors.

Entrepreneurial vision, a civic-style of competition, personal confrontations with a disintegrating political system, influence from abroad, and interaction with a reformist editor convinced Ealy to profoundly transform journalism at the newspaper in the 1990s, and in a civic direction. The parameters of the change were still being tested a decade later. However, compared to the early 1990s, *El Universal* was a more autonomous, assertive, and diverse newspaper. As the head of Periodistas de Investigación stated in 2004, Ealy "changed in time, and for the benefit of us all."[20]

By comparing *El Universal* with *Excélsior*, we can isolate the variables that explain journalistic change and its direction (see table 7.1). Both publications faced similar environmental conditions and were run by the same publisher in hierarchical fashion for decades. Here, however, the similarities end, and the variables explaining journalistic change come clearly into focus. Systemic shocks in Mexican politics and the economy in the mid-1990s were abstract for the publisher of *Excélsior* but personal for the owner of *El Universal*. While *El Universal*'s coverage of the murder of Colosio brought Ealy into direct confrontation with the regime, *Excélsior* experienced no such direct confrontation. Additionally, at *El Universal,* the support of foreign media organizations and contacts reinforced alternative ideas and sources of prestige, while no similar process happened at *Excélsior*. Finally, there was no leadership turnover at *Excélsior*, but Ealy promoted a reformist editor to run *El Universal*, was swayed by his arguments and ideas, and empowered him to transform the newsroom.

Table 7.1 Divergent Pathways

Similarities

Excélsior	El Universal
Market leader in 1990	Market leader in 1990
Faces new style of competition for readers and ads by 1995	Faces new style of competition for readers and ads by 1995
Same publisher since 1976	Same publisher since 1969
Hierarchical management	Hierarchical management

Differences

Excélsior	El Universal
Systemic shocks are abstract	Systemic shocks are personal
No direct confrontation with regime	Direct confrontation with the regime
Closed to outside ideas	Open to outside ideas
Same sources of prestige	New sources of prestige
No leadership turnover	Leadership turnover

Outcomes

Excélsior	El Universal
A frozen organizational culture and inertial authoritarianism	A transformed organizational culture and civic-oriented journalism

Adaptive Authoritarianism

Another authoritarian alternative to civic journalism in the 1990s appeared as local television station owners and directors adapted to new societal conditions by tying news organizations to state-level political leaders.[21] Several local television stations adapted the authoritarian model of journalism by serving local political elites of any party. My analysis of such cases finds further support for the importance of organizational leadership and clashing mental models of journalism in understanding journalistic change.

I chose to analyze local television because of the variation in coverage compared to national networks. While national networks produced relatively balanced news coverage by the 2000 campaign, local coverage remained slanted in ways that suggested linkages to local political elites rather than the influence of audience preferences.[22]

Table 7.2 presents the cases. They were chosen from a ninety-three-program sample of local newscasts that were monitored by the federal elections office in 2000, and come from states run by each of the top three political parties in Mexico. Three cases are privately held local news stations and three are state-owned TV stations. All of the stations produced news that

Table 7.2 Local Television Stations, 2000 Election

State	Governing Party	Station	Ownership Regime	Degree of Bias for Governing Party[a]
Baja California	PAN	Channel 66	Private	-6.8
Guanajuato	PAN	Channel 4	State	15.9
Guanajuato	PAN	Televisa del Bajío	Private	31.8
Tabasco	PRI	Televisión Tabasqueña	State	87.9
Tabasco	PRI	Channel 9	Private	36.25[b]
Tlaxcala	PRD	Televisión Tlaxcalteca	State	11.0

Notes: [a] Difference in the percentage of time allotted to the state-level governing party as compared to the percentage of time allotted to top partisan rival.
[b] Average of afternoon and evening broadcasts.

was highly biased for the state-level party in power during the 2000 presidential election with the exception of Baja California's Channel 66, which leaned slightly in favor of a state-level opposition party and provided an interesting comparison. Bias was measured only by the differences in time dedicated to the top two parties, a blunt but effective measure considering the level of differences in coverage time that was registered. The sample also includes two of the most-developed states in Mexico (Baja California and Guanajuato), as well as two where the private sector is very weak (Tlaxcala and Tabasco). By comparing across states and ownership regimes, I hoped to identify the rationales, incentives, and enforcement mechanisms of adaptive authoritarianism in the newsroom. The case studies were constructed from interviews with the managing director and the news department head in three stations and the managing director in two stations. I was unable to obtain official interviews at Tabasco's private sector station, but I interviewed two anonymous news employees, other area journalists, and an electoral institute official with a reputation for independence. I also reviewed news articles, government reports, and other ethnographic materials.

The most striking finding from the interviews was the degree of top-down control that characterized both government-owned and private sector television stations. A second finding was that rank-and-file journalists in each of the stations espoused the norms of civic-oriented journalism, but most could not practice them fully. In the most extreme cases, the underlying conflict between their professional values and journalistic behaviors caused emotional distress, and the interviews became almost confessional.

Guanajuato State Television

Like all the state television directors in the sample, the executive director of Guanajuato's state channel is always directly appointed by the government.

In Guanajuato, the director during the 2000 presidential campaign owed his office to the former state governor and then-PAN presidential candidate, Vicente Fox. Station personnel explained that the focus of news programming at Channel 4 changed with each new executive director, either focusing on the governor and his cabinet specifically or political parties generally. "If we have a governor who perhaps asks us not to touch certain interests, or more than interests, not to adversely affect his image, then he dictates a policy and the director follows it," said news director Alicia Arias Muñoz.

State-owned television stations "are part of Narcissus's mirror," said executive director Jorge Pantojo, who was appointed by newly elected governor Juan Carlos Romero Hicks in 2001. "If the governor in this moment is *panista*, everyone goes for the PAN. If he is *priísta*, everyone goes for the PRI."

When Fox was governor, the station was on a short leash because he had his eyes set on the presidency. This caused the united opposition in the state legislature to threaten to withhold additional funding from the station in 2001, which, in turn, convinced Romero Hicks to hire a new director whose mission would be to tone down pro-PAN coverage. Previously a director at the university-run Channel 11 in Mexico City, Pantojo said that he accepted the Guanajuato appointment only when Romero Hicks assured him that he wanted Channel 4 to operate in a nonpartisan manner. Pantojo understood, however, that the governor could also revoke that order.

Televisión Tabasqueña

The director of Tabasco's state television channel in 2000 answered to the state government's director of Social Communication and Public Relations, Ady Gárcia López. Gárcia was an appointee of Robert Madrazo, who became governor in a heavily disputed election in late 1994. Among the opposition's complaints that year were pro-PRI media bias and that the Madrazo campaign exceeded the legal campaign spending cap by more than 100 percent. Some of that money went to journalists and media owners in the state. In one of the more Byzantine twists in Tabasco politics, crates with original campaign documents supporting these claims were left at a PRD protest in Mexico City. Complaints of media bias surfaced again in 2000, when the newly empowered Federal Electoral Tribunal annulled Tabasco's gubernatorial election in part because biased television coverage had interfered with the public's right to freely elect their leaders.

Like Vicente Fox in Guanajuato, Roberto Madrazo has national political ambitions. He participated in the PRI's first internal presidential primary in 1999, losing a close internal election to Francisco Labastida. In 2002, Madrazo became the PRI's first popularly elected national president. In 2005 he became the PRI's presidential candidate for 2006. Madrazo brought Gárcia with him to the PRI's National Executive Committee in 2002, where she was placed in charge of party relations with media outside of the national capital. Tabasco state governor Manuel Andrade is a protégé of Madrazo. He also has the power to hire—and fire—the director of state television.

Televisión de Tlaxcala

Tlaxcala's state channel is the only source of local television news in that small state. During the 2000 elections, an engineer who had helped found several important educational stations in Mexico, Hector Parker, directed the state's broadcasting system. Governor Alfonso Sánchez Anaya of the PRD appointed Parker upon taking office in 1999, just months after leaving the PRI because the party had passed over him for the candidacy. Sánchez Anaya has been accused twice of removing journalists who refused to follow his news policies. Mexico's Fraternidad de Reporteros, a journalists' association in Mexico City, accused him of removing five radio programs from the airwaves in 1999 because they were too critical (Salas and Olivos 1999). In 2002, staff members and electoral commission members said he fired Parker and almost all the journalists in the television station's news division. According to the station manager, Romeo Peña Silva, the dismissals occurred because the journalists did not support the PRD enough during state legislative elections in 2002. "We followed the law in terms of times allotted to each of the parties. This was looked upon badly. So when the governor's expectations in the elections weren't met, he decided to fire the executive director," Peña Silva said. "The new director has told us, 'your boss is the governor and you owe your job to the governor.'"[23]

The governors of Guanajuato, Tabasco, and Tlaxcala controlled news production on state-run television during the 2000 elections. Their conception of journalism as a resource to be captured for partisan advantage meant authoritarian newsroom practices easily adapted to new political realities. The principal method of enforcement of authoritarian norms in the newsroom was through the appointment of the station's executive director. Neither electoral competition nor combative journalists guaranteed the application of a civic-oriented news model.

If top-down, executive-branch control explains adaptive authoritarianism in state-owned television, why did authoritarianism adapt in private sector news outlets that should have become more attuned to market forces as the PRI regime weakened? Quantitative analysis of ninety-three newscasts found that news bias was indeed lower on aggregate in privately owned stations compared to the previous PRI monologue found in most Mexican news, but not all private sector stations followed a commercial model. Again, the person with power in the news organization—in this case the media owner—decided the model of journalism guiding news production at a station.

Channel 9 in Tabasco

Perhaps the purest form of adaptive authoritarianism was found at Tabasco's private Channel 9. News at the station reflected all the characteristics of the traditional Mexican press institution, but its focus was at the local level rather than central regime elites in Mexico City. The family of a PRI state governor received a new federal broadcast concession and founded Channel 9 in 1979. When family members could not turn the new concession into profits, they sold the station to Ángel González, a Monterrey native who quietly built up an empire of ninety radio stations and thirty-eight television stations in six Latin American countries. In addition to Channel 9, González also owns part or all of a television station in the southern Mexican state of Chiapas.[24]

González began his career by selling Mexican TV programming abroad. He began his own television empire in Guatemala, where he now owns the only four broadcast stations in the country with a national reach. An Organization of American States report in 2000 called González's network a monopoly, criticized its links to Guatemalan politicians, and cited with concern the cancellation of "the only program critical of the government." González has spoken openly of his willingness to support politicians of any party he favors with free air time: "I award free publicity to anyone who deserves it," he said (Weissert 2002). In Tabasco, González's preference has been the governing PRI. In fact, prior to the 2000 election, even mentioning the PRD or those closely associated with it was prohibited at the station.

The owner's relationship with the local PRI appears to be purely pragmatic. Station employees were told that the state government's advertising purchases were enough to cover the payroll. Should González's preference change, however, station personnel will be expected to comply. As a news director told an employee: "Look, this is the way we are here. If the boss asks you to paint yourself yellow [the PRD's color], you paint yourself yellow. And if the boss asks you to paint yourself tricolor [the PRI's colors], you paint yourself tricolor. And if the boss asks you to paint yourself blue [the PAN's color], you paint yourself blue."[25]

Televisa del Bajio

The news philosophy under Televisa owner Emilio Azcárraga Jean in the second half of the 1990s committed the national network to a market-driven approach to the news. This model included certain limitations for democratic development, such as a tendency to emphasize conflict and crime. However, it also presented an important, affirmative influence for democratization by offering voters information about politically diverse candidates for office. Azcárraga Jean's new philosophy did not diffuse naturally to wholly owned affiliates such as Televisa del Bajio during the 2000 campaign. It had to be imposed by the central office.

Leonel Nogueda, CEO of Televisa del Bajio since November 1998, said his station was known for taking sides during previous local elections. However, the station covered the PAN more in 2000 because of campaign dynamics particular to Guanajuato that year, including Vicente Fox's candidacy. Yet when the order came from a new network vice president midway through the campaign to tone down PAN coverage, Nogueda complied by lowering pro-Fox bias by 30 percentage points.

Again, the decision to shift the news model was made by managers atop a hierarchical structure. By 2002, the local station seemed to have absorbed the market-driven approach. Nogueda projected the philosophy underpinning market journalism during an interview. He said news should not take sides, should protect advertisers, and "has to be a business. A news production structure costs a lot of money."[26]

Baja California's Channel 66

This Mexicali, Baja California, station was the only television station I studied that did not bias its newscasts in favor of the state-level ruling party (PAN), but instead inclined slightly toward the main opposition party in that state (the PRI). That skew was not the stated intention of journalists, who purposefully and with the blessing of the station's owners designed an elections coverage plan to give all candidates an equal airing. The reason the journalists felt secure in pursuing partisan diversity was their belief that the owners and CEO of the station wanted the coverage that way.

The programming of Channel 66 in Mexicali reflects the founding family's vision of journalism as a force for community service, the owners' outsider status among Mexico's media elite, and the family's tenacity in the face of the inequalities of Mexico's media politics. The station's "founding culture," as Schein might have called it, was unique among the case studies.

Channel 66 is owned by Grupo Intermedia, with family Arnoldo Cabada de la O at its head. Cabada petitioned President José López Portillo directly for his first broadcast concession in 1979 after he won a national public service prize for a local news program in Chihuahua. During the program, callers offered services and products for the poor. The show made Cabada a celebrity in Ciudad Juárez, but did not endear him to the owner of Televisa's local affiliate where he rented airtime. As the family tells it, Cabada and the station owner argued over the credit and prize money. Cabada eventually left the station and approached López Portillo for a concession to open a new station. But even with the president's blessing, the Communications and Transportation Secretariat blocked him because, son Luis Arnoldo Cabada says, he was not part of a powerful media family. When Cabada told the president, López Portillo personally ordered the secretary to award the concession.

Fourteen years after the first concession, Cabada and his sons tried to participate in the Carlos Salinas administration's privatization of the state-owned network Imevisión. The Cabadas believed the bidding was fixed in the Finance Secretariat, which was in charge of privatizing state-owned enterprises as the country moved toward a market-based economy. The family decided to go directly to the Communications and Transportation Secretariat, which oversees the awarding of concessions. Luis Arnoldo Cabada said secretariat officials tried to turn him away even though the official deadline had not passed. "I said, 'we are Mexicans and have the right,' and I said it in front of the notary and television cameraman I had brought with me. I slept in the Hotel Camino Real with the 140 applications beside me. Andrés Caso, then the assistant secretary, called us and that's how the Mexicali station was born, as well as another in Piedras Negras, Cuahuila. Only two stations, but we applied for 140."[27]

The rest of the stations went to Ricardo Salinas Pliego, a Monterrey businessman and business partner of President Carlos Salinas's brother, Raúl. They became the country's second-largest network, TV Azteca.

Like the experience of the Mexican press, local television news became more balanced only when the news philosophy of those with power inside the organization demanded it. This finding of the determinacy of hierarchical power structures supports the conclusion from earlier chapters that organizational dynamics are central to understanding why news media resist societal change or choose a particular transformative pathway, sometimes even in advance of societal change. In all cases reviewed thus far—including civic-oriented journalism, inertial authoritarianism, and adaptive authoritarianism—the mental models of those with the power to direct news organizations explains the type of news Mexicans received from their media.

The mental models of journalism and society of newsroom leaders reviewed in this chapter responded to various drivers—orthodoxy and cognitive filters on the part of Excélsior's publisher; delegitimizing political shocks with personal effects, newfound international prestige, and interaction with a civic-minded editor for the owner of *El Universal*. In local television, pragmatic calculations of partisan gain or personal profit by state governors or station owners drove adaptive authoritarianism, network dictates moved Televisa del Bajio away from adaptive authoritarianism, and the founding values of a journalist-owned news company influenced the second generation of owners of Mexicali's Channel 66.

8 Market-Driven Journalism

Asked why his network broke with custom to give better coverage to the opposition during the first-ever Mexico City mayoral election, the new president of the country's television powerhouse, Televisa, answered directly: "Democracy is a great customer."[1] And indeed it was. All three major Mexican political parties invested heavily in television ads during important federal and state elections in early 1997, thanks to more public campaign financing. Ratings for news programs and special reports such as a candidates' debate increased, meaning the networks could raise advertising rates based on the size of the viewing audience. Moreover, the cash injection came at a time when Mexico's commercial television giant was hurting. The company was heavily indebted, registering net losses, and had squandered leadership in the exploding Mexico City cable market. To top it off, a new competitor with a flamboyant anchor pounded the older network's primetime newscast. Audiences preferred two-year-old TV Azteca's *Hechos de la Noche* newscast over Televisa's staple *24 Horas* by a more than two-to-one margin.[2] All of this occurred during a decade in which private sector advertising skyrocketed and government support shriveled, changing the incentives for news production in a way never seen in modern Mexico. PRI rulers had wanted the news to produce public support, or at least acquiescence, but the largest private advertisers sought customers. Under these circumstances, the question for those wanting to understand the transformation of journalism in Mexico is not why Televisa's approach to journalism changed in the late 1990s, but what took it so long to make a switch?

An inquiry into the transformation of Mexican television journalism and the market-driven model it adopted needs to account for the multiple layers of the institutional development of the media. Societal level transformations including electoral liberalization, increasing commercial competition, and the energizing private sector advertising market set the parameters for the decision to change journalism in Mexico's mammoth Televisa network in the late 1990s. However, these contextual shifts in the political economy of news production do not explain why the network took as long as it did to change its newscasts or why the news was transformed into market-driven journalism rather than a civic-oriented or adaptive authoritarian model.

While societal transformations created new incentives for news production, organizational leadership and professional identities explain the timing and direction of journalistic transformation. In this case, new leadership at Televisa responded to societal changes that had been developing since the 1980s. Thrust into office forty-three days before his father's death, twenty-nine-year-old network president Emilio Azcárraga Jean and the young executives he brought with him were trained to recognize the profit-making potential of the news. When an anchorwoman asked whether the company would continue to support the PRI, Azcárraga Jean responded: "I inherited my father's responsibilities, not his commitments."[3] So in the spring of 1997, Televisa's news programs left a ruling party candidate to fend for himself for the first time. The PRI's subsequent loss of the capital city government, as well as its outright majority in Congress, foreshadowed the loss of the presidency and end of the PRI regime three years later.

The rise of market-driven journalism is a phenomenon in many neoliberal democracies where journalistic autonomy has eroded. Mexican television journalism, particularly, has changed by increasing the partisan balance in news coverage, while at the same time increasing its focus on crime and personalized woes. Analysis of the development of Mexican television news over the last five decades, especially on Televisa over the last quarter century, reveals the characteristics and determinants of three periods of Mexican television news: the authoritarian media institution; inertial authoritarianism; and, finally, the establishment and acceleration of a market-driven model. In each transition, the interplay of changes in the societal environment, organizational leadership, and journalists' professional identities determined the nature and timing of the transformation. Again, it is worth remembering that the market-driven model is an ideal type used for analytical purposes. As Hallin (2000a) notes, there are few "pure" representatives of any model of journalism. At various points, however, Televisa and other news organizations displayed a mix of traits that inclined toward one model more than the others. I argue that the preferred model at the network has been market-driven since 1997.

The implications of the market-driven news model for Mexican democracy are contradictory. Partisan balance on Mexican television initially encouraged electoral competition and participation, helping to phase out the single-party system.[4] The tabloidization of the news, however, took formal political participation off the agenda of mainstream newscasts and may have contributed to the political alienation Mexicans felt in 2003, when record numbers abstained from voting during the first post-PRI federal election. The people chose to express their demands on the street in a record-setting protest against crime just twelve months later.

What Is Market-Driven Journalism?

In an international study of news systems two decades ago, Altschull argued that the news media in any society can be described metaphorically as a piper playing tunes for the powerful. The pipers' paymasters might be political parties, political chieftains, or the captains of commerce. In authoritarian societies, he wrote, the state controls the news process by setting and enforcing the rules on news production. In capitalist democracies, commercial interests and their allies typically control news production, although they may be restrained by traditions of newsroom autonomy and public service (1984, 254, 259, 262).

Altschull, like others, called the U.S. media system a commercial system because news is produced largely in the private sector and is financed through advertising. Since the early 1980s, however, some researchers have contended that U.S. journalism has moved from a simple commercial news model, in which journalism norms compete with a business logic for control over the news process, into a phase where a commercial logic drives news decisions with little or no interference (McChesney 2000, 2, 3, 48–77; McManus 1994; Underwood 1993). Hallin (2000a) argues that a market-based logic became dominant in the United States in the mid-1980s. In television, this was due to increased competition, the end of government-mandated public service programming requirements, the rise of tabloid-driven local news and reality-based programming, and the purchase of media enterprises by profit-centered conglomerates.

While the market and the commercial forces it unleashes certainly influence news content in neoliberal democracies, Altschull's conceptualization requires qualification on two grounds. First, the U.S. media belong to the private sector and certainly respond to powerful commercial pressures, but also react to news management by government image-makers. Moreover, the view of journalists as pipers for the powerful must be moderated by the potential of journalistic resistance. The acknowledgement of the potential of journalists to preserve their autonomy runs counter to arguments that rely on a "system logic which assumes that state-controlled media serve the state and corporate-controlled media service business corporations" (Curran 2000, 125–26).

Journalists' resistance to encroachment on autonomous decision making is based on norms of public service and the need for legitimacy. Curran (2000) cites international examples of journalistic resistance beyond the confines of established liberal democracies and suggests that the desire for autonomy may have become a global aspiration as the ideals of democracy diffused across countries in the late twentieth century. Certainly, I heard such aspirations in newsrooms throughout Mexico from 1994 to 2004, even in the difficult atmosphere of heavily controlled newsrooms such as those in Tabasco.

Yet journalists' optimism about the potential of professionalism to moderate commercial or political encroachment on the newsroom is tempered by the hierarchical nature of newsrooms and the limited reach of professional norms. Hallin (2000a) notes in a study of U.S. journalism that public-service norms are weakest in television news stations where professionalism experienced only a brief heyday and was never fully consolidated even at its peak. Similarly, resistance in the hierarchical newsrooms of local Mexican television stations was not enough to change the overall tenor of news in stations where owners demanded certain types of coverage.

In the end, journalistic resistance to encroachment by either political or commercial figures—the rock of the state and the hard place of the market—illustrate what McManus calls the "eternal dilemma" of news. In *Market-Driven Journalism*, the professor writes: "The eternal dilemma of news is the tension between representing reality as accurately as humans can, and misrepresenting it in favor of those who control the production process—be they tribal chieftains, popes, kings, warlords, government officials or corporations" (1994, 199). Sometimes resistance works, and the news approximates reality as defined by a group working autonomously and at least partially on behalf of a broader public. Other times, the news reflects the reality of the paymaster.

The ascendance of a market logic in U.S. television newsrooms produced a number of changes in news content, frames, and forms over the past quarter century. These content characteristics are helpful in constructing a model of market-driven news to use as a reference regarding Mexican television news. In the academic literature, these trends have alternatively been referred to as market-driven journalism, sensationalism, or tabloidization. I use these labels interchangeably, although tabloidization is developing a literature of its own. My sense is that tabloidization is, as Hallin (2000a) might say, a more "pure" variant of market-driven journalism, installed without the resistance of civic journalistic norms or a need for public legitimacy.

Market-driven television journalism as practiced in the United States frames the news by focusing on personality, conflict, episodic events without context, and authority figures presented as either culprits or saviors rather than empowered citizens (Bennett 2004). In terms of news themes, stories on crime, disasters, celebrities, scandal, and individualized health problems displace public affairs coverage. While the market-driven agenda includes important topics such as domestic violence, the events usually are not treated as societal problems but individual troubles brought on by bad luck or dishonest or inept government officials. Moreover, formal politics and international news fades from the news agenda except during wars involving the United States, which are given personalized, dramatized, and fragmented treatment. Changes in form are evidenced in the packaging of news into visual stories using camera movement, fast-paced editing, dramatic music, and sometimes reenactments (Hallin 2000a; 2000b, 272; Grabe, Zhou, and Barnett 2001, 637–38; Bennett 2005, 54–59).

Academics and journalists debate the societal effects of market-driven journalism. Some argue that it is a form that depoliticizes the viewer, delegitimates government, and deforms the public agenda. Postmodernists contend, instead, that since tabloidization brings new voices and topics into elite-centered news programming, it is a form of popular resistance and expression, and that its focus on close-to-home issues such as domestic violence and consumer scams broadens the public agenda, rather than narrows it. Moreover, even "serious" journalists argue that dramatization focusing on real-life cases is a legitimate way to attract audiences' attention to societal problems (Hallin 2000b).

Echoing this argument, a TV Azteca news anchor said he uses jolting content and images in his news program *Hechos* to ensure that he is not preaching to an empty cathedral. "I come from the view that people have to tune into my program, and after that I'll worry about the content, for this, for that, for the other," he said. "Afterward I'll worry about all of that, but my fundamental preoccupation is that people watch me."[5] Similarly, former TV Azteca vice president for news Sergio Sarmiento, a prestigious columnist who became an architect of Azteca's more sensational style in the mid-1990s, told a national gathering of journalists in 1999 that sensationalism brings what every journalist wants—audience. "The fact is that sensationalism generates ratings. We have to start with the facts. This is one fact. Another fact is that all journalists want high ratings. What are ratings? Ratings are nothing more than an audience measurement. All journalists want the largest audience possible. No one likes to preach in the desert. That is why we always want to have a larger number of readers, a larger number of viewers, a larger number of listeners."[6]

However, the *Hechos* journalist mentioned previously also defended his use of sensational and sometimes shocking images on normative democratic grounds. He said his ultimate goal is to use the images to draw attention to corruption and ineptitude in the criminal justice system.

> What I want is that when there is a painful incident, when there is a shocking event that the images portray, for it to be framed as a justice issue. There is also a story behind (the images) that has to do with corruption, that has to do with the poor administration of justice, that has to do with the work of the prosecutors, and that has to do with the citizens' access to justice. Then the thing is to take this event which is so shocking, but add something to it, give it something so the citizen knows "my system of justice has become a disaster." That is, not stick with the shocking anecdote, but add force to the story.[7]

Critics of tabloid news content generally argue that the style rarely includes context for cases of individual outrages and demands for justice, depriving viewers of the information needed to debate causes and solutions to systemic problems. Instead, tabloid stories focus on common people in a way that individualizes their dilemmas and fragments social trends. In a market-driven news station, for example, a rape victim would be covered more readily than a victims' organization. Critics argue that tabloid journalism provokes emotions rather than understanding, delegitimizes participation rather than empowering citizens, and distorts the public agenda rather than reflecting problems in proportion to reality (Hallin 2000b; Sparks 1998; Grabe, Zhou, Lang, and Bolls 2000; Gross and Aday 2003).

Much of the general criticism of market-driven journalism applies to Mexican television after 1997. However, the rise of pluralism in elections coverage for the first time in Mexican history and the fact that essentially no government criticism appeared on Mexican television prior to the rise of market-driven journalism are important countervailing trends that must move the academic discussion of market-driven journalism and tabloidization beyond the realm of established democracies. The potential effects for democratic deepening are complex and contradictory, rather than black and white.

After years of discussion and limited amounts of empirical research, the debate over the effects of market-driven journalism has not been settled, and it is not my purpose to try to do so here. Ultimately, most researchers agree on two elements: the news media and the journalistic forms they employ—including tabloidization—can influence a nation's political agenda, its stock of social and political knowledge, and its style of political participation and discussion; and journalists use market-based techniques such as sensationalism in an attempt to draw viewers and thus increase the amount their organizations can charge advertisers (Hallin 2000a).

During nearly two decades of economic and political liberalization, the environment in which television news was produced in Mexico became more similar to the market-dominated landscape of U.S. television news production. As the macroenvironment of news production changed, Mexican networks hired U.S. news producers to work on TV Azteca newscasts or train Televisa technicians. In this sense, "Americanization," or the transferal of U.S. television norms, is an important element in the Mexican television transition, especially given the techniques used in news production today in Mexico.[8] However, the Mexican transition to market-driven journalism involved more than a simple adoption of U.S. norms once the news environment liberalized. The concentrated structure of the television market, its links to the transitional political system, the organizational structures and interests of individual TV networks, and the inertial and emerging cultures of the newsroom and journalistic identity all contributed to a difficult transition from an authoritarian news model toward a market-driven one that exhibits both generalizable and uniquely Mexican elements.

From about 1997 on, Mexican television newscasts increasingly produced a form of market-driven journalism that rivaled the purest of market content in the United States. More civic-oriented content appeared in some cases, but given that Mexican television journalism never went through a period during which civic norms were dominant or consistent, the dearth of party-based electoral coverage and marginalization of contextualized reporting is not surprising. Civic news norms have spread through the Mexican newspaper field only in the last twenty years, and even in the more hospitable format of print, contextualization is often lacking. Prior to 1997, civic norms were intentionally suppressed in major Mexican television. Today, civic television journalism is expressed narrowly in connection with the formal politics of sharply contested elections, such as the presidential and Mexico City mayoral races, alongside what is a dominant market approach to news production generally.

Why Market-Driven News?

The market-driven model in Mexican television is based in part on two clear trends in TV journalism over the last twenty years. The first is greater reflection of audience preferences in electoral coverage. This trend is depicted as greater pluralism among voters and in television campaign coverage in figure 8.1, which contrasts the percentage of time allotted to the opposition in network news coverage with the percentage of the opposition vote in four presidential elections. Pluralism in electoral coverage accelerated after 1988. Societal change began earlier. News coverage of the two viable opposition parties and the ruling PRI approximated the level of each party's strength in the electorate only in 2000. Qualitative studies also found a propensity to

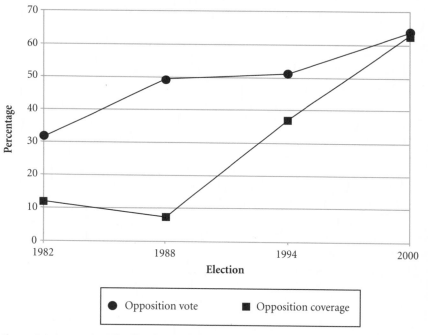

Figure 8.1 Increasing Pluralism in Electoral News: Opposition Vote (%) and Television Coverage of the Opposition (%) during Four Presidential Campaigns

Notes: PRI vote is the party's percentage of the total official vote tally. Opposition vote is all other. Percentage of coverage is based upon the top three candidates only. Coverage in 1982 is an estimate based upon observation of state Channel 13 in 1982 by Ortiz Pinchetti (1982) and general statements concerning the lack of pluralism in TV coverage. For 1988, figures are reported for *24 Horas* and *Día a Día* (Arredondo Ramírez 1990). For 1994, figures are reported for *24 Horas* (Aguayo and Acosta 1995). For 2000, figures are reported for all programs in Mexico City (Instituto Federal Electoral, Comísión de Radiodifusión 2000).

report news in a neutral manner by 2000, especially compared to attempts to skew news in favor of the PRI in earlier elections.

What are the implications of this shift toward pluralism, which for the first time presented opposition candidates to national television audiences in a balanced manner? The timing of the television transition means that the shift in television news could not have initiated democratization in Mexico—though it seems to have accelerated the process. Despite viewers' ability to read between the lines of slanted newscasts, the absence of information about the opposition probably forestalled democratization by narrowing the voices presented on the medium most Mexicans reported as their primary source of political information during the country's political transition. After 1994, however, the appearance of the opposition on television seems to have bolstered electoral pluralism. Panel studies of Mexico City voters—a repeated survey that followed a set of voters throughout the campaign—provided support for this claim. The 1997 study found that as coverage of the left opposition increased on Televisa, so did voter intentions among those participants who were watching the network. Controlling for other possible explanations for the change, the author concluded that television coverage had a powerful effect on opposition vote choices because, for the first time, viewers saw a substantially fair and balanced representation of the PRD on Mexican television (Lawson 2002; Lawson and McCann 2004).

The second general trend in Mexican television news coverage over the last two decades is the tabloidization of the news agenda, which is neglected in the data reported in table 8.1.[9] Tabloidization began in the late 1990s, about the same time as increased pluralism in electoral news. The increase in coverage of crime, security issues, and protests as public disturbances is apparent by 1998, as is the decline in the volume of political coverage generally.

Even without directly comparable data from midterm elections in 1997, the absence of electoral coverage on network newscasts during the 2003 congressional campaigns is striking.[10] Essentially, electoral politics was absent from mainstream newscasts. Interestingly, however, it was not absent from television. Much electoral information migrated to tabloid-style television formats outside the mainstream newscasts, including human interest candidate profiles. Additionally, game shows featuring candidates as contestants were aired directly after nightly news programs in an attempt to make electoral information more attractive to viewers. This strategy was successful to a degree; an *Hechos* anchor reported that ratings went up for a series of human interest electorate profiles aired on TV Azteca directly after *Hechos* in 2003.[11] Television advertising also aired in record amounts. Some of it presented information about candidates, parties, and platforms in a straightforward

Table 8.1 Tabloidization of the News Agenda: Newscast Time (%) by Subject

Coverage Topic	1994	1998–99	2003
Activities of president	9.3	4.2	6.5
Activities of ministries, federal government	11.3	8.7	6.3
Activities of legislature	2.2	4.2	0.6
Activities of parties, elections	30.9	3.5	4.2
Activities of state, local government	0.6	6.7	3.3
Official corruption, human rights	0.3	3.1	5.8
Social programs	0.4	1.9	0.8
Chiapas conflict, guerrillas	10.7	0.2	0
Colosio assassination	4.3	0.0	0.0
Total politics	70.0	32.5	27.5
Crime, security, protests	5.8	23.8	29.5
Health	0.2	5.2	8.5
Economy	4.2	10.2	5.2
Media, entertainment	4.4	2.8	3.1
Education	0.3	1.1	2.6
Church, religion	2.2	4.6	2.9
Natural disasters	0.3	5.2	3.1
Other	5.7	4.7	12.6
Accidents	3.2	1.1	0.9
High culture	3.3	1.1	2.5
Environment	0.4	2.6	0.9
Mexico City urban affairs	0.0	3.6	0.0
Human interest	0.0	1.0	0.0

Source: For source material, please see note 9 to this chapter.

manner. Others were particularly striking in their chafing, burlesque critiques of incumbent politicians.

Despite the use of info-entertainment formats and record amounts of political advertising, the first federal elections of Mexico's democratic era recorded a historic level of voter abstention. "The failure of political marketing to promote the vote was the signature of the July 6 elections," *Proceso* magazine reported, reflecting the view of many that rampant advertising and political image-making had at least contributed to voter alienation (Olmos 2003, 10). No studies systematically tested whether negative television advertising or tabloid news coverage decreased voter turnout in 2003. Disentangling the effects of watching tabloid coverage from the effects of real-world problems such as crime and governmental ineptitude is difficult even when there are well-constructed studies.[12] However, the postmodernists should not find comfort in these results. Tabloidization of the agenda, frames, and techniques of Mexican television news was at its highest levels ever during the 2003 campaign season, and yet fewer Mexicans than ever went to the polls to vote.

Analysis reveals three overlapping explanations for the direction and timing of the rise of market-driven journalism. These explanations are similar to the variables explaining the diffusion of civic journalism in the press, and lend support to the institutional model of newsroom transformation presented in figure 1.2. They are: (1) the changing incentives of the political economy of news production; (2) the power of organizational factors such as newsroom leadership and culture in a hierarchical organization; and (3) the influence of ideas from abroad.

Founding the Authoritarian Media System

The single-party system that ruled Mexico from 1929 to 2000 created a system of media control that relied much more on the carrot than the stick. In the case of television, a mutually beneficial relationship emerged based on the following incentives. First, broadcast concessions were awarded politically. The Mexican president, Miguel Alemán Valdes, granted the country's first television frequency concessions to a small number of entrepreneurial families with political connections beginning in 1949. By 1973, the industrial families had combined with the family of the former president to create the Televisa network from the networks Telesistema in Mexico City and Televisión Independíente de México in Monterrey. Televisa was a national commercial monopoly for two decades (Molina 1987). The second national commercial television network in Mexico, TV Azteca, was created in 1993 when the government sold a network of 140 state-owned stations to a family with no broadcasting experience. The brother of the then-sitting president is thought to have been a silent partner in the network (Barrera 2004; Preston 1996a, 1996b). The result of the sale was a "duopoly." Two networks now control approximately 95 percent of the television market in Mexico, according to figures from the IBOPE rating service, and make Mexico the most-concentrated television market in Latin America.[13] Moreover, until recent years programming was highly centralized in Mexico City. Approximately 80 percent of Mexico's 465 television stations simply repeat programming—news and otherwise—emanating from the two national networks' capital city stations.[14]

Government subsidies such as advertising and inputs to production were a second pillar of cooperative media-state relations during the PRI regime. Mexico had a mixed economic system from the 1940s on, but by 1982 the government came to control more than 1,500 companies, including important advertisers such as banks, the national telephone company, and airlines. The government at its peak controlled about 40 percent of total investment. Additionally, it could subsidize or block the entrance of imported technology and inputs for production important for news companies.

The third characteristic in cooperative media-state relations was protection from competition. Besides providing advertising and subsidies, the Mexican government protected Televisa from competition until 1993, when the Salinas administration privatized the state-owned television network. Competitors were discouraged, blocked, or nationalized. Protection produced a highly concentrated ownership structure that remains today. Only an estimated 15 percent of 465 stations in the country are owned by independent proprietors. Televisa owns about 60 percent of the 465 commercial stations in the country, while TV Azteca owns about 25 percent.[15]

After almost five decades of cooperation, it would be simplistic to attribute Televisa's support for the PRI-government during most of the 1990s only to a quid-pro-quo arrangement. Supporting the PRI regime became an embedded culture and a way of being at the network. From its earliest days, Televisa's corporate interests defined newsworthiness, and corporate interests were interlocked with those of the state except for two narrow issues: the possibility of greater competition in the broadcast sector and the usually latent threat of nationalization.[16] Televisa's open identity as "a *priísta* company,"[17] set and modeled by the owners, permeated company newsrooms. In his study of the corporate strategy behind Televisa news production in the mid-1980s, Molina (1987) found that news as promotion of corporate interests, and corporate interests synonymous with those of the state, became "entrenched in newsmen's occupational ideologies" (178). A news executive who started as a newsroom assistant at the company in 1978 explained in a 2003 interview that Televisa journalists normatively accepted that the news should support the PRI: "Before we were doing things as we perceived they should be done. If they had seemed wrong to us, we would have dedicated ourselves to something else, but politically it was the correct thing to do. I never had the sensation nor the belief that I was doing something I shouldn't, because if I had had this belief, surely I would not have dedicated myself to this."[18]

Television news broadcasting in Mexico always had close ties to the president and the PRI. TV news was officially inaugurated with President Miguel Alemán's third State of the Nation Address in 1949, a triumphal affair after which powerful Mexicans from all walks of life paid homage to the president. In 1958, during the Adolfo López Mateos administration, television began to cover the president's tours through the country on a regular basis. Television news programs, however, did not present a uniform view of politics until after they came under the control of corporate leadership following the Tlaltelolco Massacre in 1968, when state security forces ended a student protest movement by killing hundreds of students in Mexico City's Tlaltelolco Plaza. The extent of the confrontation was not reported in the broadcast media until several decades later. At the time, network executives worried that they did not have direct control over what newscasters said because large advertisers directly sponsored independently produced news shows. Journalists did not work directly for the network, but for the sponsors. Of special concern was the broadcast sponsored by the critical newspaper *Excélsior*, then published under the editorship of independent-minded journalist Julio Scherer (Molina 1987, 170–75). Executives at Telesistema, the forerunner to Televisa, responded to the dilemma in various ways.

Telesistema president Emilio Azcárraga Vidaurreta put President Alemán's son, Miguel Alemán Velasco, in charge of centralizing control of news broadcasts. Alemán Velasco created a single news department to report, write, and edit for all news programs on the network and placed it under a single corporate news division, the Directorate of News, from which decisions on controversial subjects could be made when necessary. The first anchor under the centralized news system was Jacobo Zabludovsky, and the first show, *24 Horas*, aired for the first time on September 7, 1970. According to *Reforma*, Zabludovsky also had coordinated radio and television affairs for President López Mateos and advised President Gustavo Díaz Ordaz on promotion and public relations. Díaz Ordaz's administration was responsible for the Tlaltelolco Massacre. Zabludovsky would remain as anchor on the stellar newscast until it closed twenty-seven years later (Molina 1987, 170–73; Meraz and del Río 1995).

The idea propelling the centralization of news production after the 1968 massacre was to strengthen Telesistema's political power by allowing the network to speak with one voice on political events. Explained Alemán Velasco: "Nineteen sixty-eight took us by surprise. Suddenly we realized that we did not have a voice, a version, a position towards those critical events which we could put forward and sustain before the nation. The problem for this enterprise was that it did not have a news program to channel its opinion" (Molina 1987, 172).

Televisa's powerful second president, Emilio Azcárraga Milmo, considered company journalists his employees and their newscasts an extension of his beliefs, especially on controversial political matters. *El Tigre,* as he was known, preapproved story lineups for many newscasts and sometimes sent down orders for how to handle controversial political issues. Azcárraga's biographers, Fernández and Paxman, believe a psychological need for control drove Azcárraga's monitoring of newscasts more than a necessity to check up on the key personnel in Televisa's newsrooms. New stars rose through the ranks and maintained their places by pleasing their boss. The troops learned loyalty to the company's interests through a mix of self-selection, socialization, reward, and sanction (Fernández and Paxman 2000, 3, 325–27, 330–31; Molina 1987, 175–80). Televisa's journalists absorbed the organization's news culture as their own, left voluntarily, or were fired (Corro 1994, 6).[19]

Authoritarian Inertia

The 1988 elections were a watershed in Mexico, featuring two strong opposition candidates who filled plazas—but not TV screens—with enthusiastic followers. In the end, many Mexicans believed the PRI held onto power through outright vote fraud when the usual mix of cooptation, claims to nationalism, targeted repression, and control of information failed to quell opposition support. Televisa stayed staunchly *priísta* during the campaign and fully backed PRI candidate Carlos Salinas. The incentives of docile journalism were still intact in 1988, but the network's support for the PRI was an embedded worldview as well. The network's owner, director of news, and star news anchor all had matured professionally during the years when PRI support underpinned network survival and growth. Moreover, *priísta* rule was legitimate to them. The PRI claimed the mantle of the 1910 Revolution, had produced economic growth for the urban middle class, and framed the opposition as extremist and "anti-Mexico." The network's newscast reflected the owners' political views, especially those of majority owner and president Emilio Azcárraga Milmo. "Company leaders' militancy in the PRI gives our communication policy a partisan line," explained Televisa's information director Félix Cortés Camarillo in 1986. "Our commentators interpret and place news items with the confidence of the company in accordance with our political tendency. All information (broadcast by the company) follows it" (Arredondo Ramírez 1990, 57).

Televisa broadcast coverage that promoted the image of an omnipotent PRI candidate even as voters switched party allegiances in record numbers. The nightly news largely ignored the opposition, but sporadically broadcast crude attacks. For instance, Televisa aired an interview with two men who assured viewers they were leftist candidate Cuauhtémoc Cárdenas's "illegitimate" half-brothers and they supported the PRI. Part of Cárdenas's popularity stemmed from the fact that his father was a revolutionary general and beloved former president. On another occasion, the network juxtaposed images of Cárdenas and Manuel Clouthier of the conservative PAN with those of Nikita Khruschev and Benito Mussolini (Fernández and Paxman 2000, 321). Sometimes Televisa journalists were even more direct. When Cárdenas said during the campaign that his government would be pluralistic but would not include members of the PRI, a Televisa anchor raised his eyebrow and opined, "Not so pluralistic" (Adler 1993a). Mostly, however, the opposition was just absent from the newscasts; both opposition candidates together commanded just 7 percent of airtime on Televisa's *24 Horas* and the newscast *Día a Día* of the state-run network Imevisión.

The campaign coverage was so slanted that the pro-business party PAN organized an advertiser boycott to pressure Televisa to open its newscasts. "We're going to stop drinking Dom Pedro Brandy and eating this and that," said PAN candidate Manuel Clouthier. More that one million bumper stickers were distributed, reading: "Do not watch *24 Horas*. They do not tell the truth," and, "This home is Catholic. We do not watch *24 Horas* here" (Fernández and Paxman 2000, 320–21). At the time, a few Mexican academics began to experiment with content analyses of television news that documented the extreme biases but were not widely distributed until after the campaigns. The most well-known was a rigorous study by Pablo Arredondo Ramírez of the University of Guadalajara, which documented the PRI's 93 percent share of coverage (Arredondo Ramírez 1990, 57).

The PAN boycott did not change Televisa's coverage, but provoked responses from the network's leadership. Azcárraga Milmo and top anchor Jacobo Zabludovsky offered different rationales for why the commercial network refused to diversify its coverage. Azcárraga Milmo told a group of political elites in January 1988: "We are of the PRI, members of the PRI. We do not believe in any other option. And as members of our party, we will do everything possible so that our candidate triumphs. This is very natural" (Albarrán de Alba 1994, 6–7). Zabludovsky, responding on camera to Clouthier, offered a less partisan rational to television audiences: "In the United States, the political parties can buy as much airtime as they want. In Televisa, we believe that the political parties should be assigned air time in the news in proportion to the quantity of votes they received in the last election," he said (Adler 1993b).

Political conditions had changed as the 1994 presidential campaign approached. Domestic and international rights groups increased pressure for less-biased media coverage at a time when the PRI government had bet long-term stability on internationalizing the economy through the North American Free Trade Agreement and slowly liberalizing the political system, favoring the free-market PAN.

Mexican civic groups with international financing, such as the Mexican Academy of Human Rights and the umbrella group Alianza Cívica, documented television news biases in detail and publicized these findings widely during the course of the campaign. Civic-oriented Mexican newspapers had strengthened by then, and joined the newsmagazine *Proceso* to report pro-PRI biases in other media. Foreign reporters coming to Mexico in record numbers because of NAFTA and the January 1994 Zapatista rebellion used civic newspapers as tip sheets for their own stories, and the opposition became more adept at alerting the foreign press to electoral trickery. Foreign news reporters and wary U.S. congressional representatives focused their attention on authoritarian practices in the United States' new trading partner, including its media. The evidence of obvious bias spread throughout U.S. academic and policy circles, as well.

At first, it looked as if Mexican television would conduct business as usual despite better-organized domestic groups and greater international scrutiny. Both networks rolled cameras after a state bureaucrat hired transvestites to interrupt a dinner held for PRD candidate Cuauhtémoc Cárdenas in Veracruz. In Mexico, charges of homosexuality are sometimes used in an attempt to discredit someone. "I do not want to give my opinion, but here are the facts," an anchor said on TV Azteca's news program *Buenos Días* before running the tape the next morning, on which the transvestites cheered "*A la bio. A la bau.* We're all with Cuauh" (Ravelo and Vera 1993, 6–7). Another cloddish attempt to sway opinion occurred when an outspoken academic, Jorge Castañeda, was caught by Televisa's cameras using foul language to say he planned "to cause a scandal" about PRI domination before a U.S. Senate committee holding hearings on NAFTA. Televisa cameras had been hired to transmit Castañeda's testimony from Mexico City to the U.S. Senate building and Castañeda didn't know he was being recorded. Castañeda was then accused by lesser-known academics of being a "traitor" and "anti-Mexico" (Garavilla 1993).

Such boorish media coverage embarrassed the Salinas administration internationally, and was subsequently modified. Under the watchful eye of newscast monitors from the Mexican Academy of Human Rights, and later the newly independent Federal Electoral Institute (Instituto Federal Electoral, or IFE), Televisa moderated the gross differences in time allotted to coverage of the top contenders compared to 1988. Yet favoritism persisted at a more subtle level, according to critics. Televisa reporters commented on immense and enthusiastic crowds greeting the PRI presidential candidate on his campaign tours of the country, framed shots in ways that suggested overwhelming PRI support, and praised the PRI candidate's sage-like solutions for local problems.[20] Analysts noted that electoral coverage was framed in ways that suggested a PRD victory would lead to violent upheaval and a PAN victory would undercut advances for women. "Television has changed, yes, but the change is in the style of presenting information," concluded journalists Karla Monica Casillas-Bermúdez and Salvador Frausto Crotte in their comparison of electoral coverage on *24 Horas* in 1988 and 1994. "Partiality persists. The facts are presented to the public in such a way that the distortion continues. The manipulation is more sophisticated" (Casillas-Bermúdez and Crotte 1998, 108; Hallin 1998).

A human rights academy qualitative comparison of coverage of the three candidates' visits to the turbulent National Autonomous University of Mexico (UNAM) in 1994 highlights the differences in news coverage. Coverage of PRI candidate Ernesto Zedillo's trip made references to a confrontation with protesting students, but never showed them on the screen. Instead, the candidate gave his version of events on-air, thanking the well-behaved students who invited him to speak to their department. Coverage of PRD candidate Cárdenas and PAN candidate Diego Fernández de Cevallos at UNAM was quite different. The report on Fernández de Cevallos's university rally focused on a group of students throwing rotten eggs at the candidate. While the anchors of both networks criticized the students involved, their reporters pointed out that the aggressors were supporters of Cárdenas and the EZLN. Other "students" who were singled out by the cameras were dirty, wild-eyed and gap-toothed (Academia Mexicana de Derechos Humanos 1994). For Cárdenas's rally, Televisa's cameras focused tightly on the candidate. A camera pan would have showed the campus's large esplanade overflowing with enthusiastic students. Televisa's editing of the candidate's speech also cut references to issues other than the armed insurrection in the state of Chiapas. TV Azteca's version of the campaign event was closer to reality, showing the size and enthusiasm of the crowd and allowing Cárdenas to speak about a wider variety of issues, such as the fairness of the election.[21] In a somewhat sloppy insertion, however, TV Azteca included a camera shot of a Zapatista supporter placing an EZLN banner above the crowd, another attempt to link the PRD to the violence in Chiapas.

Televisa president Azcárraga Milmo supported the PRI in other ways, as well. He gave the party discounts for political advertising, which was used for the first time during the 1994 campaign. He was also a big private donor to the party. Part of President Salinas's strategy for the "modernization" of PRI rule was to shift the party from reliance on under-the-table government funds to private donations. The president asked a number of the country's wealthiest businessmen for $20 million donations during a special "billionaires banquet" in the period before to the 1994 election. Azcárraga Milmo, himself a billionaire, was reported as responding enthusiastically: "I have made so much money over the years, that I commit to giving more." The amount was $70 million (Puig 1997).

Preferential framing of coverage and the ability of the PRI to tap into millions of dollars from tycoons made international elections monitors such as The Carter Center pronounce the election free, but not fair. Noting that the state spent $750 million to produce a credible voter registration list and photo identity cards, the prestigious elections monitoring group nevertheless cited: "an uneven playing field which limits the ability of all political parties to compete equitably . . . especially regarding continued bias in media coverage, the high cost of advertising, campaign spending limits beyond the reach of any party except the PRI, and great disparities in financial resources" (The Carter Center 1994, 4).

Criticism of television coverage came even more strongly from the nonpartisan Mexican observation group, Alianza Cívica. The group's media monitoring program documented a six-to-one pro-PRI bias in coverage of viable presidential candidates on top newscasts through April, casting doubts at home and abroad upon the fairness of the election. In another study, the Mexican Human Rights Academy, an Alianza Cívica member, cited Televisa's "accelerated image promotion" of the PRI's replacement candidate, Ernesto Zedillo, after the assassination of its original candidate, Luis Donaldo Colosio. As the evidence of bias mounted, the Federal Electoral Institute's new directorate, made up mostly of independent-minded academics, issued "guidelines" for television coverage of the election for the last three months of campaigning based on the notion of pluralism in coverage. Following pioneer academics and then civil society groups, the IFE then launched a media monitoring effort. The better-funded IFE analysis also found that the PRI received substantially more coverage (Albarrán de Alba 1994; Hughes 1994).

Most media critics find that TV Azteca's coverage did not differ greatly from Televisa's during the 1994 campaign. Both were pro-PRI. According to the human rights academy study, TV Azteca's newscast *Hechos* gave the PRI candidate more than twice as much coverage as either of the two strong opposition party candidates. It also made positive references to the PRI candidate 4.5 times more often than the opposition, and criticized the center-left candidate Cárdenas six times more than the PRI's Zedillo (Acosta Valverde 1996). For some, TV Azteca also was too sensationalist. However, the newly privatized network did open up its studio to interviews with opposition presidential candidates during its first year on the air. While network management was busy shoring up the entertainment side of the young network, the journalists were given freedom to experiment. Traditional stenographic reporting and passivity toward the president was "a bore," said a leading member of *Hechos* in a confidential interview. Moreover, cabinet officials would give their interviews first to Zabludovsky. The *Hechos* journalist remembered: "So I said 'no problem, we are going to turn our camera toward the people.'" Young technicians and journalists, aided by U.S. and Spanish television producers, also experimented with more dramatic, image-based story telling.[22] A few years later, Televisa would follow suit.

TV Azteca presented a new kind of Mexican television that impressed viewers. Besides, some viewers wanted to watch anything other than Televisa. Internal audience studies found that *Hechos*'s level of credibility with viewers increased after the opposition interviews, giving the program a competitive advantage. In his confidential interview, the *Hechos* journalist said:

> As a television product, my positioning, my great opportunity to generate credibility, was in '94 when Televisa still insisted in being a soldier of the PRI and openly stated this type of thing. I don't know about these studies that said our coverage was similar to Televisa's. I don't remember what Televisa did. I remember more or less the perception people had of Televisa. For me that was the great opportunity of 1994. . . . From that moment on we earned something that, for a journalist, is very important. We opened our doors to the opposition for the first time and that is what made us advance.[23]

Hechos anchor Javier Alatorre became the most popular television personality in Mexico City within two years, passing starlets and popular comedians, according to *Reforma*'s first media use survey in December 1995. Zabludovsky was not even mentioned. By the 1996 poll, capital city audiences preferred Alatorre's *Hechos* by two-to-one over Zabludovsky's *24 Horas* (López 1996; Orozco 1999). Whether the electoral monitoring numbers show it or not, there was enough of a difference in coverage that people perceived that TV Azteca better reflected their partisan preferences.

Televisa badly needed to repair its image after the election, and the network's intent to change news models initially seemed genuine. Azcárraga Milmo called upon his nephew, Alejandro Burillo, who had first met opposition leaders as his uncle's liaison after criticism of the company's coverage grew ferocious during the 1994 campaign. As Televisa's executive vice president in 1995, Burillo, a quarter-century younger than his famous uncle, modified Azcárraga's oft-repeated position as "a soldier of the PRI." He told opposition party congressional representatives, "The country has changed. We (Televisa) defend the institution of the president of the republic, but not the party of the president of the republic . . . one party and one political position no longer necessarily represent institutionalism." He convinced several opposition leaders of his sincerity (Delgado 1996).

Burillo relied upon journalist Ricardo Rocha to help with the makeover. While Zabludovsky stayed in front of *24 Horas*, Rocha took charge of a new weekend news program, *Detrás de la Noticia*. *La Jornada* reporter Ricardo Alemán, himself a regime critic, described the new program as having "a critical journalistic sensibility" and an orientation toward "public service" (Alemán Alemán 1996). Change went further in Televisa's less-centralized radio network, where stations hired journalists from Mexico's civic newspapers, such as Blanche Petriche from *La Jornada*, Carlos Ramírez from *El Financiero* and Alberto Barranco of *Reforma*.

From the beginning, the new style and its emissaries clashed with the old. Barranco spoke publicly of a number of obstacles placed in his path, including direct orders from his news producer not to include criticism of Mexico City's PRI mayor, which he ignored, and an ominous internal message delivered after he criticized the president's behavior during May Day parades in 1995 (Delgado 1996). Government officials were not happy with the new style either, especially after Rocha aired an explosive videotape in early 1996 showing state security forces in Guerrero executing seventeen farmers en route to an opposition party rally. Though *La Jornada* and the Acapulco newspaper *El Sur* had been writing extensively about the probable involvement of the state's hard-line governor in the June 1995 killings, the impact of the television images led to the governor's reticent request for a permanent leave of absence.

Airing the video gave Burillo and the Televisa reform project instant credibility among the country's leftist opposition, intellectuals, and independent journalists. But while Burillo had approved the broadcast, apparently Azcárraga Milmo had not. Coupled with other irritations, the nephew had worn out his uncle's welcome in just four months. Rocha stayed on after Azcárraga Milmo promised him the videotape was only part of the reason for Burillo's exit. Rocha's newscasts in 1997 were cited as more objective than most, but he did not air another politically explosive news program for almost three years. Barranco and others departed the radio network (Fernández and Paxman 2000, 449–50).[24]

Burillo did not have sufficient newsroom power to push through the transformation he envisioned. Again, the control of organizational resources were a crucial element in newsroom transformation. While Roberto Rock at *El Universal* was granted the authority to implement journalistic change at Mexico City's oldest newspaper, Televisa's Alejandro Burillo did not have the backing of the network's powerful owner and so his efforts ultimately failed.

Televisa's thaw after the 1994 presidential campaign lasted only about four months, but the next electoral season would belong to a new Emilio Azcárraga. Two years after Burillo's short-lived attempt to move the company's news model in a more civic direction, new owner Emilio Azcárraga Jean decided it was time to try again. This attempt at journalistic transformation would follow the market. Unlike Burillo, Azcárraga Jean had the organizational power to make it happen.

The Rise of the Market

By 1997, television coverage reflected the electorate's pluralism more completely during important campaigns for the mayor of Mexico City, the federal Congress, and four state governorships. Television news programs essentially gave equal time to coverage of the top parties and covered them in a more neutral tone. In fact, the strongest opposition party at the time, the PRD, received slightly more coverage than the PRI.[25] The PRD's Cuauhtémoc Cárdenas won the Mexico City mayor's position with support from 47 percent of the electorate, while the PRI's candidate received 25 percent of the vote in the country's mammoth capital of eleven million people. Outside of the capital, the PAN took two of four contested governor's posts from the ruling party, including the industrial state of Nuevo León. This was a historic shift in political power in Mexico, and one that was finally reflected in the Mexican news media.

Opinion polls conducted in Mexico City, the country's largest television market by far, documented how the electorate was turning strongly in favor of Cárdenas and the PRD during the course of the campaign. Election polls were conducted more regularly, promoted more widely, and had more legitimacy than in any previous Mexican election. Figure 8.2 shows the electoral polls published on the front page of *Reforma*. This is what Televisa executives saw as they made programming decisions. The newspaper's prestigious polling unit became the reference point for voters and politicians during the campaign. Moreover, in 1996, the IBOPE ratings firm increased its three-year-old "people meter" measurement service for television usage to national coverage in twenty-seven Mexican cities. The increased coverage by the Brazilian firm, better known in Latin America than the U.S. Nielsen Ratings, responded to advertiser requests for better TV audience data.[26] Thanks to IBOPE's minute-by-minute audience measures and the polls of *Reforma* and others, market-driven journalists could follow the preferences of their audience and advertisers could demand higher ratings in return for their purchases.

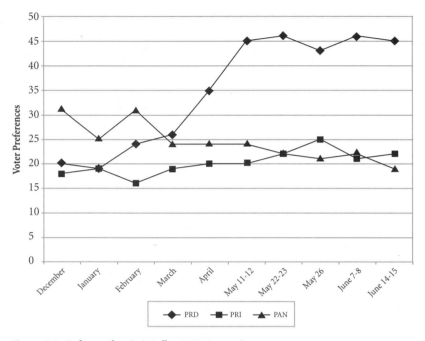

Figure 8.2 *Reforma* Election Polls, 1997 Campaign
Source: Giménez and Romero (1997a, 1997b, 1997c, 1997d).

Partisan balance at Televisa and TV Azteca was not evident at the start of the election campaigns. Media monitors at the Mexican Academy of Human Rights documented a dramatic shift in television coverage of the elections between early April and late May. In the first two weeks of April, Televisa's primetime newscast *24 Horas* heavily favored the PRI candidate. The newscast devoted almost three times more coverage to the PRI than to either opposition candidate. By the last two weeks of May, Televisa journalists had reversed this tendency: *24 Horas* gave Cárdenas 79 percent more time than the ruling party's Alfredo del Mazo, and 9 percent more time than Carlos Castillo Peraza of the PAN. Suddenly, Televisa's journalists had switched sides. TV Azteca's electoral coverage also became more balanced in May, but the network took a more antagonistic stance toward Cárdenas. TV Azteca's *Hechos* devoted about twice as much coverage to the PRI candidate in the first half of April, but moderated the disparity later in May to 31 minutes, 17 seconds for the PRI; 30 minutes, 5 seconds for the PAN; and 26 minutes, 59 seconds for the front-running PRD (Academia Mexicana de Derechos Humanos 1994).

As programs became more balanced, the tone of the newscasts became more neutral. A Mexican Academy of Human Rights qualitative study found that only 5 percent of the total TV news coverage dedicated to the candidates contained comments viewed as slanted in favor or against a candidate. Journalists on *Hechos* issued most of these slanted statements, with nine slanted comments for every one made by a journalist on *24 Horas* (Acosta Valverde 1998).

Televisa's news programs became more balanced and neutral, but there was some variation between programs, indicating differing views of journalism were at work. A human rights academy analysis of coverage of the televised debate between the front-running PRD and PRI mayoral candidates found that the weekend Televisa newscast led by Ricardo Rocha, the would-be reformist, was most objective and fair to both debaters. The Televisa morning weekday newscast, anchored by Abraham Zabludovsky, Jacobo Zabludovsky's son, was slightly partial to del Mazo. TV Azteca's coverage of the debate focused on del Mazo's attacks on Cárdenas and did not allow the PRD candidate an opportunity to respond (Academia Mexicana de Derechos Humanos 1994).

There are several possible explanations for TV Azteca's aversion to Cárdenas's candidacy beyond loyalty to the PRI. Network owner Ricardo Salinas Pliego held a strong, free-market philosophy that clashed with Cárdenas's views on the economy, and it was apparent by 1997 that Salinas Pliego had business ties to the family of Cárdenas's old political rival, Carlos Salinas. These connections helped Salinas Pliego purchase the network from the government in what was supposed to be an unbiased auction of the state-owned stations in 1993. Moreover, Cárdenas's party decided not to purchase political advertising on TV Azteca in 1997, the first election in which the opposition spent many millions of dollars on television ads.

For Televisa, more balanced and neutral political coverage represented a sea change that responded directly to new rules laid down by the network's president and majority owner when he took over the company six weeks before his father's death in April 1997. New network president Emilio Azcárraga Jean quickly made it clear in the newsroom and the boardroom that his father's vision of journalism was not his own. He told news executives and anchors in a meeting just after his father's death that the company would no longer be *priísta*. The same week, he told political parties and voters—who were also advertisers and viewers—that times had changed. "What we are looking for today in Televisa's news programs is the truth. And what is important is to provide a space so people say their truth. The trick is that people say what they think, not that Jacobo [Zabludovsky] says it. If such and such congressman or such and such official has something important to say, they should say it. They should say it, understand? Jacobo shouldn't say it. I think news programs are to inform, not to build images or power centers" (Puig 1997, 31).

Azcárraga Jean turned twenty-one during the turbulent 1988 presidential campaign, took business courses in the United States, learned the practical side of the television business in network affiliates across the border from the commercialized media of San Diego, and earned his father's rare praise when he represented the company at a New York shareholders' meeting in 1995 (Fernández and Paxman 2000). When he took over Televisa, the company owed $1.3 billion and its ratings were at record lows. Azcárraga Jean called himself a businessman, and he decided that listening to the market was the only way to save his company. "My lawyers told me one of my options was to sell," he said. "But I looked at it this way. I am 29 years old and in 10 years if I haven't done anything, then I'll sell in 10 years. But before that, I am going to try" (Arreola 2000; Fernández 2001).

Azcárraga Jean promised quick action. He begged Wall Street investors during a conference call in May of 1997 to stick with the ailing giant essentially as an act of faith. To calm investors' fears, Azcárraga Jean hired experienced outside executives with financial credibility. Cost-cutter Gilberto Pérezalonso came to Televisa as vice president for finance after nineteen years with Mexico's giant retailer Cifra, a stock market darling and the Mexican partner of Wal-Mart. Pérezalonso implemented a company-wide restructuring that slashed six thousand of the twenty thousand jobs at the network, including the retirement of executives who had served Azcárraga Jean's father for years. Along with Pérezalonso, Azcárraga Jean brought in the former president of the United States' largest Spanish-language network, *Univisión*, as executive vice president for operations. Jaime Dávila reoriented the entire range of programming at Televisa to improve ratings, focusing on *telenovelas* and newscasts. Dávila also ended the network's unpopular monopoly-era sales program requiring advertisers to pay ahead of time, thus making prices more sensitive to ratings. With Wall Street comforted by Pérezalonso and Dávila, Azcárraga Jean rounded off his group of closest collaborators with old friends who, like him, were young businessmen under age thirty-five (Arreola 2000; Fernández 2001).

One of the first things Azcárraga Jean did as head of Televisa was order a study of the company's image. He did not like what it said. Even company trucks made people mad because they double-parked on public streets. But the image of the network's newscasts was particularly troubling and more difficult to remedy. "In news, the credibility issue was very sensitive," Azcárraga Jean recalled a few years later. "The ratings we had were about 9 or 10 points, when Azteca was about 20 or 21 points. We had a very grave problem here" (Arreola 2000). Azcárraga Jean entrusted the task of transforming the newscasts to a childhood friend, twenty-nine-year-old Bernardo Gómez. In the course of three years, Gómez changed anchors twice. To cool critics, he invited some of the network's most vocal and credible intellectuals into the studios and gave them sixty seconds of free airtime to offer an opinion on any issue they chose. Personalities such as Elena Poniatowska and Carlos Monsiváis, ferocious cultural critics of the PRI regime and its ally Televisa, began to appear on the new newscast feature called "In the Opinion of . . ." Televisa also changed the form of their news programs. Younger photojournalists and editors brought ideas about camera movement, music, and editing from the networks' first tabloidized newsmagazines to the primetime newscasts, and network managers brought in a U.S. consultant and sent network technicians to CNN and local networks to learn tabloidization techniques in the United States.[27]

The 1997 mayoral campaign was a watershed not only for the country, but for journalism at Mexico's largest commercial network. New campaign financing and continued decline in viewers suggested a shift toward a style of journalism that reacted to audience and advertiser preferences to help make the company profitable again. These trends did not suddenly appear in April 1997, but a new company owner did. "If you are looking for a watershed at Televisa," said a news executive and longtime Televisa journalist, "the watershed is found in the change in administration in Televisa, in the death of one Mr. Azcárraga and the ascension to the presidency of another Mr. Azcárraga."[28]

Such a profound change in journalistic values and behaviors was not so easy to institutionalize. Ultimately, personnel change and outside training—as in the *El Universal* transition—was necessary to overcome inertial values, assumptions, and behaviors. The network's journalists reverted to more familiar, authoritarian behaviors on at least four occasions leading up to and during the 2000 presidential campaign, when Azcárraga Jean again bet his company's credibility with viewers on balanced political coverage. On two of these occasions, network journalists appeared to be reacting to residual pressure from the PRI government. The other two cases appeared to be journalists' instinctive responses to unscripted news events that brought the traditional culture of the Televisa newsroom directly into conflict with the new culture Azcárraga Jean wanted to install.

The first reversal involved criticism of the likely PRD presidential candidate, then Mexico City mayor Cuauhtémoc Cárdenas, after a popular variety show host was gunned down in the capital in June 1999. Television journalists intended to hold Cárdenas personally responsible for the attack by suggesting it was a random street crime in a city that was out of control. Though Cárdenas had been in office about eighteen months, the coverage suggested the city's four-year-old crime wave was completely his fault. Coverage of the murder was thoroughly tabloidized, featuring tearful starlets and moralistic condemnations of the Mexico City authorities. This criticism was part of 11.5 nonstop hours of coverage on the top two networks—5.5 hours on Televisa and 6 hours on TV Azteca—that began immediately after the curbside shooting.[29] While Televisa joined in the condemnations, the network modified its stance once evidence of a drug connection emerged. TV Azteca, however, continued its political attacks. The majority owner of the country's second commercial network went so far as to question whether the country's democratic transition was a good idea in the face of rising crime. "Why do we pay taxes? Why do we have elections? Why do we have three branches of government? Why so much government when there is no authority?" Ricardo Salinas Pliego asked viewers.[30]

A city press spokesman who worked on media relations as the case unfolded provided the following account of how dismayed city officials viewed the television coverage.

> Hours after the Paco Stanley murder, the (Mexico City) public security secretary was talking to both TV networks. He was giving a first presentation to the media and the media, especially television, continued with a witch hunt. That same day, we presented an artist's sketch of the killer and we said what was going on. The next day, and I do not think there has been a similar situation with a PRI government, we said that this gentleman (Stanley) was carrying cocaine, to provide access to information, not for revenge as you might think because of the media campaign on 24 hours a day. I believe that the people, the citizenry, understood that a death like that with so many gunshots was not due to just any hold-up.[31]

The decision to launch personal attacks on the Mexico City mayor initially may have been a gut reaction to the crime. The victim was a popular TV personality who had worked for both networks, and TV Azteca's aversion to Cárdenas's political agenda was by then well known.[32] The attacks also could have responded to ratings, though TV Azteca's decision to downplay the drug connection and continue coverage suggests that something more than ratings was driving news decisions. According to IBOPE ratings data, noon newscast ratings for TV Azteca jumped more than threefold less than ten minutes after journalist Jorge Garraldo began to demand Cárdenas's resignation at 12:15 p.m. Ratings topped out at 3:15 p.m., and the networks discontinued uninterrupted broadcast a short time later. In summary, the attacks may have been driven by the market, an ideological aversion to the Cárdenas government, internal political considerations at TV Azteca, or, most likely, a mixture of all three. In any case, once the initial ratings spike was over, Televisa moderated its tone, while TV Azteca did not.

The clash between news models at Televisa revealed itself again during coverage of President Ernesto Zedillo's State of the Nation Address on September 1, 1999, the president's last annual address before the 2000 election. Historically, the State of the Nation Address in Mexico presented the president's unchallenged view of the nation's progress during the previous year. The media gave live coverage to the address, the president's triumphal entrance and exit, and other events during most of the day. Often, coverage reflected a paternalistic vision. The president's press office encouraged this. In 1993, for example, a president's office press release told reporters what the president ate before the speech should they care to include it in their commentary—eggs, refried beans, and *nopales* (cactus salad), a traditional Mexican breakfast. In 1999, as a bow to increasing pluralism in Congress, Zedillo remained in the congressional chamber as a representative selected by opposition parties read a response to his message.

The opposition, given a national television platform in 1999 for the first time since the 1994 presidential debate, was unrestrained. Delivered emotionally by PAN senator Carlos Medina, the response roundly criticized both Zedillo and the PRI. The press published key points of the senator's speech the next day, along with narratives of the sometimes comical free-for-all it caused among congressional representatives. Televisa, however, omitted Medina's response and the resulting chaos in Congress from its newscast. Even without airing the response, however, primetime anchor Guillermo Ortega directly criticized Medina on his program *El Noticiero,* which replaced *24 Horas* in 1998. In the style of his predecessor Zabludovsky, Ortega faced the camera full-frame and called the senator's statement "an embarrassment for the Mexican people." While Zedillo was "tolerant and respectful," Ortega said, Medina took it upon himself "to disqualify the address on his own behalf, converting the legislative chambers into a market." TV Azteca aired the response, but brought in former vice president for news Sergio Sarmiento to issue an opinion. The speech, he said, was disrespectful and "full of intolerance" ("Omiten noticieros" 1999). [33]

The clash in journalistic paradigms at Televisa became obvious when Azcárraga Jean publicly chastised his new primetime anchor at a university forum one week later. Azcárraga Jean promised communications students at his alma mater, the Ibero-American University in Mexico City, that "a commercial model" would drive Televisa's coverage of the 2000 campaign. The coverage would be balanced, he promised. Ortega said later at the same forum that he had made a mistake by criticizing the opposition.

In earlier days, Televisa anchors had virtually been able to read the mind of the company's *priísta* owner Emilio Azcárraga Milmo, and tailored their coverage accordingly. In this time of journalistic transition, the new rules were more fuzzy. Like his father, Azcárraga Jean expected adherence to company policy, but apparently the harsh criticism of the sitting president had confused Ortega. He forgot that his boss wanted a network that reflected his customers' political preferences, even when that meant broadcasting an opposition representative directly criticizing the cornerstone of the PRI regime. Azcárraga Jean replaced Ortega as lead anchor during the heat of the campaign season the following spring. Neither would say publicly how important a clash in journalistic vision was in driving the departure. Ortega's viewer levels in 1998 had improved greatly over Zabludovsky's in 1997, but were eroding in 1999.[34] "His departure could have been for a deeply held reason or that he didn't share the idea we had of the news," Azcárraga Jean said, obliquely (Arreola 2000).

Another incident suggests Televisa was willing to sacrifice pluralism when the government pressed the point, although it did not lead a charge in defense of the regime as was its custom in earlier years. The incident involved coverage of the initial refusal of the country's radio and television networks to broadcast a political ad criticizing the PRI, the sitting president, and five former presidents just prior to the ruling party's first-ever presidential primary in November 1999. The refusal was first revealed the same day by the PAN's presidential candidate, Vicente Fox, during a campaign speech. Radio reporters told *La Jornada* that they were prohibited from including Fox's criticism in their dispatches. Once foreign reporters became interested, some PAN sources believe, the government backed off its initial "recommendation" not to run the ad.

While the print media widely reported the incident, including Fox's denunciation of the episode as an order to censor the party, broadcast stations focused on statements from the Interior Secretariat and the president of the broadcast station owners association, the CIRT, of which both networks are members. Association president Joaquín Vargas stood next to Assistant Interior Secretary Javier Lozano and denied having received an order to hold back the ad. In fact, it turned out later that the "order" was a "suggestion" from the secretary, but Vargas and Lozano's choice of words implied that no statement was made and that the PAN was using the incident to discredit the government (Intentó SG 1999).

By the 2000 campaign, the monitoring of television elections coverage by the Federal Electoral Institute, academics, and the independent press had become more frequent, rigorous, and detailed, with some measuring both volume and tone of electoral coverage on a daily basis. Overall, they found that Azcárraga Jean had done what he promised. Content on both Televisa and TV Azteca, in the words of Lawson and McCann (2004), was "fairly even-handed." However, their study of visual images on Televisa documented a strong tendency during the last half of the campaign to broadcast positive images of the PRI and PRD candidates while portraying Fox negatively. Similarly, *Reforma*'s measure of positive, negative, or neutral verbal characterizations of the candidates found that the network's roughly equal treatment of the two frontrunners began to shift dramatically in the last three months of the campaign. Fox's portrayal first became more positive in April, then much more negative in May. Positive coverage of the PRD's Cárdenas and the PRI's Labastida surged in May. Figure 8.3 depicts the change in tone found in *Reforma*'s study.[35]

The shift in coverage was at least in part driven by events as they unfolded in the campaign. According to the *Reforma* study, the timing of the change coincided with live coverage on May 23 of Fox's stubborn insistence on an immediate second candidates' debate— "Today! Today!" he exclaimed. He even went to an empty TV Azteca studio to symbolically wait for his

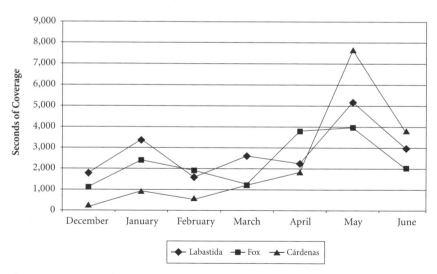

Figure 8.3 Positive Election Coverage on Televisa, 2000

Source: Reforma media use surveys

opponents, a publicity stunt by the campaign and the network that backfired. However, negative coverage of Fox endured beyond the failed second debate story. Hence, two other dynamics may have been at work. The change in tone suggests that pressure from the government following Labastida's poor performance in the first debate on April 25 caused Televisa to abandon its adherence to market-driven news in favor of a slant toward the PRI candidate. The alternative explanation has commercial origins. Televisa's executives certainly did not like that Fox went to their commercial rival, TV Azteca, to demand a new candidates' debate on-air. Executives may have decided to let him know of their displeasure through their own newscasts.

The market-driven news model that emerged at Televisa during the 1997 election continued during the campaign leading up to the regime-ending 2000 presidential election. It responded to the changing macroenvironment of news production, greater competition from a new style of competitor, and the diffusion of ideas from abroad. Change in television journalism also, and importantly, responded to a change in leadership at a hierarchical news organization. The immediate effect was to increase the diversity of voices presented in the network's electoral coverage, offering citizens an opportunity to judge the candidates' proposals and credibility for themselves. The shift in news models and the increasing pluralism it produced was not yet institutionalized, however. At crucial moments when journalists reacted impulsively, when commercial rivalries flared, or when the regime flexed its remaining muscle, authoritarian behaviors reappeared in the news and pluralism diminished.

Azcárraga Jean's turn to market-driven journalism served the investors who stuck with Televisa during its difficult times in the late 1990s. By the end of 1999, the network's new generation of managers had met and passed their commercial goals. They slashed $227 million through cuts and layoffs; renegotiated the company's $1.3 billion debt; made advertising plans more flexible, client-friendly, and ratings sensitive; and, most importantly, installed a new approach to programming that included not only more balanced coverage but also the tabloidization of the news. Grupo Televisa reported income of $2.1 billion in 2000, 60 percent of which was from its television business. TV Azteca reported income that year of just $558 million, almost all of that from television. Most importantly, Televisa had regained its near-monopoly market share of viewers. Figure 8.4 plots the network's rebound in audience preferences. TV Azteca commentator Sergio Sarmiento's positive assessment of sensationalism and ratings in 1999 may have reversed by early 2004, when tabloidization of the news agenda on both networks was at record levels and yet *Reforma*'s annual media use survey found that viewers defected from

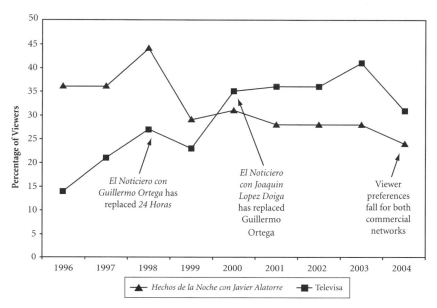

Figure 8.4 Shifts in Mexico City Newscast Audience Preferences

Note: In 2004, two smaller networks received 15 percent of audience preferences, a historic high.
Source: Reforma media use surveys.

Televisa and TV Azteca newscasts for smaller networks in numbers greater than ever before.

Responding to viewers' demands for more balanced electoral coverage was not the only way that Azcárraga Jean remade his network to attract viewers and advertisers. Televisa's newscasts—like TV Azteca's—focused much more on crime and related issues by 1999. However, during the 2003 campaign for Congress and several governor's posts, the main nightly newscasts essentially stopped covering the election. Mediated political campaigns became more personality focused, and migrated to new programming genres that profiled politicians at home and even placed them as opponents in a quiz show. These programs asked politicians about their personal lives and policy stands, offering voters valuable information, but produced electoral information that was closer to propaganda. The shows rarely contested politicians' answers and almost never verified the information they offered.[36]

In the postauthoritarian era, conflict- and personality-driven news content became more important. The on-camera lynching of two undercover narcotics agents by an enraged crowd in 2004 came to symbolize the incompetence of security forces and the dangers of political alienation turned violent. An attempt to knock the frontrunning presidential candidate out of the election—for moving slowly to comply with a judge's order for the Mexico City government to vacate a strip of commercial land, a small matter for some—reached all the way to the Supreme Court. The media's role, if any, in accentuating conflict was debated among intellectuals and media critics who worried about the lack of deliberation and reflection as the 2006 presidential elections approached.

Television news coverage also came to be used by politicians who sought to harm rivals by leaking highly explosive information. The most famous examples were the "video scandals" that rocked the small Mexican Green Party, the larger PRD, and Mexico City's government as the popular mayor prepared his presidential bid.

The Clown, the Videotape, and Politics by Other Means

When Televisa news executives wanted to increase their ratings with young men in 2002,[37] they decided to offer a morning newscast anchored by "El Brozo," a foul-mouthed, sexist clown who quickly got a reputation for straight talk in the language of the street. They called his early morning newscast *El Mañanero*, or "The Morning Quickie." Interestingly, the red-nosed, green-haired Brozo quickly became the preferred news personality of Mexican politicians. Even First Lady Marta Sahagún de Fox tried to buff her tarnished image on his show. Brozo's claim to fame, however, came four years into Mexico's fledgling democracy, when a PAN assemblyman told Televisa news executives that he wanted to show a videotape on the clown's newscast the next morning. It would be "a bomb," he promised.

As Mexico City assemblyman Federico Doring handed the videotape to the clown on March 3, the politician said it was a present for his saint's day. The tape showed Mexico City assemblyman Rene Bejarano, a PRD member and political operator of Mexico City mayor Andrés Manuel López Obrador, the country's most popular opposition politician, accepting thousands of dollars from a city contractor who dated the PRD's party president. The cash overflowed, so Bejarano stuffed it into his pockets. Bejarano, it would turn out, happened to be next door in the studio of a more traditional morning newscast. Brozo invited him over. As the videotape played, viewers watched live on a split screen as the politician sweated. "This is going to be the worst day of your life," the clown told him. "I believe it is," Bejarano responded.[38]

The Bejarano video was the last of a trio of *videoescándalos* that shook Mexico in the spring of 2004. The first showed the president of the Mexican Green Party, the country's fourth-largest party, purportedly negotiating a $2 million payment in exchange for the party's support for a zoning change in Cancun. The second showed the Mexico City finance secretary betting thousands of dollars in the VIP room of the Bellagio Hotel Casino in Las Vegas. Apparently, he was a regular there.

Television's role in airing the videos was hotly debated in Mexico during the spring of 2004. Always present political corruption now made its way into every living room. So did cutthroat politics. Was Mexican democracy better for it? Public confidence in politics generally plummeted. Following record-level abstention in the 2003 congressional elections, some analysts worried that faith in democracy itself would go with it. Pollster Dan Lund interviewed 1,200 Mexicans about democracy as part of the Latinobarometer study in November 2003. A slim majority, 53 percent, said democracy "is preferable to all other forms of government." Thirty percent said that "for people like me, a democratic or nondemocratic regime makes no difference" (MUND Américas 2003).

However, one thing that most Mexicans agreed on was that the sort of corruption that appeared on the videotapes had gone on for decades in Mexico. It had just never been seen by the public. In this sense, perhaps Televisa's airing of the Bejarano videotape was a small step toward accountability. The videotapes are another sign of the ambiguous relationship between market-driven journalism and democracy. As Spanish author Arturo Pérez Riverte told *Reforma* a few days after the Bejarano video aired: "Whoever made those videos public did it for reasons that are as dirty as the others, but it doesn't matter because from here on the politicians will have to be more careful." As for whether he personally wanted to watch such disdainful behavior, he said, "I'd rather be lucid than an imbecile" (Bucio 2003).

Part IV

PROSPECTS FOR CIVIC JOURNALISM AND DEMOCRACY

9 The Durability of Civic Journalism

When a group of farmwomen approached the tall, mustached president early in 2003, they teased softly that he was as good looking in person as he appeared on television.

"Ah," said Vicente Fox, playing along. "How do I look?"

"Handsome," they replied, "and your government is moving along nicely too."

"Moving along, are we? You obviously don't read the newspapers," the president said.

"No, I can't read at all, but I watch you on TV," responded one of the women.

"You are better off that way," the president told her. "You'll be happier" (Venegas 2003; Castillo 2003).

While Fox's comment contradicted the president's charge to eradicate illiteracy, this was not the first time the president had said that reading Mexican newspapers was depressing. In fact, he said it so often during his first four years in office that a top editor investigated whether he took anti-depressives. But when one read the headlines, Fox's sour mood was more understandable, if not the expected reaction of a weathered politician. Newspapers criticized everything from the president's exorbitant expenditures on his clothing and living quarters—including four hundred dollars each for a set of embroidered towels—to his mispronunciation of the last name of author Jorge Luis Borges in front of the Second International Congress of the Spanish Language in Spain. "The press focuses on *babosadas*, childish drivel, and not on my accomplishments," Fox complained one year into his term. "I know that the citizens, who watch, listen and read the media, will make their own evaluations and in the end will stop reading those newspapers that don't appeal to them, as I have stopped reading a good number of newspapers, because, frankly, they sour my day a bit" (Sistema Internet de la Presidencia 2001).

Fox's distinction between the depressing press and more cheery television coverage should not have come as a surprise to those who watched both media closely. A detailed content analysis of three months of coverage in 2003, as well as a review of numerous media scandals during the first four years of Fox's term, found notable differences in the way market-driven television and more civic-oriented newspapers covered the first democratically elected Mexican president.[1]

The Press and Television—Different Approaches

Tables 9.1, 9.2, and 9.3 compare the coverage of Fox during three months in 2003 by the top two commercial television networks with coverage by two of the largest-circulation civic newspapers in the country, *El Universal* and *Reforma*. The differences Fox noticed between newspapers and television are borne out by the data, which were drawn from a sample of twelve dates selected as "constructed weeks," or sequential days of the week spread over three months. To ensure greater reliability in the coding, ten percent of the

Table 9.1 Tone of Presidential Coverage, 2003

Television *(El Noticiero* and *Hechos)*

Treatment of the President	Number of Items	% Coverage in TV Seconds
Negative	1	.9
Balanced	5	20.7
Positive	9	25.2
Neutral	12	53.2
Total	27	100

Print *(El Universal* and *Reforma)*

Treatment of the President	Number of Items	% Coverage in Press Words
Negative	55	31.8
Balanced	45	30.5
Positive	48	29
Neutral	17	8.7
Total	165	100

Table 9.2 Reporting Assertiveness for Presidential News, 2003

Television (*El Noticiero* and *Hechos*)

Type	Number of Items	% Coverage in TV Seconds
Passive	16	53.3
Breaking news	3	15.4
Assertive	7	31.3
Total	26	100

Print (*El Universal* and *Reforma*)

Type	Number of Items	% Coverage in Print Words
Passive	71	45
Breaking news	6	4.7
Assertive	65	50.3
Total	143	100

Table 9.3 Framing Assertiveness for Presidential News, 2003

Television (*El Noticiero* and *Hechos*)

Who Set the Frame?	Number of Items	% Coverage in TV Seconds
Networks	3	14.6
Government source	20	78.9
Political party	1	1.2
Other actor	3	5.3
Total	27	100

Print (*El Universal* and *Reforma*)

Who Set the Frame?	Number of Items	% Coverage in Print Words
Newspapers	27	15.6
Government source	74	45.5
Foreign media	9	2.8
Political party	23	13.5
Other actor	32	22.6
Total	165	100

larger database of television cases were double-coded and determined to have an inter-coder agreement of 0.920 when controlling for chance.[2]

Despite the transformation of coverage of elections and political parties, most of the news Mexicans saw about the president on the two networks after the fall of the PRI regime was either neutral or positive.[3] On most occasions, *El Noticiero* and *Hechos* limited the majority of coverage to summaries of Fox's speeches, ceremonies, and press conferences. In the three months under analysis in table 9.1, presidential coverage was neutral in more than half of all coverage, 53 percent, and positive 25 percent of the time. Only about 1 percent of presidential coverage was negative, while about 21 percent contained both negative and positive information about the president.

While criticism of the president was relatively rare, it crept into news about the president when the networks covered both positive and negative aspects of a story in a balanced fashion or when an event itself was inherently negative for Fox, such as when protesting public school teachers marched on the presidential residence or when school children tripped the president while he swatted a Christmas piñata during a press event. Negative coverage of the president infrequently criticized policy. The occasional negative broadcast story usually highlighted the personal failings, sharpened conflict, or dramatic visuals that are characteristic of tabloidized television news. Such images may have been too strong to pass up even though they reflected poorly on the sitting president. On balance, however, any negative television story involving the president was few and far between when compared to the daily drone of presidential ceremonies, press conferences, and pronouncements.

The networks' relatively hands-off approach to criticism of Fox has to be qualified historically, however. Coverage of the president during the study period was relatively infrequent, taking up just 6.5 percent of newscast time. That was about 30 percent less than in 1994 and probably represented an even bigger decline from still earlier news programming, when coverage of the president dominated political news.[4] Moreover, prior to the mid-1990s there was no criticism at all of the sitting president on television. Finally, images of the president have always been a touchy subject, so the broadcast of a president tumbled by school children represents a dramatic change from the days of the reverential media. During the Miguel Alemán administration (1946–1952), for instance, a magazine was forced to close after its editors ran a questionable picture of Alemán's son in a Paris nightclub. A decade later, a newspaper was closed during the Gustavo Díaz Ordaz administration (1964–1970) when it inadvertently swapped a caption intended for a picture of a gorilla with one of the sitting president. As late as 1999, Televisa's main anchor chastised an opposition congressman for criticizing the president to his face—even though the network had omitted footage of the criticism itself from the broadcast. So we should not underestimate the fact that Televisa and TV Azteca ran the incident of the stumbling president.

The networks' reporting methods during this time period largely remained passive. More than half of coverage of Fox in the content analysis, 53 percent, came from press conferences, statements, or ceremonies where reporters were spoon-fed the news.[5] Only 31 percent came from more assertive methods of reporting such as personal interviews or the consultation of multiple sources. Moreover, network journalists selected how to interpret, or frame, a news event in only 15 percent of coverage. Eighty percent of coverage presented government interpretations of events.[6]

Market-driven journalism in postauthoritarian Mexico had replaced the authoritarian PRI system's lavish praise of a God-like president with moderated coverage of a slightly more fallible chief executive. Television coverage of the president was largely neutral and sparse, reflected government framing of events, and was reported passively, but criticism sometimes crept into the newscasts indirectly via the issues themselves or balanced reporting that covered positive and negative aspects of a story.

Newspaper coverage, on the other hand, was more critical of the president. Two of the top newspapers in the Mexico City market were more likely to publish information critical of the president in articles that were either balanced (30.5 percent) or solely negative (31.8 percent). Newspapers also were more assertive in their reporting about the president, using personal interviews, documents, their own polls or multiple sources in half of coverage. Finally, newspapers were more likely than television to use independent interpretations or frames of news events or to use frames set by sources outside of government to guide news narratives. Yet newspapers remained passive in most cases. Government sources still were able to control framing of news events three times as often as the newspapers themselves.

How roughly the press treated the president depended to a degree on the ideological stance of the newspaper. *Reforma*, which has a center-right editorial line similar to the ideology of Fox's party, PAN, treated the president somewhat more positively than the essentially centrist *El Universal*. Had the *La Jornada* been included in the study, the tone would have been much more critical. The left-leaning daily had little good to say about the president during his six years in office. The reverse was true of the leftist Mexico City mayor, Andrés Manuel López Obrador. *Reforma* had little good to say about the mayor, while *La Jornada* rarely, if ever, criticized him.[7]

Several storylines that arose in news coverage during the three months of detailed content analysis further highlight the differences in press and television treatment of the president. The networks gave relatively little coverage to the scandal surrounding the investigation of illegal donations to Fox's private campaign organization, Amigos de Fox. The issue was bad news for the president, so any reporting of it reflected negatively on Fox. The two networks covered the issue on just one day during the period of detailed analysis, while the scandal was in the press almost every day. Another controversial issue, the purported political ambitions of First Lady Marta Sahagún de Fox and whether her charitable group was really preparing the ground for a presidential bid, received a lot of print coverage but was presented in the newscasts only once—and in a positive manner—during the study.

Over the course of the Fox presidency, the networks' coverage of the presidency was much more restrained than what appeared in the press. Besides titillating *scandalitos* such as the president's extravagant expenditures for linen and clothing, newspapers also covered far-reaching ethical breaches and policy failures. The press wrote stories about an indigenous reform law rejected by the largest indigenous groups, the president's failure to pass a much-needed tax reform or generate jobs in a stalled economy, the continuing wave of violent crime, fierce infighting among cabinet members, the failure of the president's special prosecutor to indict a former president some considered the author of the killing of protesters in 1971, and possible links between Fox and a controversial developer. Television news covered the same issues, but much less frequently and vociferously.

Comparing television and press coverage of the most important actor in Mexican politics provides evidence that a hybrid media system replaced the authoritarian Mexican media institution after the fall of the PRI regime. One of the two dominant forms of journalism in Mexico in the 2000s can be described as approaching the market-driven model—diverse and assertive enough to raise ratings, but no more. Most TV news programs either presented neutral summaries of orchestrated presidential events or, more infrequently, focused on conflict, personal failings, or compelling images. The other journalistic form practiced in Mexico after the fall of the authoritarian political system approached civic-oriented journalism. Civic-oriented newspapers were more diverse and assertive than the commercial networks, often greatly so. Policy issues and allegations of corruption or incompetence received ample coverage. Adaptive authoritarianism—passive and nondiverse journalism, sometimes sold to the highest partisan bidder—still existed in pockets outside the major cities or in capital city newspapers with few readers whose owners used the publications to pursue personal projects, while even the civic newspapers protected owners' personal interests, such as a hands-off approach to the church. The authoritarian form was waning as a normatively accepted and instrumentally efficient manner to run a news organization, however. The most successful news organizations no longer followed its tenets.

Institutionalizing Civic Journalism

Have civic values and behaviors become institutionalized in a field of media organizations operating within a hybrid media system? Can civic-oriented journalism survive as more than a marginal form within a commercial media setting as the electoral transition slows, commercial pressures continue or increase, and new cohorts of print journalists take control of Mexican newsrooms? The answers to those questions are vital as the country exits its electoral transition and enters the crucial phase of building democratic institutions, among them the institutionalization of a free and citizen-focused press. Institutionalization is a process of continuous solidification of the norms, frameworks, and organizations that regulate social transactions (Eisenstadt 1968, 415; Jepperson 1991). Has that happened in civic newsrooms after the elections of 2000 formally ended the PRI regime?

The evidence supports the argument that the uneven but far-reaching transformation of the Mexican media from an authoritarian institution in the early 1980s into a hybrid media system by the 2000s followed the institutional model of media development presented in chapter 1. While the direction of media transitions hinged upon change agents' mental models of journalism and society, change itself responded to conditions in four interacting institutional domains: the environment of news production outside of media organizations; the trans-organizational institution of media organizations; a social-psychological domain encompassing journalists' values, professional identities, and mental models of journalism and society; and the organizational nexus of the newsroom. To gauge the survivability of civic journalism in postauthoritarian Mexico, we must assess conditions in each of these four institutional domains.

Journalists and the organizations in which they work operate within a broader societal context that sets the parameters for news production. A number of characteristics of the Mexican news environment had already changed substantially by the end of the 1990s—relations with sources, the threat of drug trafficking, and pressures from wealthy individuals and companies. Journalists and media owners by the 2000s knew how to interact with politicians of many partisan stripes. They reported on drug traffickers and other entities operating outside of the law. They worked in a society where wealth was extremely concentrated and the economy had moved in and out of recession for at least two decades. While new circumstances eroded the authoritarian media institution, they posed both opportunities and constraints for the consolidation of civic journalism during the Fox presidency.

In one of the most positive developments for the institutionalization of assertive journalism, the political climate immediately after Fox's election enabled a coalition of independent newspapers, academics, and NGOs to convince opposition politicians to push through a broad access to information law that was seized upon by thousands of citizens as a tool to monitor their government. The development of the law began when Fox lost control of a campaign proposal for an anticorruption measure. More than one hundred independent newspapers, academics, and NGOs promoted the cause and turned it into a proposal for a new law that would open up the executive branch to citizen petitions for information for the first time in Mexican history. How did the pro-access civic coalition come into being, and how did it successfully lobby for the law?

Mexico's civil sphere had strengthened over two decades of political and economic liberalization, creating conditions for the emergence in 2001 of a powerful alliance of newspapers, academic experts in law and communication, nongovernmental organizations working in human rights and the environment, and, ultimately, opposition legislators. Together, in a pragmatic partnership that responded strategically to government delays and antagonism, the Oaxaca Group promoted the Federal Law for Transparency and Access to Information. The law emanated in civil society, and passed Congress despite the initial resistance of Fox and the ruling PAN, who won the presidency in 2000 by promising to reform the Mexican state along democratic lines. Instead, as Milton (2001) found in his study of stunted media reform in Eastern Europe, the Fox administration's prodemocratic promises on legal reform for the media stayed largely at the rhetorical level once it gained the privileges of presidential power.

The newspapers *El Universal* and *Reforma* put aside commercial rivalries to push for the law in a pragmatic partnership. These two newspapers were joined by more than one hundred other publications, including the influential *La Jornada*, but became the law's most powerful proponents because of their stature as political points of reference and unyielding positions in favor of the law. They used their public news pages and behind-the-scenes lobbying power to promote openness and counteract government attempts to limit the scope of the civic groups' proposal (Escobedo 2003; Villanueva 2003).

Insider accounts suggest that the formation of the pro-access alliance was incremental and entirely pragmatic. Academics, activists, and newspaper journalists, who four years earlier had publicly accused one another of either manipulating the public or trying to "gag" the press, decided to agree that an access to information law was beneficial and possible in the current political climate. A strategy of cooperation on points of consensus then evolved incrementally through a series of private and public meetings.[8] As Ernesto Villanueva, a member of the group and professor at UNAM, has written, "esprit de corps formed because of a shared concern" (Villanueva 2003, 133).

Coalition member and scholar Juan Francisco Escobedo described several phases of development of the access coalition that became known as the

Oaxaca Group, taking its name from the city in which these actors first met at an academic conference in May 2001 (Escobedo 2003). At this inaugural meeting, the newspapers put aside past disputes and, for the first time, reached out to NGOs and previously antagonistic academics to work on a consensus agenda for media reform. On the top of the list was access to information. The coalition formed a working group that wrote the Oaxaca Declaration in favor of an access to information law. It was published in more than one hundred newspapers across the country. By using the resources of the press, the group sought to frame the public debate and turn public opinion in favor of an access to information law that contained guarantees of access and enforcement. In the meantime, the working group employed the intellectual resources of the coalition. Its legal experts wrote a legislative proposal for an access law, based on international models, which they presented to congressional representatives in September.

A second stage of action began when someone leaked a draft law, written by the Fox administration, which was eventually filed in November. Coalition members considered the government's powers to deny petitions too broad. They decided to lobby friendly opposition lawmakers to make the group's earlier proposal a formal legislative proposal. This was a key moment. The group convinced the unified opposition to support the bill.[9] The civic coalition's ability to sway public opinion through the news pages and the opportunity to use the issue against the ruling PAN helped the coalition gain even the necessary support of the PRI, which had established the norm of government secrecy during its seven decades in power.

The newspapers kept up the public pressure. As the Fox administration pushed for public hearings on a more restrictive version of the law, *Reforma* dedicated a page of coverage on November 24, 2001 under the headline "No to the Government Hearings." On the same day, *El Universal* published on its front page: "The Mexican Editors' Association . . . expressed its 'public condemnation before the evident signs that the government seeks to chill citizen enthusiasm for learning on what and how the government spends the public's money.'"

The coalition finally convinced opposition lawmakers and ultimately Fox himself to enact this legislation. After intense negotiations, most of the group's proposal passed Congress without change (Escobedo 2003). Fox signed the law with flourish, in an attempt to win back some of the public relations appeal. Mexicans gained the right to know the workings of their government on June 12, 2003. International experts consider the law well designed; it included time limits for government response to petitions for information, restrictions on the type of information that can be withheld from public scrutiny, and an independent oversight authority to ensure compliance. In the first nine months of operation of the Federal Law for Transparency and Access to Information, 26,673 Mexicans asked for and received information from an executive branch agency, something unheard of just five years earlier. Traditionally, government information had been reserved for the personal use of the country's governors, not Mexican citizens with a right to know what their government was doing.

Mexican citizens have mostly wanted to learn about the everyday stuff of democratic governance—budgets and salaries, personnel openings, contracts, programs, and policy effectiveness. Table 9.4 reports the type of information sought by Mexico's empowered citizenry. Academics (21 percent of total petitions), lawyers and business people (16 percent), and government officials themselves (9 percent) used the law more than journalists (7 percent).[10] Most requests from citizens were fairly ordinary, but a few were splashy enough to make it into the press. After fifteen years of protests, physicist Bernardo Salas Mar received information about the country of origin of uranium used in the Laguna Verde Nuclear Power Plant so he could investigate complaints of its poor quality. Pro-choice NGOs learned that the lion's share of government money dedicated for reproductive health support was going to an anti-abortion group, and that it was being spent in a shady manner. And communications scholar Raúl Trejo Delarbe, who had requested a list of the country's broadcast licenses for more than a decade, finally forced the Com-

Table 9.4 Material Requested under the Federal Law for Transparency and Access to Information (June–December 2003)

Type of Request	Number	%
Agency-level statistics, forms, concessions, and survey results	5,811	24.1
Institutional activities: agendas, calendars, results, other	3,841	15.9
Organizational structure, directories, job openings	2,802	11.6
Expenditures	2,381	9.9
Contracts	1,690	7.0
Salaries and other remuneration	1,412	5.8
Program design, budget, beneficiaries, impact	1,233	5.1
Personnel data	966	4.0
Audits	155	0.6
Repeated or unreadable	120	0.5
Incorrect agency	1,454	6.0
Other	2,293	9.5
Total	24,158	100

Source: For source information, please see note 10 to this chapter.

munications and Transportation Secretariat to publish the list online (Salas Mar 2004; Bordon and Hernández 2004; Mejía Barquera 2003).

Journalists have now begun to use the law to level the playing field with sources who once held the upper hand when they released public information on a friendship basis or leaked information to harm rivals or further their own interests. Most journalists do not use the access law on a regular basis, but those who do have pried open public entities like never before. One is Jorge Alejandro Medellín, the armed forces reporter for *El Universal*, who received a complete report on the Mexican Navy's internal structure, ranks, salaries, and advisors after his newspaper challenged the secretariat's denial through the independent Federal Access to Information Institute (IFAI). He has also received information on soldiers expelled from the services after contracting the HIV virus and ex-soldiers who joined the federal police forces. Another *El Universal* reporter, Anabel Hernández, requested and eventually received a list of prices and purchases of wardrobe for the president and first lady, again after the newspaper appealed to the IFAI. Hernández later wrote a hard-hitting book on the presidential family's wealth, *La Familia Presidencial*, with radio reporter Arelí Quintero.

Reforma reporters also have used the law. Business reporter Verónica Galán found out through a request that budget surpluses President Fox said had gone to school construction and other social programs had actually paid salaries from a general fund. Her colleague Armando Talamantes learned that the Finance Secretariat had no idea how the billions of pesos from the national lottery—also supposedly earmarked for social programs—were actually spent. *Reforma* benefited indirectly from the access law when the pro-choice NGOs got records showing that the government was sending healthcare funds to an anti-abortion group that appeared to be misspending the public money. The NGOs turned the documents over to the newspaper, which then produced a number of front-page stories.

While many have benefited from the law, there are shortcomings. The law's implementing regulations only cover the executive branch. Initially, the Mexico City government, the Mexican Congress, and the federal courts all balked at implementing their own laws or regulations. Supreme Court justices finally enacted a regulatory code for the federal courts in March 2004 after severe criticism in the press and heated debates with newspaper editors at public forums. Judicial decisions in criminal and family court, once handed to reporters as favors or leaks, are now considered public records. However, no independent body hears challenges to Supreme Court decisions to seal sentences (Fuentes 2004). Another limitation is that most newspapers have not institutionalized access law petitions as a routine part of daily reporting practices, although there has been slow progress. Nongovernmental organizations such as the pro-access group Libertad de Información-Mexico, A.C., the journalists' professional organization Periodistas de Investigación, and the Knight Center for Journalism in the Americas at the University of Texas conducted training sessions around the country after the law went into effect. Despite the shortcomings, the advances in opening government have been spectacular when compared to the culture of secrecy that prevailed only recently in Mexico.

In other areas, however, media reform has stalled. A proposal to create a nonpartisan, public board to grant broadcast frequency concessions failed to get a vote in Congress in 2005. News reports suggested that lobbying by media owners' associations and large commercial networks derailed the proposal. Said a senator who sponsored the reform: "They have spoken to practically all of the legislators. To our legislative whip, the president of our party, the chairmen of all of the Senate committees. . . . They have told us that the politician who approves of the proposal is burned with the industry, that this isn't in his best interest, that businessmen know how to return a favor" (Audiffred 2005).

While the access to information law makes the quid-pro-quo award of the lucrative broadcast concessions more risky, a nonpartisan board could make sure the practice of exchanging licenses for favorable coverage came to an end. However, network lobbyists pushed through their own version of media reform—which made the only criteria for television concessions financial wherewithal, thus assuring their control of the airwaves for decades. The proposal was halted in the Senate, but network pressure on legislators continued.

Moreover, the Fox administration's relationship with the commercial networks seemed closer than ever as the election neared. The outgoing interior secretary, Santiago Creel, granted licenses for sixty-five gambling centers to an affiliate of Televisa just five days before leaving office and beginning a multimillion dollar advertising campaign in favor of his presidential bid. He did not explain where the money for the ads came from, but newspapers reported that networks gave him an enormous discount that other presidential hopefuls soon clamored for. As for TV Azteca, the network's former director of government relations became the President's office liaison with the broadcast media, while continuing to receive payments from his former employer (López 2005; Aponte 2005; Barajas 2005).

On another front, a coalition of newspapers led by *El Universal* began in 2003 to promote a shield law to protect journalists from police orders to divulge their sources. As the print media's assertiveness increased and the old forms of control decreased, police had begun issuing orders and threats for journalists to reveal their sources. Police even entered the daily *La Jornada* newsroom in Mexico City and threatened journalists there. The situation was complicated because the cases of corruption and violent crime investigated by the journalists sometimes involved law enforcement officers. After the *La Jornada* scandal and reaction from press groups nationally and internationally, the Mexico City Attorney General's Office created guidelines for subpoenaing journalists. A proposed law granting journalists the right to protect their sources passed the Senate in April 2005, but then stalled in the Chamber of Deputies (Martínez, Soto, and Martínez 2004; Otero 2004). Fox and the National Human Rights Commission publicly support the legislation, but violent events after its passage overshadowed the movement for reform.

More journalists were killed in Mexico from November through April 2005 than in any other Latin American country. Three were assassinated openly. The fourth disappeared. All reported about drug trafficking and local corruption. A team from the Paris-based group Reporters Without Borders documented 16 deaths or disappearances of local reporters on the U.S. border or the Gulf during the Fox administration. The Mexican Network for the Protection of Journalists documented 421 instances of attacks, threats, or murders of journalists from 2000 to 2004. The violence came amid drug gang turf battles and sometimes the complicity of police. Frequently, prosecutions were slow, stalled, quashed, or misdirected. The Mexican Network believed nearly one-quarter of the attacks and threats in 2004 were carried out by police forces themselves.

Journalists' ability to protect themselves under such circumstances are limited. Nevertheless, in a second instance of cross-media professional development following the successful efforts of the Oaxaca Group, they responded by organizing to pressure the government. Journalists in sixteen cities marched to protest attacks and impunity in late 2004, chanting "*Ni uno más*" (not one more). They turned out again on World Free Press Day, May 3, 2005. The Center for Journalism and Public Ethics, run by former *Reforma* reporter Leonarda Reyes with initial funding from the Knight Center, redirected its program objectives toward pressuring for a federal response and training journalists for work under dangerous conditions. On August 31, 2005, forty newspaper editors and owners signed a declaration pushing Fox to make attacks on journalists a federal crime so that state-level police would no longer lead investigations. The owners and editors pledged to hold regular training sessions and vowed to create a team of reporters to investigate attacks on their colleagues themselves (Otero 2005). This followed the example of *Zeta* in Tijuana, which published the names of gunmen that journalists believed killed their editor in 2004, and *El Periódico* in Guatemala, which published the names of an armed squad that invaded the home and psychologically tortured the publication's editor in 2003. In both cases, the newspapers investigated because they felt the authorities would not.

Other responses were more problematic for participatory democracy. Understandably, newspapers increased caution and self-censorship. Frontera in Tijuana implemented review of all drug-related stories to anticipate possible reactions and decide whether it sufficiently advances information the public needs to be worth the risk of publication. *Frontera*'s sister newspaper, *El Imparcial* in nearby Sonora, lost reporters Alfredo Jiménez Mota and Francisco Arratia Saldierna in less than a year. Arratia was murdered and Jiménez disappeared on the way to meet a news source. At the radio station where crime reporter Dolores Guadalupe García Escamilla was executed in a barrage of gunfire April 1, 2005, her replacement now covers press conferences and no more. Mexican newspapers launched the new investigative team in early 2006 in Nuevo Laredo on the U.S. border. One week later, a group armed with rifles and grenades attached the newsroom of El Mañana, the local host of the event. Reporter Jaime Orozco Tey was seriously injured. Press groups around the world condemned the attack.

The largest civic newspapers around the country remained on stable financial footing into the 2000s despite economic stagnation from 2001 to 2004. Even in this environment, *El Universal* and *Reforma* increased sales of "popular" versions of their more expensive daily newspapers. *El Universal*'s growth was spectacular. Its revamped afternoon tabloid, *El Gráfico*, cost less than half of the morning newspaper's price and highlighted *El Universal* stories that appealed to a more working-class, male audience. The newspaper reported its circulation increased from 12,000 to 200,000 copies in just one year.[11] While *El Gráfico*'s advertising income was only a fraction of what the morning publication brought in, the circulation gain challenged the traditional adage that Mexicans do not read newspapers. It seems more likely they just could not afford them.[12]

Advertising in the top three newspapers by 2003 was much more dependent upon the private sector than it had been one decade earlier. The government's ability to control newspapers had disappeared. At the same time, however, newspaper editors had to fend off pressure from private-sector advertisers. Both *El Universal* and *Reforma*'s owners were in a position to do so if they wanted to, as neither had a single client who controlled more than about 5 percent of total ads. *La Jornada*'s case is exceptional among the three. While the publication still relies heavily on government advertising, by 2003

Table 9.5 Private Sector and Government Advertising in Civic Newspapers

Newspaper	Private Sector (%)	Government (%)	Political Party (Electoral Year) (%)
El Universal	96	4	4
Reforma	97	3	1
La Jornada	60	40	10

Sources: Data reported by newspaper editors in confidential interviews by author, June 10, 12, and 18, 2003, Mexico City.

private-sector advertising had for the first time become more important.[13] Table 9.5 presents self-reported advertising ratios for the country's top three newspapers in mid-2003.

As of 2003, there was little competition for these top newspapers in the capital with the exception of the financial press, especially *El Financiero*. The daily *Milenio*, owned by a Monterrey media group, was still read mostly by political junkies. Many of its best reporters and editors had left because of staff disputes. Traditional, PRI-oriented newspapers had little impact and few readers. At least one inertial authoritarian newspaper in Mexico City, *Novedades*, closed after Fox was elected. *Excélsior* held on with an inconsistent editorial line, a skeleton staff, and its million-dollar downtown real estate. It was finally sold in early 2006, but its future was unclear. *El Heraldo de México*, purchased by a radio entrepreneur with private financial backing, struggled to reorient its style of journalism. Finally, *El Independiente*, founded by a politically connected developer, had to close within two years when its owner became embroiled in a bribery scandal.

Mental Models and Professional Identities

Evidence of the institutionalization of the civic model among the nation's leading newspapers was less ambiguous when viewed at the cognitive level of mental models and professional identities. The conceptualization of the financial and normative superiority of civic journalism appeared well consolidated in 2004 in the country's leading newspapers. To reach this judgment, I analyzed confidential interviews with editors who directed or were role models for reporters at *El Universal*, *Reforma*, and *La Jornada*. The sample included editors-in-chief at two newspapers and the managing editor at the third newspaper, as well as two other top editors in each newspaper. I also analyzed interviews with seven political reporters from these newspapers.[14] Table 9.6 presents excerpts from editors' responses to the question: "What is the role of the press in Mexican society?"

The civic attitudes expressed by the sixteen journalists came out clearly in the interviews. The majority of newsroom leaders and role models in the three largest newspapers in Mexico expressed conceptions of journalism that support the institutionalization of a civic role for the press—monitoring government and giving citizens the information they need to debate, deliberate, and act politically. Monitoring economic and cultural power was less notable in the interviews, but also present. The only cleavage detected was on the issue of whether a journalist should act as a protagonist in news events, especially political ones. This conflict appeared between the views of the oldest editor, who assumed a more activist role for journalists against the injustices of laissez-faire economics, and two editors and a younger reporter who rejected this role without prompting to bring up the issue. The remaining journalists did not mention the issue.

This implies a profound cultural change has taken place among the leaders of Mexican newspapers. Questions remained, however, about the steadfastness of media owners as the 2006 presidential election approached. Their personal and business interests might influence coverage, even where civic-minded editors hoped to work in the public interest.

Will civic-oriented journalism survive in postauthoritarian Mexico? Can it be more than a marginal journalistic form subsumed within a commercial or oligarchic news system? The answer depends not only on continued structural reforms after the passage of the country's new access to information law. Reforms such as a shield law protecting journalists' confidential sources and federal prosecutors for crimes committed against journalists could make journalistic autonomy and assertiveness more possible. A nonpartisan, transparent board to oversee broadcast licenses could give civic journalism a chance to take root in at least some rogue organizations within the market-driven broadcast media. However, the survivability of civic journalism also requires the continued institutionalization of civic beliefs and practices in Mexican newsrooms.

My interviews with editors and surveys of journalists suggest that civic leaders and role models are in place now in the major newspapers, so civic journalism has a foothold at least for the next decade if media owners cooperate. Mexican journalists' conceptualizations of their profession and its role in society were forged during a specific moment in time when journalists had to choose sides between an increasingly illegitimate regime or an emerging civil society. The decision to resist state encroachment and work on behalf of a nascent citizenry required an intense struggle to assert professional autonomy from an authoritarian regime and forged a new professional identity within

Table 9.6 Conceptions of the Role of Journalism among Editors in Leading Mexican Newspapers, 2003

El Universal

What is the role of journalism in Mexican society?	Years in journalism (2003)
The press as "watchdog," the concept of the press as a pain in the neck versus the government	26
Intermediaries between the facts and the readers so they have information to decide their vote, their way of life, even to be entertained once in awhile	26
The absolute counterweight of power, of political power, economic power, cultural power, power in a broad sense	20

Reforma

What is the role of journalism in Mexican society?	Years in journalism (2003)
Inform and as a consequence of that, monitor or criticize. Sometimes reporters mix themselves in politics. I have learned to be less protagonist and have more of a public responsibility.	20
The press should inform so that society itself naturally becomes vigilant, by contrasting statements with reality.	16
Be sure that the laws are respected and denounce it when government or the private sector act incorrectly. Then the society will know what to do.	15

La Jornada

What is the role of journalism in Mexican society?	Years in journalism (2003)
Neoliberalism or "The Washington Consensus" on market economics was a fundamental rupture globally that affected journalistic activity. We think this was not the right path. What we must do is be militant journalists.	27
The press should monitor the state because its fundamental role is to serve society, the citizenry. I believe there is no country that can consider itself strong if its citizenry is not well informed.	26
The better informed a society, the more capable this society will be to make important decisions such as electing who governs it. It is imperative that we keep going out to the streets to tell people what is happening in the country.	24

those who lived through it. Many of these journalists are mentors in civic newsrooms and professors who pass the new norms on to their students.

There are many reasons why these norms, even deeply ingrained, may not produce news coverage on behalf of Mexico's nascent citizenry, however. An international comparison will help to better ascertain where those pressures may develop.

10 Media Transformation in Comparative Perspective

Mexico's transition from an authoritarian media institution to a hybrid system in which civic, market driven, and authoritarian elements of the press compete and conflict can be formulated as an institutional model of media transformation generating hypotheses about journalistic change. Application of the model in other national contexts will allow us to test the generalizability of the model, probe the relative strength of the levels of institutional action, and seek clues about whether civic impulses that awaken during democratic transitions can consolidate as more than a marginalized form of journalism or an unfulfilled desire when societal power centers reconfigure.

I apply the model to three other Latin American press systems—Guatemala, Chile, and Argentina—where innovative newspapers prompted change in the press field during transitions from various forms of authoritarianism. This is an adaptation of a most-similar system comparative design because we are analyzing other national media systems that have previously passed through transitions from authoritarian rule for clues about the causes of media transformation and the ultimate outcome of civic media transformation in the Mexican case. The comparison is general and based upon secondary sources because ethnographic data at the level of detail collected for the Mexican case is not available for the other cases. Moreover, the degree to which these cases display civic tendencies varies. All the founding civic newspapers in the cases strove for autonomy and assertiveness. The degree of diversity of the perspectives and voices they offered to readers varied, although their creators usually voiced a commitment to diversity.

Nevertheless, the comparison of the development of postauthoritarian media systems is highly instructive. It supports the model's proposition that only by understanding the interaction of environmental opening, the institutional field, organizational culture, and professional values and norms can we understand how media systems transform. The comparison also strongly suggests that the normative arena is what matters most for media opening when political and economic pressures on the subordinate media begin to lift. Finally, the comparison suggests that the consolidation of civic journalism is closely linked to civic participation and diversity. For all of these countries, including Mexico, consolidation of civic journalism after the romance of democracy fades will be extremely difficult.

The institutional model presented in table 10.1 envisions four levels of action and interaction that together produce stability and change in a media system: the environmental, the institutional field, the organizational, and the level of the social-psychological or change agent. An opening in the news production environment allows professional identities stemming from new ideas about journalism and alternative political values to assert themselves in an organizational form. Organizational expression of the new identity occurs when change agents possess sufficient newsroom power to effect change through mentoring, retraining, altered incentives, and personnel replacement. The relationship between the environmental opening and the expression of new identities in newsroom behavior is interactive and incremental. Change in one sphere engenders change in the other, and the line of influence runs in both directions.

The cases of journalistic change that I analyze are the newspaper *La*

Table 10.1: The Institutional Model of Media Transformation

Environment shifts*	Institutional field	Innovative news organizations	Change agents
· Open political space · Open economic space · May create systemic shocks	· Innovative organizations change referents, influence others that mimic the early innovators · Conflicting models of journalism and society develop · Personnel networks develop and spread	· Change agents obtain organizational power in the form of decision making autonomy, and leadership skills · Change agents transform the organizational culture via mentoring, retraining, replacement, or new incentives	· Harbor oppositional political values · Learn alternative ideas about journalism · Develop new professional identities · Obtain control of the newsroom

Note: *In Latin America, environmental shifts refer to political and economic liberalization.

Epoca during Chile's delayed transition from a personalized variant of bureaucratic authoritarianism, the newspaper *Página/12* in Argentina during democratic consolidation after that country's transition from bureaucratic authoritarian rule, and Guatemala's *Siglo Veintiuno* during the consolidation of electoral democracy after a prolonged civil conflict. Each of these countries are now considered electoral democracies, but have serious deficiencies in respect for human rights, political representation, governmental accountability, and general adherence to the rule of law. Each of the aforementioned newspapers were standard-setting innovators within the press fields of their respective countries as authoritarianism waned or democracy consolidated. Writes Rosental Alves, a Brazilian editor who now runs the Knight Center for Journalism in the Americas: "These daily newspapers played a very important role in opposing and resisting authoritarian regimes. They acted as spearheads of democratic forces, openly defying oppressive political systems and even other media outlets that have been tamed or [entered into] mutually beneficial collusion with governments. Perhaps their most important common trait is that the newspapers set an example for the rest of the media, strongly influencing them to change their editorial lines and reporting styles, to adapt themselves to the new times of political openness and democracy" (Alves 1997).

These publications' innovative approaches to journalism—all anti-authoritarian, autonomous, and to a greater or lesser degree civic in orientation—were not sustained after their countries' respective political transitions ended and the arduous work of deepening and consolidating democratic rights and institutions began. Since the end of the political transitions in which these newspapers played important roles by transforming journalistic thought and behavior, each has either closed or substantially changed its orientation toward political power and the citizenry. Only in Guatemala did the autonomous style survive. It was directly transferred to a new newspaper, *elPeriódico*, which resists financial pressure and physical repression.

The demise of civic-like journalism occurred as independent newspapers faced varied political and economic pressures from the external environment and within the newspaper field. In particular, the concentration of media ownership in a few hands, holdover market strength from the predemocratic era, trading of economic favors for news coverage, advertising boycotts, psychological repression, and physical threats limit civic behavior. The constant variable in all of the failed cases, however, was the reemergence of newsroom leaders' ideological identities when political leaders who shared the journalists' ideological views took office. Once a commitment to journalism that enabled participatory participation was lost, the three civic pioneers reviewed here all lost their autonomy and assertiveness on reporting about centrally important issues and actors.

Independent, assertive, and diverse journalism in each of the countries is worse off for the demise of these newspapers and the deterioration of the ethic they fostered, but the story is not all discouraging. While the original newspapers ceased to be the powerful motors of participation that they once were, they have left legacies. They changed or moderated the behaviors of other newspapers, spawned networks of like-minded journalists, and helped instill a set of norms and values in the generations of journalists that followed them. Should environment pressures subside and civic-minded newsroom leaders again regain control of these newsrooms, civic journalism may reassert itself more vigorously in these countries.

Chile's *La Epoca*

The environment for journalism under the dictatorship of General Augusto Pinochet was highly restrictive in the years immediately after the military violently ended the polarizing, but legitimately elected, government of Socialist Salvador Allende in 1973. Autonomous, assertive, and diverse journalism could not be practiced openly, but a number of opposition periodicals attempted to crack the military's media-protected image. In the early years, critical publications relied on subtle wit and allusion. Later, hard-hitting investigative reports appeared. Many journalists paid dearly for their efforts. Forty journalists or media workers died or disappeared at the hands of the military regime in place from 1973 to 1990 in Chile, while three hundred went into exile and about one thousand more were unable to find work (Uribe 1998, 31; Bresnahan 2003). In addition to physical repression, authoritarian laws and separate military statutes punished journalists criminally for disrespect of government officials and soldiers. When publications became too feisty, they were shut down or "encouraged" to sell to regime supporters. Censors frequented newsrooms, but self-censorship reigned in the publications that did not openly support the regime. With few exceptions, advertisers in the government and private sector shunned critical publications. Restaurants provided free meals to opposition journalists whose work they supported, but could not openly advertise (Agüero 2003, 316; Bresnahan 2003, 44–46; Graham 1987; Ungar 1988; Leon-Dermota 2003, 32).

The "trench" publications, from which critical reporters sniped at the dictatorship, had small circulations numbering a few thousand at best. Word of mouth certainly increased their impact, but they could not match the reach of the mass-circulation newspapers that became a duopoly with the dictatorship's support, the *El Mercurio* and *La Tercera* chains.[1] The largest publications in Chile had supported the takeover and were satisfied with military rule as long as they prospered financially. Regime-friendly publications amassed wealth in the neoliberal environment imposed by the dictatorship. Other strategies, more oligarchic in nature, included buying up anti-regime publications with international loans made cheap by the government-supported peso. These same pro-regime media were bailed out with government loans after the Chilean peso crashed in 1981–1982.[2]

As in Mexico, the relationship between the Chilean authoritarian regime and its supporters in the press was not based entirely on an instrumental calculation of possible benefits. Orthodox economic thought, as well as a conservative and antidemocratic philosophy called *gremialismo*, unified some newspaper executives with the military during the coup and its initial decade in power. Publishers' enthusiasm waned only after economic failure and international outrage at human rights abuses undercut regime legitimacy (León Dermota 2003).

The opening of the news production environment to more autonomous and assertive journalism came after the economy soured in the early 1980s. León Dermota (2003) writes that Pinochet "had bet heavily on justifying his regime with the economy." To regain his footing in the wake of the economic crisis, he temporarily fired orthodox economic advisors and jailed the most notoriously corrupt "Piranhas." The Piranhas were regime-affiliated bankers who gobbled up companies, including media companies out of favor with the government, by borrowing money at cheap international rates with the overvalued peso. The economic crash and corruption made Pinochet feel vulnerable. Public protests erupted in 1983 for the first time since the coup. Top labor organizations demanded and received policy consideration, and there was an incremental thaw in relations with the critical press.

A number of opposition publications were born in this period and others increased their criticism. All critical publications lived precariously and most were financed at least partly from abroad. Most "opposition" publications were small-circulation weekly magazines, but the innovators also included a wider circulation daily newspaper, *La Epoca*, which sold 150,000 copies of its first edition in March 11, 1987. When it settled in a month later at 55,000 daily circulation, the newspaper became the third-largest newspaper in the capital following the regime-supported establishment publications (León Dermota 2003, 27, 28, 40–42; Christian 1987; Germani 1987).[3]

La Epoca became the newspaper of reference during the political transition. It crystallized opposition action around the campaign to oust the military from power via a referendum on continued rule in 1988.[4] *La Epoca* stood out from larger pro-regime competitors because of its intent to be assertive and, at least in its early years, politically plural. While *El Mercurio* placed Pinochet's color photograph and speeches on the front page nearly every day, *La Epoca* covered all of the political parties. One of the newspaper's early scoops was simply to report honestly that Pope John Paul II had called the Pinochet government "dictatorial" while en route to visit Santiago. The front-page story, reported from international wire services, contrasted sharply with coverage in *El Mercurio*. *El Mercurio* had two reporters on the Pope's plane, but the newspaper ignored the statement. Other pro-regime newspapers buried the story, if they covered it as all (Alves 1997; Germani 1987; Ungar 1988). The establishment newspaper's censorship by omission was not only striking, but thanks to *La Epoca*, it also was obvious.

An editorial from the first issue of *La Epoca* explained that the Chilean public deserved "not just one side of the coin," referring to other newspapers' alliance with the dictatorship. *La Epoca* was the first newspaper in thirteen years to profess an anti-regime stance, but its founders resisted the label "opposition." "Chile lacks a newspaper with four basic characteristics: professional, independent, pluralist, and democratic," founder Emilio Filippi told a *Los Angeles Times* correspondent. "We offer access to ideas of all kinds: left, right and center, resisting identification with one of them. This kind of newspaper is essential for Chile if democracy is to return. Explain the options and let people decide for themselves. That's what good newspapers do all over the world." When asked on another occasion what headline he would most like to run in his newspaper, he answered: "Chile returned to full democracy" (Montalbano 1987; Christian 1987).

Many of *La Epoca*'s founding journalists had come of age after the 1973 coup against Allende. The first editor-in-chief took over in 1987 at age twenty-nine (Alves 1997). Although they had formal access only to authoritarian ideas about journalism in newspapers, press laws, and military controlled universities, the new generation of reporters clearly harbored ideas about journalism and society that conflicted with pro-regime competitors. The most obvious source for these ideas at *La Epoca* was the Christian Democratic philosophy of Filippi and some of the original twenty-four investors in the publication, but other ideas probably came from the Spanish model of *El País* and the tradition of Chilean opposition journalism that survived stubbornly, if mutedly, under the harsh repression of the 1970s. As the newspaper developed, some compared its role as aggregator of opposition opinions and actions to the work of *El País* following the death of Francisco Franco in Spain.

The driving force of *La Epoca*, Filippi was a well-known journalist who had suffered professionally under the military regime. According to Alves

(1997), Filippi initially was sympathetic to the coup as a way to end the chaos of the Allende government, but he quickly became disillusioned because of human rights abuses and Pinochet's ambition to stay in power. Filippi's critical stance earned retribution. He was forced out of his job as editor of the magazine *Ercilla*, which was the first independent voice allowed to publish after the coup because of its moderate Christian Democrat ownership. Only *El Mercurio*'s publications were allowed on the street immediately. Soon after *Ercilla* resumed circulation, Filippi's boss was told to fire the editor or face closure. At the same time, the regime's allies at the Banco Hipotecario de Chile offered the owner a better deal: sell to them. The magazine was sold and Filippi quit rather than work for the pro-regime bankers. Most of the editors went with him (León Dermota 2003, 22–23).

Filippi then launched *Hoy* magazine, which quickly garnered six thousand readers in Chile and another six thousand abroad. Its coverage also pushed the parameters set by the regime. When Filippi published interviews with two Socialist leaders in 1979, military censors shuttered the magazine. But wide segments of Chilean society that had come to depend on *Hoy* as an opinion leader and agenda setter pressured for its return. *Hoy* appeared on the newsstands two months later full of ads from domestic and multinational companies. In the wake of the thaw spawned by the economic crash, Filippi applied for a government license to open *La Epoca*. It took three years for him to receive it (León Dermota 2003, 22–23; Alves 1997).

As in the Mexican case, there is evidence that *La Epoca* created networks of like-minded Chilean journalists that spread outward to influence other publications. A few, including Fernando Paulsen, who became the editor of *La Tercera*, went to work for mainstream publications after the military left office (Alves 1997). *La Epoca*'s journalists also helped create at least two other independent or quasi-independent publications that carried on the tradition of critical, assertive, and diverse journalism. One of the first, a Sunday supplement of the quasi-governmental newspaper *La Nación*, called *La Nación Domingo,* had a separate staff and was one of few places where newspaper readers could encounter investigative journalism in Chile in the 2000s. The experiment failed in 2003 when all of the journalists walked off the job rather than allow management to carry through with censorship of a story about corruption in an agricultural development agency. Soon the journalists, led by former *La Epoca* reporter Alejandra Matus, created another publication. Appropriately, they named it *Plan B* (Bresnahan 2003, 49). The bimonthly publication lasted eighteen months; it never earned enough to pay its writers, who worked in other jobs as well. Matus, whose investigative book on the Chilean judicial system had sent her into exile for three years after the return to electoral democracy, said the unwillingness of advertisers to appear in a publication that made waves was part of the reason for its demise. Another was the tendency of Chilean journalists, advertisers, politicians, and readers to take sides politically rather than support a nonpartisan, critical publication. She was doubtful that independent journalism could survive given current environmental conditions in Chile.[5]

Most analysts of Chilean journalism credit *La Epoca* and other critical magazines with a role in forcing *El Mercurio* and *La Tercera* to change their coverage. The publications, in conjunction with changing cues from the liberalizing environment, spurred journalistic change within the newspaper field. A political thaw was underway in the late 1980s and the executives of pro-regime newspapers would have been blind not to see that civilians would soon replace generals in the presidential palace.

León Dermota calls the change that occurred in coverage at pro-regime newspapers "calculated pluralism," and attributes it to competition from *La Epoca* and other critical publications in a market that was becoming more free politically and economically. After Chileans voted to remove Pinochet from office, the dominant chain *El Mercurio* began to cover all of the political parties, invited left-of-center politicians to write opinion columns, and reported on social issues in special supplements. At the same time, analysts have noted that the chain's newspapers did not end all of its old behaviors. For example, it supported political candidates from pro-Pinochet parties and negatively framed news about demands from marginalized citizens, such as indigenous peoples' claims to land and political rights. An apparent consensus around laissez-faire economics made decisions on how to cover the economy easier. The winning center-left coalition that entered the presidency in 1990, the Concertación, continued Pinochet's orthodox economic policies that had been germinated domestically in an *El Mercurio*-affiliated think tank.

Besides increasing partisan pluralism, the pro-regime newspapers reacted to the critical, politically focused publications by "depoliticizing" their content after the return to democracy. *El Mercurio*, especially, now offers a wide range of coverage beyond politics, including a strong classified advertising section, sports coverage, and lifestyle reports. *La Tercera*, a tabloid, focuses on urban issues for Santiago's middle class. Chilean media executives call this change "re-tasking the product" (León Dermota 2003, 32–34, 39).[6]

Alves, as well as some opposition politicians at the time of the plebiscite on regime change, suggested that *La Epoca*'s coverage innovations were more important than wider democratization and market forces as explanations for change at pro-regime newspapers. The leader of the centrist Christian Democratic Party, Juan Gabriel Valdés, said in late 1987 that *La Epoca* had "forced (other newspapers) to improve their political coverage in order to be more competitive" and believed the pro-regime newspapers would "reduce by half the number of articles they print on the opposition" should *La Epoca* not exist (qtd. in Bridges 1987b).

Matus said she witnessed the impact of *La Epoca* in a small way when she covered the courts with five *El Mercurio* reporters. They told her that editors had complained when they missed stories, which she had covered, about the reopened investigation into the 1976 assassination of Orlando Letelier, Allende's U.S. ambassador. "*El Mercurio* was accustomed to covering court cases when, according to them, the case had reached a resolution," she said. "Not the witness that gave testimony, not the pressures that were brought to bear. So, when they saw that *La Epoca* published relevant information everyday, they began to do the same."[7] It is difficult to determine how much of the change in authoritarian newspapers was attributable to environmental conditions and how much was due to innovative, anti-regime competitors, but it is clear these variables are interlinked and that *La Epoca* set a new standard against which the authoritarian newspapers would be judged.

The story of *La Epoca* and Chilean journalism thus far fits the predictions of the institutional model derived from the Mexican experience in media transformation. An environmental opening gave change agents harboring alternative political values and different ideas about Chilean journalism an opportunity to express a new professional identity in the organizational form of the newsroom. Once the innovative organization produced news based upon the new identity, a new form of journalism that promoted civic participation against an authoritarian regime conflicted with the dominant, authoritarian form of journalism. This innovated model of journalism set a new standard that, in interaction with changes in the environment, forced authoritarian newspapers to adapt.

What do the institutional model's propositions tell us about whether autonomous, assertive, and diverse journalism at *La Epoca* or similar organizations could survive past Chile's founding democratic election? What about the limits to the institutional transformational of the media? The answers are not heartening for proponents of citizen-focused journalism. *La Epoca* no longer exists, nor do offspring created in the style of the newspaper by journalists formed there. In general, most analysts of Chilean journalism note that there is *less* assertiveness and diversity in the Chilean press today than at the end of the dictatorship. Otano and Sunkel (2003) write that the "paradox" of Chile's media transition is that: "a supposedly democratizing process has been depleting the ideological and cultural diversity of the media in comparison with what existed in the last years of the military regime, with the result that not a few journalists who were in the opposition in the 1980s denounce with disillusion that currently certain types of information, criticism or viewpoints cannot be expressed."

How could that happen? Again, environmental, institutional, organizational, and social-psychological dynamics interacted to produce, in this case, an unhappy result for the survival of civic journalism. Environmental factors include the dictatorship's legacy of concentrated media ownership and the new government's failure to support with advertising or legal reform what Bresnahan (2003, 40) calls "a major democratic resource" of diverse and critical media. However, the loss of a civic identity prizing autonomy and assertiveness also was important.

After the news production environment loosened in the last years of the dictatorship, leaders of *La Epoca* believed a democratically elected government would favor their style of journalism with at least an equal share of government advertising. Certainly, many hoped the most draconian press laws would be repealed as well. This was not to be the case. Although critics say the newspaper was financially mismanaged, *La Epoca* had the cards stacked against it. The new Concertación coalition, although it produced two successive Christian Democratic presidents from 1990 to 2000, did little to change the distribution of government advertising that supported the "establishment" newspapers, in which coalition politicians now sought to appear as columnists and news sources. The best media policy was to leave the ownership structure and advertising distribution unchanged, they decided. Meanwhile, private sector advertisers remained loyal to the wider-circulating regime newspapers, which came out of the dictatorship as market giants and in a much stronger financial position than their oppositional rivals. Both chains had received millions of dollars of government loans to survive the economic crisis of the 1980s. *El Mercurio*'s empire went from eight newspapers prior to the coup to fourteen in 1999 (León Dermota 2003, 35, 36, 54–56).

Moreover, holdover authoritarian press laws did not help journalistic assertiveness. National security statutes and special military laws punished journalistic "contempt" (*desacato*) criminally long into the democratic period. More than thirty journalists were prosecuted under this law after the return of elections, including Matus. Only in the third democratically elected government was Section 6b of the State Internal Security Law, the source of many of the authoritarian restrictions, eliminated. This came eleven years after the return to democracy and while the government was under intense pressure from international human rights and journalist organizations because of the Matus case. Even after the repeal of the law in 2001, however, the Supreme Court cobbled together other statutes to charge a television commentator who had described the Chilean justice system as "immoral, cowardly, and corrupt" for wrongly convicting a woman and failing to apologize to her (Bresnahan 2003, 45; Agüero 2003, 316).

With advertisers and the law set against civic-oriented journalism, the cultural climate of the postauthoritarian period offered few incentives to assertive publications. The years immediately after the military removed itself from government were a nervous time in Chile. The democratically elected government of Patricio Aylwin (1990–1995) decided not to confront the still-powerful generals on issues that academics and activists believed would have successfully completed Chile's political transition, including: clarification of nearly one thousand pending cases of disappeared people; reconciliation of the regime and its victims through apology, pardon, and a shared interpretation of the military's violent rule; and reform of the authoritarian constitution that left many undemocratic laws in place and gave Pinochet the position of senator for life. Instead, "the government of the transition" decided to declare the transition over and focus its work and discourse on the consensus around economic policies (Agüero 2003).

Agüero writes: "A seemingly all-embracing consensus in (economic policy) helped to push the constitutional divide to the wayside. The consensus facilitated the view that the transition was over, and thus led the government to give in to the Right's discourse on the matter . . . if the government charged with ending the transition declared the mission accomplished, there was little to prevent this view from becoming dominant. An important consequence was the emergence of a climate that discouraged divisive views and issues, which were perceived like skunks at a garden party" (2003, 297).

When *La Epoca* published stories about human rights abuses or judicial investigations on the front page, circulation actually dropped. Matus remarked:

> For me it was frustrating as a journalist that the editors would put on the front page things that we all thought were super important and there was a sort of rejection from the public. So there was a historic period where it was difficult to report on these issues. Maybe because the people had suffered for seventeen years and didn't want to hear about any more suffering. I don't know the social reasons for what happened but that was how it happened. *La Epoca* was a newspaper that focused on those issues, judicial cases, political issues, human rights, which were the least appreciated by the society.

However, the erosion of civic identities among those who controlled the direction of *La Epoca*'s news content cannot be discounted as a powerful explanation for the demise of autonomous, assertive, and diverse journalism at the publication. Observers believe that the reemergence of a Christian Democrat partisan identity at *La Epoca* after the urgency of regime change diminished the publication's critical edge. Filippi even accepted a position as ambassador to Portugal under Aylwin as the newspaper foundered financially; 50 percent was eventually sold to a former regime official and banker who earlier had bought part of the *La Tercera* chain. Other journalists, who had lived on minimum wages, also experienced economic fatigue as they reached their forties. Mónica González, a journalist jailed for her investigative reporting during the dictatorship, said she quintupled her salary when she moved from the opposition magazine *Análisis* to *La Nación* (León Dermota 2003, 32, 66, 96, 110–11; Alves 1997). She has recently become an editor of an independent magazine that sold a portion of its shares to the *La Tercera* chain as a way to survive financially.[8]

Otano and Sunkel, an experienced Chilean journalist and sociologist, respectively, describe the creation of a culture of "journalistically correct" behavior in the environment of imposed consensus that emerged after the 1989 election (2003). The passive, don't-rock-the-boat journalistic culture prevents journalists from broadening news agendas and sources away from officially presented ones. The researchers describe Chilean newspapers as highly penetrated by external economic, political, and religious powers, who act in collusion with owners who look instrumentally to the market and the political establishment to determine news coverage. Owners, on the other hand, blame journalistic passivity on reporters themselves (León Dermota 2003, 112). However, it is unlikely that reporters' norms are the origin of a docile press, given that Chilean newsrooms are perhaps even more hierarchical than Mexican newsrooms, and professional autonomy is described as extremely limited. More likely is that the majority of young journalists are not encouraged to make waves, have few employment options, and, according to Otano and Sunkel, have no collective memory of the Chilean tradition of journalism as a counterweight to even the most repressive form of power.

In the end, the upsurge of civic journalism that happened with the political thaw following the 1981–1982 economic crisis helped propel Chilean society toward democracy by crystallizing and reaffirming the opposition to Pinochet, but could not create the conditions under which autonomous, assertive, and diverse journalism would flourish. What survives of civic journalism is due to the legacy of opposition journalism of *La Epoca* and other publications, but in the current environment there is no sustainable civic organization that can endure as more than a marginalized island in a sea of commercial and oligarchic complacency.

"I think that things happen in their moment," Matus said. "Perhaps one cannot escape the hand of history. Perhaps that's the lesson in Chile that we have learned the hard way. When society is ready for a certain type of journalism, to listen to these voices, an enormous variety of media that reflect this emerge and flourish. But perhaps Chilean society is not ready to cross that barrier."[9]

Matus's career, like those of many journalists in transitional Mexico, reflects the willingness to risk her livelihood rather than work in a publication that contradicts her vision of journalistic purpose. However, her case would be extraordinary in the Mexican context because of the number of times she left a publication in order to protect her professional autonomy. From *La Epoca* she went to *La Nación*, from *La Nación* to exile, from exile to *La Tercera*, from *La Tercera* to *La Nación Domingo*, and from *La Nación Domingo* to *Plan B*. As of mid-2005, she was working as a freelancer for a women's magazine and plotting ways to finance another assertive publication.

Argentina's *Página/12*

Another Latin American newspaper frequently mentioned as part of "democracy's vanguard" is the tabloid *Página/12* in the Argentine capital, Buenos Aires. *Página/12* reinaugurated investigative journalism after the fall of the disgraced military junta that brutally ruled the country from 1976 to 1983. The daily newspaper published or prompted others to expose the slew of press scandals that hit the administration of Carlos Menem in the 1990s. In part because of press exposés, more than seventy government officials were accused in court of corruption by the end of Menem's first term. Few would be jailed, but most lost their positions and were publicly shamed. Even Menem, by then ex-president, was placed under house arrest for a time (Waisbord 1994, 1998, 56; 2000). *Página/12*, known for irreverence as much as investigative journalism, shook up Argentina's staid mainstream newspapers. Waisbord believes that *Página/12* played a pivotal role in the reawakening of the Argentine press: "An appreciation of the emergence of the daily *Página/12* in 1987 is central to understanding the emergence of scandal politics. It has had a remarkable impact on the Argentine political communication landscape: Other newspapers have adopted what is called a *Página/12*-like style, and the daily has become almost obligatory reading among policymakers" (1994, 28).[10]

Argentine journalism in the early 1970s included investigative elements and was considered one of the most combative press systems in Latin America. "The military in 1976 inherited a press to be reckoned with," wrote press historian Jerry Knudson (1997, 107). Most assertive publications and individual journalists were killed, silenced by fear, or co-opted when the Argentine military took power following the death of strongman Juan Domingo Perón. The rest went underground, distributing newsletters and cables through the mail and by other means to foreign reporters and domestic newsrooms under censorship. Perón had returned from an eighteen-year exile in 1973 to become president, but died just months later. As vice president, his wife, María Estela Martínez, took over the presidency, but could not control the factious politics that provoked political violence from groups on both the Left and Right. The military overthrew her with support from most of the press in March 1976.

This was the latest of a long line of military coups in Argentina. As in Chile in 1973, the Argentine generals decided they would not return the government to civilian politicians, but Argentine authoritarianism never moved toward personalistic military rule to the degree that the Chilean armed forces did. Instead, each military branch was represented within a ruling *junta* that carved up the bureaucratic pie, including control of a state television channel. Disorganization, infighting, and jealousy between the branches increased the chaos of military rule, but its brutality was described as a systematic purge of anyone suspected of dissidence.

Prompted by intellectual extremism, isolation from civil society, and anti-Semitism, Argentine generals became convinced that an international communist conspiracy was playing out on their soil. They unleashed a methodical and brutal campaign of repression. "First we will kill all of the subversives; then . . . we will kill their sympathizers; then . . . those who remain undecided, and finally we will kill the indifferent ones," said General Ibérico Saint-Jean, military governor of Buenos Aires, on May 26, 1977. In the decades since, his statement has become emblematic of the repression during Argentina's dirty war.[11] Among the nine thousand to thirty thousand Argentines who died under the dictatorship were almost one hundred journalists.[12] An estimated five hundred went into exile and seventy were jailed (Alves 1997; Ward 1983).

The military repressed journalists along with other cultural producers in order to "pull up by the roots" any possibility of public criticism, according to the government's National Commission on the Disappearance of Persons, which investigated the dirty war after electoral democracy was reestablished.[13] Journalist Jacobo Timerman, publisher of a liberal newspaper that criticized human rights abuses after the coup, wrote a powerful account of his detention and torture by a military faction in his book, *Prisoner without a Name, Cell without a Number* (1981). His disappearance came one month after publishing a special supplement questioning politicians' silence on disappearances. After forty months in clandestine jails, international pressure forced his release. Timerman was one of the luckier detainees.

The only other mainstream newspaper to openly question the authoritarian regime was the English-language *Buenos Aires Herald*. Its editor, Robert Cox, fled the country with his family after receiving death threats for the coverage. Cox had begun to look into cases of the missing, but determined that investigative reporting was impossible given the repression (Knudson 1997, 99, 101, 102; Ward 1983). Openly leftist newspapers, a few of which had circulations above 100,000 when the coup occurred, were targeted for repression and closed. Editor Rodolfo Walsh, a founder of investigative journalism in Argentina in the 1960s, went underground and produced clandestine reports delivered surreptitiously to foreign reporters and domestic newsrooms. Among his colleagues was friend Horacio Verbitsky, a founding member of *Página/12* a decade later.

Walsh was kidnapped and assassinated by a squadron of the Navy School of Mechanics on March 25, 1977, according to Verbitsky's investigations. Walsh's underground news service, ANCLA (La Agencia Clandestina de Noticias, or The Clandestine News Agency), ceased publication for a month during heightened repression after his disappearance and some contributors fled the country. The news service was the communication branch of the armed Montoneros movement, which had links to a faction of the old Peronist party. In mainstream newsrooms, however, many journalists considered the cables the "other side of the story" rather than straight Montoneros propaganda. *Le Monde* in Paris and *Cambio 16* in Spain were among the newspapers that published the reports (Millman 1992; Rodríguez Yebra 2005; Verbitsky 1997; Vinelli 2002).

Despite the torrent of physical repression unleashed against journalists and publishers, Argentine journalists say that physical threat was only part of what made autonomy and assertiveness difficult, if not impossible, during military rule. A culture of fear permeated newsrooms and psychological terror prompted self-censorship. Vague death threats and warnings to journalists circulated in newsrooms. The military heightened uncertainties by spreading rumors about the disappeared and sending unsigned directives on plain paper to intimidate editors. It ordered them to censor information about violence or disappearances. The *Buenos Aires Herald* published a directive on its front page of April 22, 1976, in protest. It read: "As of today it is forbidden to inform, comment or make reference to the death of subversive elements/or the armed and security forces in these incidents, unless they are reported by a responsible official source." Not all the newspapers were as resistant as the *Herald*. The newspaper *Clarín* responded with a full-page article stating there were no press restrictions in Argentina. Near the end of the dictatorship, *Clarín* criticized other publications that printed "disruptive . . . pernicious and destabilizing" information.[14]

Newspaper companies also had financial incentives to support the new regime, although it does not seem that they were as financially intertwined with the authoritarian regime as the mainstream press in Chile. Top dailies *Clarín* and *La Nación* co-owned a newsprint production plant together with the government, thus receiving a substantial subsidy on a costly element production. Similar to the situation in Mexico, the Argentine government at that time controlled 40 percent of industrial output, making it the country's largest advertiser and giving the military financial leverage as well. While television broadcasting was state-owned during the authoritarian regime, a holdover from earlier periods, newspapers were privately held by families that at least acquiesced to the military. Timerman was the only openly combative mainstream newspaper publisher, but his publication was shut down after his detention. Some analysts also argue that the mainstream press was ideologically in tune with what the military was doing, especially in the first months of the authoritarian government before the number of killings mounted and economic turmoil continued. *La Nación* fired at least one columnist on the military's blacklist (Knudson 1997, 94, 107, 108).

Of the mainstream newspapers, only *La Opinión* and the *Buenos Aires Herald* printed notices placed by relatives of the disappeared before they were shut down. When relatives came to other newspapers seeking help, they were sent instead to a labyrinth of government offices. Recalling those days before journalists gathered to cover human rights trials in 1985, the president of the Mothers of the Plaza de Mayo, which protested for the return of missing loved ones throughout the seven-year dictatorship, stated: "We Mothers . . . [have] suffered in our own flesh the vileness of that despicable press that today pretends to be democratic but only wants to make business with our pain and with the horror of the tragedy of the 'disappeared'" (Knudson 1997, 105).

Scholars of military rule and retreat in Latin America write that the Chilean military relinquished government control while in a strong position, thus retaining control of "reserve domains" of influence such as human rights prosecutions that have only recently been breached. Argentina's military, on the other hand, was demoralized when it left the government. It never overcame interforce disorganization, never produced sustained economic growth, and was humiliated by its loss of the Falklands/Malvinas War to the British (Valenzuela 1992, 64–66; Agüero 2003). Buffeted by economic collapse and reviled internationally and at home because of brutality, Argentina's generals hoped that occupying the islands long claimed from England would increase legitimacy. Indeed, nationalistic pride surfaced during the war. When the truth seeped in from returning prisoners of war, however, both the military and the press that had trumpeted war propaganda were humiliated. In this context, leaders of what remained of the country's tattered political parties negotiated a transition that led to elections in October 1983. The newly elected president, Raúl Alfonsín, was not a Peronist, but a fatherly figure from the Radical Party. Alfonsín took office in December 1983 and the transition to democracy was underway.

It is easy to understand why the news production environment during a vicious military dictatorship precluded autonomous and assertive reporting, but the memory of investigative journalism did not perish as the military had hoped. Some of the older combative journalists survived in exile or underground at home. Some ambitious younger journalists looked up to them and sought their aid when experiencing press freedom for the first time in the late 1980s. New boldness began to surface in magazines even before the military's departure, much of it wrapped in texts about human rights and highbrow culture. Tentatively, the mainstream dailies attempted to excise their past. *Clarín*, for example, published a series of investigative reports on what had really happened during the war (Alves 1997; Ward 1983; Proa 2003).

The development of journalism in postauthoritarian Argentina, like in Mexico and Chile, supports the proposition that greater press freedom on its own does not account for media transitions. While an environmental opening was necessary to a greater or lesser degree in each of these countries, individual and organizational action did not follow mechanistically from greater slack in the environment. Human agency in journalism is expressed within organizational and cultural boundaries, which are, in turn, embedded in the wider crosscurrents of the environment of news production. The necessary but insufficient role of environmental opening suggested by the institutional model surfaces clearly in the reemergence and then decline of assertive journalism in Argentina.

After presidential elections in October 1983, Argentine press and society experienced liberties and constitutional guarantees for the first time in seven years. Alfonsín's government (1983–1989) moved forward boldly to investigate and prosecute human rights abusers. The press took on a more assertive role in the initial postauthoritarian period, but assertiveness was bounded by old attitudes and behaviors. Some journalists think that it took time for the old fears and ingrained passivity to subside. Whatever the reason, the mainstream press avoided sensitive areas of coverage, including investigation of disappearances. Criticism of the current government surfaced, but was timid compared to what would come just a few years later. Waisbord writes that the Argentine press during the first years of electoral democracy "moderately versus actively pursued the biggest scandal in Argentine contemporary history . . . it merely observed rather than stimulated revelations on abuses of human rights" (1994, 26–27).

Verbitsky, who became the Walsh of the 1990s for many young Argentines, said the new free press environment was "terra incognita" for the journalists who emerged from the dirty war. They cautiously explored their new roles and boundaries. Much of civil society experienced similar uncertainty in the shell-shocked years immediately following the democratic transition, with perhaps the only exceptions being steadfast human rights activists and the vocal organizations of relatives of the disappeared (Verbitsky 1995, 10).

Press assertiveness, timid at first, surged after Carlos Menem (1989–1999) took office and responded to a confluence of factors. Some have called it "ironic" that press assertiveness occurred as the political environment worsened considerably during the Menem administration. At one point, 140 instances of physical attacks on the press had been reported, none of which had been cleared up. Menem himself got so angry with the press that he called reporters "vandals" and dubbed *Página/12* reporters "delinquents." He said journalists investigating local corruption would have to put up with physical threats as "an occupational hazard." The government proposed a press gag law and boycotted advertising at *Página/12* for two weeks, rescinding the proposal and boycott only in the face of unified protest and a well-timed editorial in the *New York Times* (Waisbord 1994, 27; Sims 1995, 10).

On the other hand, changes in the economic environment offer part of the explanation for the increase in assertiveness that became emblematic of the Argentine press of the 1990s. Under pressure from the private sector, Menem began to sell off state media even before his economic program embarked full-speed on the privatization of state-owned companies. The sale of state television and radio stations to private companies, as well as the modernization and deregulation of cable and satellite technologies, created media conglomerates that became financially strong enough to take on the government without fear of economic reprisals, especially when the government lost control of the largest advertisers through privatization.

The new media conglomerates owned major dailies along with newly acquired electronic media and non-media enterprises. Grupo Clarín benefited most and by the 2000s held provincial newspapers, radio stations, broadcast TV stations, a cable provider, and a satellite franchise. Its broadsheet currently has the largest circulation in the country. *La Nación* acquired cable and domestic satellite properties, but its main business remained the newspaper, which is number one among elite readers (Rodríguez Yebra 2005; Waisbord 1998). As media competition for readers and advertisers heightened, one way to attract them was by exposing corruption and other scandalous behavior. Competition for aggressive reporters increased. Reporters were told to "rev up" their copy. In literary Argentina, sitting at a café and reading about the latest salacious scandal became one of the country's favorite pastimes (Guillermoprieto 1991).

Market forces decoupled the media from state economic control in the 1990s and unleashed a series of incentives that increased press assertiveness despite worsening political conditions for press freedom. But there was more to it than that. To argue that financial security and increased competition explains assertiveness fully would be wrong. It was not the financially strongest newspaper that reinitiated investigative journalism in postauthoritarian Argentina, setting a new standard others emulated. It was, initially, one of the weakest. Nor did mainstream Argentine newspapers fully express the dormant tradition of investigative journalism until they were pushed by the innovative publication. Even then, as in Mexico, some newspapers never adopted an assertive stance. Waisbord explains: "Only one daily (*Página/12*) was initially interested in breaking stories and covering delicate issues; another (*Clarín*) later decided to take a more confrontational line, partially (according to my interviews) in response to *Página/12*'s rising sales among actual and potential *Clarín* readers. Other newspapers, even when having the same information, did not seem eager to break news about sensitive matters; instead, they adopted a cautious position, speculating that revelations implicating government officials could hurt relations with both the Menem administration and advertisers" (1994, 28).

The investigative tradition in Argentine journalism that went underground during the authoritarian government needed an organizational structure from which to express itself after the return to democracy. *Página/12* pushed mainstream newspapers beyond timid experimentation and split the newspaper field. A small tabloid, *Página/12* could afford to print only twelve pages for its first edition—hence its name. It rose to the third circulation spot in Buenos Aires as readers responded to its style, following only the giants *Clarín* and *La Nación,* which began to mimic its content.

Rather than financial strength or competitive strategy, *Página/12*'s autonomy and assertiveness initially sprung from the professional identity of its founders. These identities came from values that were inherited from the Argentine tradition of investigative journalism, Europe's leftist press, and Mexico's own civic pioneers. Two young journalists and a progressive businessman with interests in human rights thought that Argentines needed a more critical voice in the press in the mid-1980s. They founded *Página/12* in May 1987. Like the staff of Chile's *La Epoca*, *Página/12*'s journalists worked for salaries far under those of mainstream dailies, but earned respect when they mentioned their employer. In interviews in 2005, newspaper founder Jorge Lanata recalled what pushed him, assistant editor Ernesto Tiffenberg, and businessman Fernando Sokolowicz to open *Página*.[15]

Lanata had been the managing editor of *El Porteño*, a monthly magazine that began to produce investigative pieces on issues sensitive to the military in the waning years of the dictatorship, but disguised them with humor and cultural affairs reporting. *El Porteño* covered taboo topics such as AIDS, the gay community, and the appropriation of the children of the disappeared. The last topic made it the target of a bomber in 1983. The attackers were never found. Tiffenberg, meanwhile, had been studying at the National Autonomous University of Mexico until 1984, where he also wrote for *El Porteño* and edited cultural and entertainment supplements for *Unomásuno* (Periodistas 1998).

Lanata explained that the assertiveness of *Página/12* incubated in an investigative section in *El Porteño*, which ran under an inscription declaring: "everything that the other media know, but aren't willing to publish." Many of the *El Porteño* journalists who worked there soon transferred their efforts to the daily *Página/12*. "This spirit of investigation and press independence was basic in the founding of the daily," Lanata said. "I thought that we had come out of years of dictatorship and several generations of journalists had formed professionally under military influence, and we were a generation that had not had teachers because they had been disappeared or were forced into exile. I was twenty-six years old at the time and had nothing to do with either the leftist [reporting] generation of the 1970s or the passivity of those who had formed during the military."

Lanata had covered cultural affairs on and off since he was fourteen. He received editorial advice from the novelist and journalist Osvaldo Soriano, who had spent the dictatorship in exile in Belgium and France writing fiction and coediting the magazine *Sin Censura* (Without Censorship). Lanata's vision of journalism became "to tell all that we can know and can prove, and do it in a creative and entertaining way." He called his thinking about journalism "orthodox and liberal," rejecting partisanship on behalf of a responsibility to society as embodied by the reader. "A journalist cannot be linked to any party or government administration, and should always be on the side of the readers. The objective in the worst of cases is cathartic: it's always better to know that something is happening than not know it, because knowing makes us responsible."

Lanata and Soriano discussed foreign models for the young paper, including center-left *El País* in Spain and the once-militant *Libération* in France. In the end, they produced a mix of punchy and sophisticated prose, sarcastic humor, offbeat design, and muckraking exposés of human rights abuses and government corruption.

Página/12 reinaugurated Argentina's tradition of investigative newspaper journalism by hiring some of the famous journalists still alive from the 1970s and commingling them with enthusiastic novices. The main government reporter covering Menem for *Página/12* in 1991 was "an ebullient twenty-five-year-old who could pass for seventeen," wrote Alma Guillermoprieto of the *New Yorker* (1991, 68). However, the staff also included figures of impressive stature: the dean of reporters and star *Página/12* muckraker quickly became Horacio Verbitsky, who emerged from underground once the military returned to its barracks. He says he formed professionally in "the militant, rancorous, aggressive, unforgiving tradition of the 1970s" (70).

While Verbitsky has readily identified himself with the political left and foreign reporters in the early 1990s repeatedly called *Página/12* "unabashedly leftist," Lanata rejected that. He said in 1992: "we are not a left- or a right-wing newspaper. I say we are a liberal newspaper. The left attacks us for belonging to the new right and the right attacks us for being on the left" (Barham 1992). The newspaper in the Menem era was definitely adversarial toward the government, however. Noted the *Financial Times* of London, "*Página/12* rarely finds anything praiseworthy in Mr. Menem's government."

Verbitsky's reporting became the newspaper's calling card. He focused on government corruption and the disappeared. His reporting exposed attempts by Menem officials to extort bribes from international corporations, corruption in the sell-off of the army's steel works, and the sale of contaminated cheese to underprivileged children. Government whistleblowers, angry about Menem's centralized governing style as much as his government's excesses, learned that *Página/12* reporters would not reveal their sources and made the newspaper a repository of high-level leaks. Verbitsky's human rights scoops were equally as shocking. They included the confession of a Navy captain who confessed to Verbitsky that he personally assisted in drugging and dumping thirty live prisoners from aircraft into the ocean during the dictatorship. Overcome with guilt, the officer chose to confess to Verbitsky after the Navy rejected his plea to publish a full list of the disappeared. This was the first time a participant in dirty war atrocities had come forward out of guilt (Millman 1992; Verbitsky 1995; Waisbord 1994).

Besides assertiveness and financial insecurity, *Página/12* differed from *Clarín* and *La Nación* in a number of important ways. *Página/12*'s editors clearly had ideological differences with Menem, including his neoliberal economic policies and the increasing concentration of presidential power. Menem often used presidential decrees to bypass Congress and, at one point, stacked the Supreme Court in his favor by increasing the number of justices. His unsuccessful attempt to change the constitution to run for a consecutive third term in office worried observers that he would try to illegally prolong his power, but he was blocked by a steadfast congressional-court alliance. Menem's centralized decision-making style, the rampant allegations of corruption in his administration, and the oncoming economic downturn cut into his popularity. Menem left office in 1999.

Another difference between the upstart tabloid and the two older, mainstream newspapers was that it had few financial connections to the government or the country's dominant commercial groups. *Página/12* was an independent entity with a sole owner who did not interfere in editorial operations. It suffered only one short advertising boycott during Menem's two terms in office, but never received a lion's share of government advertising, either. The newspaper's irreverent and assertive reporting secured its survival; it became required reading for upper-middle-class policymakers, military officers, and business owners in addition to its staple audience of starving intellectuals and college students. This allowed the publication to survive mostly on private sector ads and newsstand sales. The publication also broke into the shady entertainment advertising market after refusing to accept ads in return for positive movie reviews. Cinemas decided to advertise anyway when they saw how the newspaper could fill up movie houses when it hosted its own previews. The *Financial Times* called the publication "entrepreneurial" (Barham 1992).

Argentina's press transformation in the 1990s responded to the institutional model's proposition that journalistic change results from interaction between four domains. Environmental conditions opened, but an innovative organization was necessary to push change beyond timid reaction to changing incentives and transform the institutional field. Unlike Mexico's early civic innovators, the Argentine change agents initiated transition after the founding democratic election and as neoliberal economic reform transformed the media structure. Within the institutional and organizational domains, the story is very much like Mexico's. Change agents with power in the newsroom—informed by values in opposition to authoritarianism and harboring ideas about journalism from abroad and from Argentina's own investigative tradition—sparked change in the newspaper field.

But how permanent was this change? Had Argentine journalism institutionalized assertiveness as a robust and enduring feature existing across time and space? The model of media transformation suggests the sources of stability and change of media institutions. In the Argentine case, the desire to practice assertive journalism could not survive a new round of shocks in the news environment; thus, the new democracy was deprived of an important incentive for governmental accountability. Since the Argentine crisis of the early 2000s was so severe, perhaps the lesson is not that the Argentine press stopped practicing investigative journalism, but that the desire to do so has survived.

The journalistic identities and practices that were expressed in assertive news content in Argentina of the 1990s were suppressed again when the news environment closed toward the end of the decade. Instead of renewed authoritarianism, this time an economic collapse closed space for media autonomy and assertiveness. Investigative journalism sputtered to a halt. The economic shock and ensuing political and social crises were tremendous. After averaging 6.2 percent annual growth between 1991 and 1998, the economy fell into a protracted recession in 1999 from which it did not begin to emerge until 2003. The economic recession was the worst in Argentine history. The currency devalued 70 percent and unemployment rose 11 percentage points. GNI per capita shrunk 47 percent between 2001 and 2003. Poverty persisted even after the return of macroeconomic growth. The percentage of Argentines in poverty more than doubled between 1996 and 2004, afflicting 46 percent of the population. During this period, total media advertising contracted 40 percent between 2001 and 2002, according to the Argentine Journalism Business Association. Daily newspapers printed per 1,000 people fell from a high of 124 in 1995 to 37 in 2001 (Levitsky 2003; Rodríguez Yebra 2005; World Bank 2005a, 2005b).

Social reaction was enormous. Screaming crowds banging pots and pans surrounded every branch of government, shouting *"que se vayan todos"* (throw them all out). Protesting crowds of unemployed workers—known as *piqueteros*—blocked an estimated two hundred roads in sixteen provinces in just one month. Two presidents resigned before Eduardo Duhalde restored governability. President Nestor Kirchner, a Peronist outsider handpicked by Duhalde, took office in April 2003 with just 22 percent of the vote.

Dubbed an improbable hero, Kirchner surprised everyone. He took bold action and within two years became wildly popular. A child of the 1970s, he quickly fired a swath of military officials associated with the 1976–1983 dictatorship and voiced support for stripping dirty war abusers of a blanket amnesty granted by Menem. He peppered his leftist rhetoric with outrage at the IMF and foreign creditors who played a role in deepening the country's economic collapse. At the same time, he pressured those creditors into the biggest debt-reduction deal ever achieved by a developing country. Perhaps most importantly, he produced two straight years of 8 percent economic growth. The debt swap saved the country $67 billion, and Argentina in 2004 posted its biggest fiscal surplus in a half-century. The *Financial Times* noted that the Kirchner government had amassed lots of money, and "if you have money in Argentina, you are the boss" (Thomson 2005).

In the years since the beginning of the crash, Argentina's famous watch-dog press ceased to bark. *Página/12* did not publish one serious press scandal touching a high administration official between Kirchner's election and mid-2005. One of the newspaper's most respected columnists, Julio Nudler, quit over what he claimed was censorship of an article linking Kirchner's power-ful cabinet chief minister to government corruption. *La Nación* and *Clarín*, which had opened investigative units in the mid-1990s, cut back severely on investigative reporting as well (Rodríguez Yebra 2005).

What happened to press assertiveness? Obviously, the government's eco-nomic power and the collapse of the private sector played important roles. Pressure on the media worked in two ways. The Kirchner government be-came a very powerful advertiser and used advertising to reward supportive publications, specifically, *Página/12*. This situation repeated itself in most of the country's twenty-three provinces through local governors (Committee to Protect Journalists 2005; Gallo 2004a, 2004b; Inter-American Press Associa-tion 2005; Poder Ciudadano 2004). Less obvious was how the federal gov-ernment supported newspaper companies' other holdings, especially those of Grupo Clarín. Media companies that had contracted dollar-denominated debt abroad were on the verge of bankruptcy when Kirchner took office. One of his first acts was to promote a law in Congress that prohibited foreign firms from buying Argentine media in case of bankruptcy. The peso devalu-ation had lowered Argentine companies' values to the point that media own-ers feared hostile takeovers from abroad. The government supported their position with the new law, effectively protecting them from foreign takeover. Later, by presidential decree, the government extended broadcast conces-sions by ten years so that owners could refinance their loans at better inter-est rates, effectively bailing them out. Rodríguez Yebra notes that, like all presidential decrees, the extension of the concessions was granted with only the president's signature. They could be revoked in the same way (Rodríguez Yebra 2005).

What happened to *Página/12* is even more stunning given the heights from which the paper's investigative tradition has fallen. The newspaper went from government disdain under Menem to government support under Kirchner. According to an audit of the federal government budget by the civic group Poder Ciudadano, *Página/12* received the same level of government advertising as *La Nación* between January and November 2004, even though its circulation is far inferior. *La Nación*'s circulation is audited externally at 144,000 weekdays, 253,000 Sundays. *Página/12* reports unaudited circulation figures of 95,000 weekdays and 136,000 Sundays, but civic groups put the circulation at only 10,000 on weekdays (Poder Ciudadano 2004). The relationship is not only cordial on the business side. Journalists repeat the rumor that Verbitsky has become an unofficial advisor to the president, which he denies, because so many of his proposals have been quickly put into place. Lanata long ago left the newspaper, saying it had been sold secretly to Grupo Clarín, something neither *Clarín* or *Página/12*'s managers have confirmed or denied.[16]

The identities of the newspaper's leading journalists also play a role in the new, friendly relationship with the government. Rather than a commitment to autonomy and assertiveness, political ideology guides coverage of the presidency. Verbitsky defends the newspaper's editorial affinity with the Kirchner government this way: "*Página/12* has a coherent editorial policy. It questioned a large number of things about the policies of Menem and Duhalde. When there is a government that does things different from how they used to do things, naturally it suits [the newspaper]. There is a coherence in the editorial policy of the daily" (Wiñazki 2005, 29).

Lanata said recently that he discussed the future of the publication with Soriano in the months after its founding. Would it follow the path of *El País* in Spain, which retained its autonomy while following a center-left orientation and building an influential media and publishing enterprise, or that of *Libération* of France, which now counts leading capitalists among its stockholders and is criticized for moderating its positions on social change? Lanata now believes *Libération* was the model: "I think we have ended up being more similar to the second because there was no democratic bourgeoisie [in Argentina] that was convinced of pluralism and who would support a project like *Página* economically."[17]

Guatemala's *Siglo Veintiuno* and *el Periódico*

The development of Guatemala's innovative daily *Siglo Veintiuno* and its impact on the wider Guatemalan press in the early 1990s resembles the other cases of vanguard civic-oriented newspapers in several respects. *Siglo Veintiuno* pioneered a civic form of journalism during an opening in an authoritarian regime, and in the process pushed behavioral change at traditional newspapers and drove a cultural transformation among younger journalists. The difference in the Guatemalan case is that when *Siglo Veintiuno* began to lose its civic identity, for reasons similar to *La Epoca* and *Página/12*, most of its journalists were able to create a new newspaper founded on civic principles. Business owners, nongovernmental organizations, and an international organization dedicated to supporting independent media backed this venture financially, creating an societal alliance for civic journalism that other countries lacked. The Mexican press exhibited a similar pattern when journalists left Mexico's *Unomásuno* to form *La Jornada* in 1984 and departed *Siglo 21* in Guadalajara to form *Público* in 1997, in each case because the owner made deals with the government that undermined the newspaper's autonomy.

Guatemala was in the waning years of a thirty-six-year civil war when a group of business owners formed *Siglo Veintiuno* in 1990. A series of personalistic dictatorships had ruled the country during most of the conflict. Democracy, even the oligarchic kind that involved only the elite sectors, was the exception more than the rule. "The state of the press was dismal" when *Siglo Veintiuno* was founded, said publisher Lionel Torriello Najera in 1997. "We were different in that we were committed to changes that the society desperately needs. We present a position that is unabashedly pro-democratic and pro-free market" (Alves 1997).

In its early years, the newspaper published muckraking articles on corruption and human rights violations. Led by José Rubén Zamora, a young editor from a journalistic family with a tradition of social progressivism, *Siglo Veintiuno* covered social issues such as the abuse of street children and opened its opinion pages to guerilla leaders and trade unionists as well as bankers and business owners (Reid 1993). The assertiveness of *Siglo Veintiuno*'s founding staff stood "in marked contrast" to the historically passive and narrow Guatemalan press, write Rockwell and Janus in their book *Media Power in Latin America* (2003, 100). The country's political and economic elite responded to the new style, and readership in the economically coveted sector of the population rose. The largest newspaper in the country, *Prensa Libre*, changed its editorial line to respond to the competition and the rise of a new generation of family owners. *Prensa Libre*, founded by five elite families in 1951, was known as a newspaper that published moderate to conservative content in support of the government (102). In the early 1990s, decades of coziness with the government became a liability. Alves writes: "*Siglo Veintiuno* became a leader of more critical and investigative journalism and was followed by other papers, despite constant threats, assassinations, kidnappings, harassment and even bombings. The leading Guatemalan paper, *Prensa Libre,* responded to the new competition by changing its automatic alliance with the government, regardless of whether it was legitimate" (1997, 17–18).

The long civil war had roots in the U.S.-backed overthrow of the freely elected, left-leaning government of Jacobo Arbenz. Arbenz's supporters took to the countryside and founded guerilla organizations that waged war on the series of governments that followed the overthrow. Formal peace accords were signed in 1996. The war claimed an estimated two hundred thousand lives, almost all at the hands of the military, according to government and church-sponsored truth commissions (Bureau of Western Hemisphere Affairs 2004). The indigenous people of Guatemala suffered terrible brutality. The worst period of repression, sometimes reaching the level of an attempted genocide, occurred under the brief reign of General Efraín Ríos Montt (1982–1983). Indigenous people either had to join rural defense patrols or be considered guerilla sympathizers. The Guatemalan military based much of its legitimacy on Cold War rhetoric, targeting opposition intellectuals and journalists for repression, disappearance, and assassination. An estimated eighty journalists died. "The violence in my country reached unparalleled levels of violence and horror," said Zamora of *Siglo Veintiuno.* "They said we were defending democracy, but the slogan they applied was: 'whoever is not with me is against me'" (Bureau of Western Hemisphere Affairs 2004; Zamora 2004).

Ríos Montt was deposed by his own defense minister, and a three-year transition toward electoral democracy ensued. President Vinicio Cerezo's government (1986–1990) was marked by corruption and widespread protests over the failing economy, but also decreased political violence. Freedom House's annual surveys note an improvement in the conditions for press freedom after Río's Montt's departure, but still called the Guatemalan press environment only "partly free" (Karkelar 2002, 2003, 2004). Journalists in Guatemala self-censored or openly supported the government, military or elected, having learned the hard way that resistance was either bad for business or downright dangerous. Even when conditions changed to allow more questioning, the self-censorship and fear persisted.

In 1990, a group of fourteen business owners professing free market and prodemocratic ideals decided it was time to found a new type of newspaper in the small country They named it *Siglo Veintiuno* (Century 21), in the hope that Guatemala was leaving behind an era of repression and intolerance. The test of *Siglo Veintiuno*'s support for democracy came just three years after its founding when President Jorge Serrano, Cerezo's elected successor, suspended the constitution and dissolved Congress and the judiciary in an attempt to take absolute power in the style of Peruvian President Alberto Fujimori's self-coup. Zamora was tipped off at 4 a.m. that Serrano had suspended the constitution and had dispatched troops to shut down the legislative and judicial branches. Zamora quickly roused his staff and produced a special edition of sixty thousand copies before the military surrounded his offices and printing plant, demanding that censors enter. Zamora, then thirty-five, and his grandfather, Oscar Marroquín Rojas, publisher of the smaller daily *La Hora*, ran the only two newspapers that refused to submit to the censorship. *La Hora*'s reporters smuggled copies of the newspaper out in their underwear. The troops surrounded *Siglo Veintiuno*'s printing plant and blocked publication.

For four days, *Siglo Veintiuno*'s staff wrote stories and faxed sections of the newspaper to political and civic leaders domestically and abroad in defiance of the censorship. When the newspaper agreed to allow in the censors, Zamora ran blank boxes in place of censored stories and changed the masthead to *Siglo Catorce* (Century 14), because "it was the last century of obscurantism, when the authorities didn't want the population to be informed" (Reid 1993). *Prensa Libre* adhered to the censors' wishes, placing a short notice on page two that the newspaper was under censorship. An editor told foreign correspondents that the newspaper complied because it had an obligation to advertisers (Reid 1993).

After seven days, the military deserted President Serrano and he had to flee the country in the face of a broad civil opposition. Foreign correspondents credit *Siglo Veintiuno*, *La Hora,* and the muckraking news magazine *Crónica* with crystallizing early opposition to the censorship and reaffirming opposition values that otherwise might have gone unexpressed. Zamora was not thinking of advertisers when he resisted the troops: "If we hadn't begun to engage in civil disobedience, people might have felt they had to accept what happened," he said. "But seeing we were defiant, they took heart" (Reid 1993). The episode raised the prestige of *Siglo Veintiuno* among Guatemala's journalists. A few years later several told Rockwell and Janus they could not completely forgive *Prensa Libre,* the only major newspaper to submit to censorship (Reid 1993; Rockwell and Janus 2003, 100). *Siglo Veintinuno* soon trailed only *Prensa Libre* in the country's small readership market.

Prensa Libre went through management turmoil in the first half of 1990s as *Siglo Veintiuno*'s circulation rose. *Prensa Libre*'s readership draw included broad coverage about issues and events far beyond politics, similar to *El Mercurio* in Chile and *Clarín* in Argentina. However, *Prensa Libre* was losing readers who cared about politics. The newspaper had five executive editors in four years after the founding editor retired in 1992. In 1996, the five elite families that own *Prensa Libre* hired Zamora's cousin, Gonzalo Marroquín, to be their executive editor. This was the first outsider to run the newspaper. Marroquín had been the executive editor in the more progressive atmosphere of the family newspaper *La Hora*. He had also been a correspondent for foreign press outlets, including Agence-France Press and CBS News. Marroquín brought younger journalists to *Siglo Veintiuno* and increased newsroom autonomy and assertiveness (Edición Conmemorativa 2001). He has survived owners' battles over the commitment to a more autonomous style of journalism; ultimately, however, he serves at the will of those owners.

The development of *Siglo Veintiuno* thus far follows the propositions of the institutional model. Owners and an editor with alternative ideas about journalism and society founded an innovative newspaper that practiced autonomous, assertive, and pluralistic journalism. By resonating with society during an opening in an authoritarian regime, the publication became both prestigious and successful financially, pressuring the traditional press into mimicking its style. In this case, the positive impact of the newspaper on the country's democratic transition is clear, helping crystallize opposition to a return to authoritarianism.

Like the other newsrooms studied, the journalistic model of *Siglo Veintiuno* depended on the acquiescence—if not the leadership—of its owners. Newsroom cultures can buffer changes of many sorts, but cannot forestall them if owners are intent on transforming a publication. *Siglo Veintiuno*'s owners lost their civic impulse when Zamora began to criticize the military too often and a new presidential administration more in tune with their free-market ideology came into power.

The civic identity of journalists working at *Siglo Veintiuno* could not stop a top-down transformation of the publication's journalistic orientation, but their models of journalism and society were so ingrained that most of the staff decided to resign rather than accept infringement of their professional ethics. "They didn't accept the pressures to abandon the struggle for freedom of expression, pluralism, respect for human rights, tolerance, de-militarization of society and the purge of governmental offices, officials and dignitaries who respond to criminal interests," Zamora said.[18]

Analysts of the Guatemalan media say *Siglo Veintiuno*'s editorial independence began to decline when a new president, who shared the same free-market ideals of the newspaper's business owners, was elected in 1996. The newspaper was one of few unscathed by an advertising boycott that President Alvaro Arzú (1996–2000) unleashed against press critics. *Crónica*, the critical newsmagazine, had to fold under financial pressure in 1998. *La Hora* was reduced to only a few thousand copies. Zamora, however, said that the spark that ignited the departure of seventy staffers at *Siglo Veintiuno* was his dismissal for publishing investigations that alienated the Guatemalan military, factions of which have aligned with organized crime and remain the power behind the new electoral environment. Zamora recounted how he and the journalists who went with him forged a new newspaper, *elPeriódico*, based on support from a broad swath of society, including businessmen and NGOs.

ZAMORA: Those of us who are here were working before in *Siglo Veintiuno*. There was a crisis there based on the fact that the newspaper attacked the army a lot. And finally they got tired of this focus and asked me to leave. So we started *elPeriódico*. There's no capital market here [in Guatemala], but I went into the street in search of friends. We put together a list of 300 friends, most of whom bought stock worth $10,000. Of those of us who work here, 80 are partners. In total we are 300 partners.

AUTHOR: Was this your idea or had you seen it done before elsewhere?

ZAMORA: It was necessity. Thinking one night that 80 people had resigned with me and no longer had a job. I didn't want to do journalism anymore, but it was the only thing we all knew how to do together. And one morning at dawn, thinking that I needed $3 million, I said, "Do I have 300 friends?" I made a list, found phone numbers, and visited them. Some said yes, others no. And survival has been difficult because we have had the last two governments against us, including an advertising boycott. Now is the first time that we have a small presence of government advertising. For eight years we didn't have even one advertisement from the government. And aside from that President Arzú formed a group of high-ranking business owners who visited my private sector advertisers so they would withdraw their ads from the newspaper. So it has cost us a great deal to survive.[19]

For a time, Zamora had to sell part of the newspaper to *Prensa Libre*. He was able to buy it back by selling the popular tabloid newspaper *Nuestro Diario* to the larger paper and because of a loan by The Media Development Loan Fund, a nongovernment organization funded by philanthropists and international media foundations that supports independent press projects in economically underdeveloped countries.

Financial difficulty has not been the only pressure on Zamora and his staff. Threats and physical repression reached a crescendo during the government of President Alfonso Portillo (2000–2004), a protégé of Ríos Montt. After *elPeriódico* published an investigative article that named military officers and government officials who profited from mafia activities, including trafficking in drugs, kidnapping, and extortion, the Portillo government sent tax auditors to the newspaper for forty days. After a related column directly criticized Ríos Montt, twelve well-organized assailants invaded Zamora's home and terrorized him and his family for two hours. On multiple occasions, they performed mock executions on Zamora while holding a gun to the head of his eldest son. Zamora sent his family to Miami and then, in typical fashion, investigated his assailants and named them in an exposé. Many had connections to the president's staff, military intelligence, and state security offices. Only two were brought to trial, and only one was convicted. During the ordeal, *Prensa Libre* lent editorial support to Zamora.

ElPeriódico has started a training center for investigative journalism; its stated goal is to give readers information so that they can analyze issues and events from different perspectives. The Guatemalan press, including the improved *Prensa Libre*, now helps set the public agenda in the country and has become much more assertive despite a surge in press attacks before Portillo left office. Press investigations into organized crime have called attention to what *New York Times* guest columnist Francisco Goldman called "the real power behind a hijacked state" (Goldman 2003). *Siglo Veintiuno* remains a widely read newspaper by Guatemalan standards, but no longer is counted among the country's autonomous press. Most observers in the early 2000s named three independent newspapers: *elPeriódico, Prensa Libre,* and *Nuestro Diario.*

While the number of cases is too small to draw solid conclusions, the press systems reviewed in this chapter offer initial support for the establishment of a model of institutional transformation of the press with applications beyond the process of media transformation in Mexico. In each of the cases, an opening in an authoritarian environment created conditions for the expression of a form of journalism that was autonomous, assertive, and, to a greater or lesser degree, diverse on issues of regime change and governance. However, it was not the financially strong press in any of these countries that took on the mantle of an emergent civil society and produced journalism that enabled civic participation. In each case, journalistic entrepreneurs guided more by ideas and values than financial fortitude or the search for profits founded innovative publications that later pushed change in the larger newspaper field.

Environmental and social-psychological variables interacted during and after the development of civic journalism, but the comparative cases suggest that the social-psychological component of the model is the more powerful

Table 10.2 Civic Newspaper Networks, Influence, and Decline in Four Countries

Country	Innovators	Reactive Newspapers	Linked Newspapers
México	*El Norte* (Y)	*El Universal* (Y)	*Reforma* (Y)
	La Jornada (Y)		*El Sur* (Y)
	El Imparcial (Y)		*Frontera* (Y)
	Others		Others
Chile	*La Epoca* (N)	*El Mercurio* (Q)	*La Nación Domingo* (N)
		La Tercera (Q)	*Plan B* (N)
Argentina	*Página/12* (Q)	*La Nación* (Y)	
		El Clarín (Y)	
Guatemala	*Siglo 21* (Q)	*La Prensa Libre* (Y)	*El Periódico* (Y)

Notes: Y=yes; N=no; Q=yes, but civic tendencies are questioned. Responses in answer to: "Publication survived in 2005?"

level of institutional action once a threshold of economic and political open-ing is established. The loss of identity in leaders of founding publications was an originating cause of civic decline at all of the early innovators reviewed here, while the importance and makeup of economic and political pressures varied. Similarly, again considering the limitation of the small number of cases, economic and ideological pressures seem to be more powerful than physical threat or violence in subduing the civic press once electoral democ-racy is reestablished.

The comparative cases also provide a cautionary tale for the survivability of civic journalism in all contexts, but specifically in Mexico as it transverses a pivotal juncture with the first electoral alternation of presidential power since the PRI lost control of the presidency and Congress. In each country studied here, founding civic newspapers lost their identity when new govern-ments sharing the ideological and programmatic priorities of media owners or newsroom leaders took power. Civic-oriented journalism was able to sur-vive within these newsrooms only when civil society supported the efforts of journalists to reestablish themselves as different media organizations. This occurred in Guatemala, but so far has failed in Chile and has not occurred in Argentina. In a sense, this brings civic journalism in Mexico full circle. Mexico's civic journalism pioneers rode a crest of civic participation in the 1980s and 1990s. Their survival is linked to whether Mexican society can re-gain its participatory dynamic.

The news is not all bad for journalism and participatory democracy, however. The civic journalism movement that emerged from authoritar-ian transitions in Guatemala, Chile, Argentina, and Mexico left a legacy in each press field. Table 10.2 shows the newspapers that were directly or indi-rectly influenced by the early civic innovators in each country. While change seems to have stopped short of the potential of the original, change-oriented manifestation, journalistic standards and practices are not the same in any of these countries as they were during authoritarianism, transitional periods, or previous periods of democratic rule. The values of younger journalists, especially, have undergone a cultural revolution. Their ability to act on those values remains constricted by the organizational structures and environmental pressures in which they work, however. The strength of the civic journalism legacy in Chile, Argentina, Guatemala, and Mexico will depend upon on the conditions of civil society as well as upon who controls the newsrooms.

APPENDIX: CODING INSTRUMENT

1. NEWSPAPER

1 *Reforma*

2 *El Universal*

3 *La Jornada*

4 *Excélsior*

2. DATE

3. CASE NUMBER

4. ACTOR	**5.** NEWS REALM (RECODE)
1 PRESIDENT	1 ELECTORAL
2 OPPOSITION GOVERNMENTS (RUN BY FEDERAL-LEVEL OPPOSITION PARTIES)	
3 PRI	
4 OPPOSITION PARTIES (FEDERAL LEVEL)	
5 MILITARY	2 RULE OF LAW
6 DRUG DEALERS	
7 CORRUPTION INVESTIGATORS, SUSPECTS	
8 HUMAN RIGHTS ABUSERS, VICTIMS	
9 BUSINESS ELITES	3 COMMERCIAL
10 PRIVATE SECTOR ACTORS	
11 ECONOMIC SECRETARIATS	
12 OTHER ECONOMIC MODEL/POLICY ACTORS	
13 CHURCH	4 CULTURAL
14 FAMILY	
15 SEXUALITY	
16 GENDER (if relevant)	
17 INDEPENDENT JOURNALISTS	5 CIVIL SOCIETY
18 NGOs	

19 UNARMED PROTEST MOVEMENTS	
20 ARMED PROTEST MOVEMENTS, ZAPATISTAS	
25 AVERAGE FOLKS NOT RELATED TO OFFICIAL GROUP, OR PERSON. NOT A CELEBRITY	

6. ACTOR EMPHASIS

Is the actor mentioned in the headline or the first six lines of the text?

0 NO

1 YES

7. TYPE OF NEWS ITEM

0 ARTICLE

1 HEADLINE ONLY

2 CAPTION WITH PHOTO

3 GRAPHIC ELEMENT

8. TONE

The actor is portrayed . . .

0 NEGATIVELY

Tone considers: a. language used to describe the actor and the actor's actions, b. whether the actor's version of events is contradicted or accepted as truth, c. the position and space the actor gets in the story/paper, and d. whether there is an implied criticism in the meaning of the language.

1 BALANCED

A roughly equal amount of both positive and negative information is included about the actor.

2 POSITIVELY

Tone considers: a. language used to describe the actor and the actor's actions, b. whether the actor's version of events is contradicted or accepted as truth, c. the position and space the actor gets in the story/paper, and d. whether there is an implied criticism in the meaning of the language.

98 NEUTRALLY

Neither positive nor negative information is presented, or none of the indicators is sufficient to tilt the story's balance sufficiently in favor of the actor in question.

99 NA

9. PLACEMENT

1 ABOVE FOLD

0 BELOW FOLD

10. SIZE OF HEADLINE (by columns, standard eight columns per page)

11. EMPOWER

If the actor is an "average" Mexican, was he or she treated in a passive or empowered manner? Empowered means the actor spoke for herself or took action to improve or change her situation.

0 PASSIVE

1 EMPOWERED

12. FRAME CONTENT

What is dominant frame?

13. FRAME-DIVERSITY

0 ONE FRAME—a perspective of an issue or actor that is unchallenged

1 ONE FRAME DOMINANT

Frames must be contrasting perspectives of an issue or actor. One is dominant in terms of space and placement.

2 DIVERSE, TWO OR MORE FRAMES

Frames must be contrasting perspectives of an issue or actor. They are roughly equivalent in terms of space and placement.

14. FRAME ORIENTATION (LEGITIMACY)

The dominant frame portrays the point of view of the . . .

0 TRADITIONAL SOCIAL FORCES OR ACTORS (PRESIDENT, BUSINESS ELITE, PRI, MILITARY, CONSERVATIVE CHURCH, ECONOMIC ELITES)

1 NEW SOCIAL FORCES OR ACTORS (NATIONAL POLITICAL OPPOSITION, INDEPENDENT ECONOMIC ANALYSTS, DEBTORS, INDEPENDENT LABOR, HUMAN RIGHTS ACTIVISTS, GAYS, LIBERATION THEOLOGISTS, EMPOWERED WOMEN, INDIGENOUS PEOPLE, INDEPENDENT NEWSPAPERS, ETC.)

2 OTHER

3 BOTH TRADITIONAL AND NEW

4 TRADITIONAL ACTOR TAKING ON NEW ROLE (PRI MEMBERS CRITICIZING PARTY, BUSINESS SECTOR CRITICIZING PRI OR PRESIDENT DIRECTLY RATHER THAN JUST DISAGREEMENTS ON POLICY, CHURCH IN CIVIC CAMPAIGNS, ETC.)

15. CRITICISM

Does coverage include criticism of . . . ?

0 TRADITIONAL ACTOR

1 NEW ACTOR

2 NOT CRITICAL OF ANYONE

3 BOTH TRADITIONAL AND NEW ACTORS

4 OTHER

16. AGENDA—ASSERTIVE

Who set the agenda of the story?

When a newspaper item follows an event (e.g., a press conference or staged news event), it is letting an outside actor set the agenda.

When the newspaper changes the frame of the original event by adding perspectives of others actors or following up the event with a story taking a conflicting angle, then the newspaper is setting the agenda of the story.

If a newspaper seeks out an interview on a critical subject and it is a news item of the newspaper's choice, the newspaper sets the agenda.

0 OUTSIDE ACTOR

1 NEWSPAPER

17. REPORTING SOURCES

Principle information for story came from . . .

0 STAGED EVENT

1 PAID NEWS STORY (GACETILLA)

2 PRESS CONFERENCE, PRESS RELEASE, OR GROUP/CURBSIDE INTERVIEW

3 UNSTAGED EVENT (BREAKING NEWS)

4 PERSONAL INTERVIEW

5 DOCUMENTS

6 NEWSPAPER POLL

7 MULTIPLE SOURCES (DOCUMENTS, INTERVIEWS, ETC.)

8 ARTICLES REQUESTED FROM NEWSMAKERS BY NEWSPAPER

9 LETTER TO THE EDITOR

97 NEWSPAPER EDITORIAL, NO SOURCES

98 NOT STATED IN STORY

99 OPINION COLUMN WITH NO SOURCES

18. NUMBER OF SOURCES

How many sources does the story cite?

Direct observation is counted as one source.

A photo counts as one source if it implies direct observation.

When opinion columns do not mention sources, then note "zero" sources.

19. REPORTING STYLE

Recode of reporting sources

0 = PASSIVE—STAGED EVENT, PRESS CONFERENCE, PRESS RELEASE, CURBSIDE INTERVIEW, OPINION COLUMN (WITH NO SOURCES), LETTER TO THE EDITOR

1 = MIXED—UNSTAGED EVENT (BREAKING NEWS), PERSONAL INTERVIEW, DOCUMENT (NOT A PRESS RELEASE), ARTICLE, OR RESPONSE SPECIFICALLY REQUESTED BY NEWSPAPER

2 = ASSERTIVE—MULTIPLE SOURCES, OPINION POLL CONDUCTED BY NEWSPAPER

NOTES

Throughout the text, all translations from the Spanish, including translation from print and television media sources, are by the author unless otherwise indicated. All interviews conducted by the author and by Juliet Gill and all responses to survey questions have also been translated by the author.

Chapter 1:
Civic Journalism and the Transformation of an Authoritarian Media Institution

1. Alejandra Xanic, e-mail to author, February 16, 2006. Jorge Zepeda (former executive editor, *Siglo 21* and *Público*), interview by author, October 19–20, 1999, Mexico City.

2. See Waisbord (2000) for analysis of the rise of "watchdog" journalism in South America after the return to democracy in the late 1980s. Watchdog journalism addresses one of the two dimensions of the civic press, accountability.

3. Lázaro Ríos (editor, *Reforma*), interview by author, August 26–27, 1999, Mexico City; Ignacio Rodríguez Reyna (deputy editor, *El Universal*), interview by author, July 18, 2003, Mexico City; Josetxo Zaldúa, (managing editor, *La Jornada*), interview by author, June 12, 2003, Mexico City.

4. *Imágenes intencionadas*, Mexican Academy of Human Rights (1997).

5. Subcommander Marcos (spokesman, EZLN), interview by Saul Landau, quoted in *The Sixth Sun: Mayan Uprising in Chiapas* (1996). Directed by Saul Landau. New York: Cinema Guild. Translation provided by the film.

6. Interview with *Reforma* reporter by Juliet Gill, Mexico City, July 17, 2003. Name withheld by prior agreement.

7. Alejandro Paez, interview by author, August 3, 1999, Mexico City.

8. The remainder said "other." Author's survey of 126 journalists from fourteen newspapers in ten Mexican cities by mail or personal interview, March–November 1999.

9. My interviews with older journalists and a review of journalists' speeches from the era also confirm this statement.

10. Lawson's panel study during the 1997 congressional elections supports this statement. See Lawson (1999).

11. Twenty of 104 investigative projects selected as the best in the region by Transparency International and Peru's Press and Society Institute were published as books rather than print or electronic media reports (Flor Zapler 2005).

Chapter 2: Media Transformation through Institutional Lenses

1. The newsroom construct is based on ideas from Cook (1998, 61–84). The definition of an organization comes from Torow (1992), especially chap. 2. For more on organizational fields and their "shared cultural rules and meaning systems," see DiMaggio and Powell (1991b, 64–65); Scott (1995, 55–56; 1998, 129–30).

2. This statement is based on many sources, including Altschull (1984); Fox and Waisbord (2002); Curran and Park (2000b); Skidmore (1993); Hughes and Lawson (2004, 2005); Karkelar (2003, 2004); León Dermota (2003); Rockwell and Janus (2003).

3. For an overview of the early organizational studies, see Schudson (2000).

4. Author interview with former *El Financiero* reporter, Mexico City, 1999. Name and date withheld by request.

5. Alejandro Junco (publisher, *El Norte* and *Reforma*), interview by author, June 2, 1999, Mexico City; Maria Idalia Gómez (reporter, *Reforma*), interview by author, April 27, 1999, Mexico City.

6. Author interview with Televisa News executive, July 23, 2003, Mexico City. Name withheld by author, per University of Miami regulation.

7. Rafael Cardona to Manuel Alonso, July 3, 2000, published in Albarrán de Alba (2001).

Chapter 3: Authoritarian and Democratic Models of News Production

The epigraph is from Ricardo Hernández (reporter, *El Universal*), interview by author, April 1, 1999, Mexico City. Hernández is speaking of his experience covering opposition candidate protests of the fraud-filled 1988 presidential election at the Mexico City newspaper *El Día*. After the experience, he left political reporting.

1. For a description of the developmental model, see Hachten and Hachten (1996, 34–38). Other studies consulted for the creation of the alternative models include: McQuail (1987, 2000); Ansolobehere, Behr, and Iyengar (1993); Curran and Park (2000b); Jakubowicz (1998–99), McManus (1994); Sparks and Tulloch (2000); and Splichal (1994).

2. I constructed the description of the institutionalized worldview, values, coverage norms, and behaviors that guided Mexican journalism from the 1940s to the 1990s from interviews with Mexican journalists and press officers, descriptive accounts of Mexican media, and an informal analysis of news content from the period.

3. Angel Gómez Granados (reporter for *El Universal*), 1983, cited in Castañeda (1993, 235–36).

4. Roberto Rock (editor, *El Universal*), interview by author, March 19, 1999, Mexico City.

5. Carlos Ferreira (former senate press officer), interview by author, May 24, 1999, Mexico City.

6. Please see chapter 1 for a discussion of how I use the term "civic" in reference to Mexican journalism.

7. The coder was Dr. Roberto Dominguez Rivera of Suffolk University. Dr. Dominguez worked in the press office of the Mexican Foreign Relations Secretariat during the 1990s and has in-depth knowledge of Mexican press behavior during

the period under study. The following list includes: (1) the measures from which the tables were constructed; (2) the simple agreement between the coders in percentages; and (3) agreement between the coders controlling for chance (Cohen's Kappa): actor: 98.1, 0.959; frames-diversity, 92.3, 0.884; tone, 91.5, 0.880; reporting style, 93.4, 0.859; sources, 92.5, 0.884; agenda setting, 99.1, 0.967; and legitimacy, 94.3 (all categories), 0.926 (more- and less-powerful actor categories only). The average simple agreement for all other variables was 94.5.

Chapter 4: Ending the Monologue

1. This is a synthesis of the work of several scholars. See the following works for more detail on the 1980s and 1990s: Camp (2002b); Cook, Middlebrook, and Molinar (1994); Cornelius (1987); Cornelius, Craig, and Fox (1994); Lustig (1992); Morris (1995); Semo (1993).

2. Fox was the first opposition party candidate to win the Mexican presidency during the twentieth century in a competitive election and take office in a peaceful transferal of power.

3. See Bruhn (1997) on the PRD; and Shirk (2004) and Middlebrook (2002) for overviews of the PAN.

4. Subcommander Marcos, identified as Rafael Sebastián Guillén, recounted the intellectuals' first years in the rainforest in an interview given to a U.S. film crew. Saul Landau, director, *The Sixth Sun. Mayan Uprising in Chiapas*, 1996. On social movements, see the following: Fox (2000) and Haber (1994). PRD leader Andrés Manuel López Obrador, *La Jornada*'s Maribel Gutierrez, and independent congressman Adolfo Aguilar-Zinser (now deceased) produced informative books from the period. See Aguilar Zinser (1995); Gutiérrez (1998); and Lopez Obrador (1995).

5. Raúl Salinas was acquitted of the murder of Ruiz Massieu and liberated on almost $3 million bond on June 14, 2005. He still faced corruption-related charges.

6. Camp (2002b, 186) reports congressional races through 1997. Figures from 2000 come from the Federal Electoral Institute. (Instituto Federal Electoral 2002).

7. Adler (1993a, 1993b) discusses media use in the 1980s, while Aguilar Zinser (1995), Lawson (2001, 2002) and Moreno (2001) discuss its later effects.

8. The original Spanish headlines read: "JLP contra el engaño al campesino: CNC"; "Oscura panorama electoral con la alianza AN-clero"; and "Plagada de cobardes, tibios, ilusos y comodinos, la izquierda: Falcon."

9. The original Spanish headlines read: "Exigen garantías para los turistas," and "Desalojan Alcaldías: Mueren 20."

10. After ninety-nine audits, he was found guilty of one charge, for which the company paid a $2,400 fine. Roberto Rock (editor, *El Universal*), interviews by author, March 19 and April 7, 1999, Mexico City.

11. Focus group interview with editors from *Reforma*, *La Jornada*, *Excélsior*, *Novedades*, and *El Universal*, July 30, 1999, Mexico City. The group was conducted by Mori de México (now MUND Américas) and sponsored by the *Dallas Morning News*.

12. The military was mentioned only twice in the 1980 sample. This was not a high enough number of cases to include results in the analysis.

Chapter 5: The Limits to Civic Journalism

1. Author interview with newspaper editor, June 2003, Mexico City. Name withheld by author, per University of Miami regulation.

2. Altschull (1984) discusses a number of conceptual constraints on journalism worldwide. Karkelar (2003, 2004) provides country-specific examples of political, economic, and legal obstacles.

3. This is lore among Mexican journalists. See also Wager and Schulz (1995).

4. Statistical tests support this relationship. A Pearson's R test for agenda-setting differences in coverage of electoral and societal actors was significant at the .10 level (sig.=.061; p= −.164; n=132).

5. The three negative items in the sample were: David Aponte, "Fox recula: en la crisis, la banca 'se despacho con la cuchara grande,'" *La Jornada*, March 9, 2000; Jorge Herrera, "Fox elogia a banqueros; Cárdenas los cuestiona," *El Universal*, March 5, 2000; Juan Antonio Zuñiga, "Son minoría los banqueros que rechazan más de lo mismo: Cárdenas," *La Jornada*, March 6, 2000.

6. The original Spanish headlines read: "Fox: el narco, en el PRI; Labastida le exige pruebas," and "Contratan a sicarios para desestabilizar."

7. Hermann Bellinghausen, "Ocupan mujeres zaptistas durante 60 minutos una radiofusora oficial" [Women Zapatistas occupy an official radio station for 60 minutes], *La Jornada*, March 9, 2000, p. 1; Hermann Bellinghausen, "'Apresurado' avance militar, denuncian en zonas zapatistas" [A quick military advance is denounced], *La Jornada*, March 10, 2000, p. 1; Justino Miranda, "Roban expedientes sobre Carrillo" [Carillo files are stolen], *El Universal*, March 4, 2000, p. 1A.

8. *La Jornada*, "Vaiven Carioca" [Carioca swing], March 6, 2000, p. 1. José Luís Ruiz and Sergio Jiménez, "Da Gobierno beneplácito a Sandri como nuevo nuncio" [The government welcomes Sandri as the new nuncio], *El Universal*, March 1, 2000, p. 1A.

9. Mexican Advertising Agency Association figures are available at www.amap .com.mx.

10. Multinational corporations controlled 60 percent of national advertising and the remaining 7 percent was controlled by other Mexican firms and a media company foundation. See the *Forbes* list reproduced in Casteñeda (2003).

11. Author interviews at *El Universal, Reforma,* and *La Jornada*, June 2003.

12. Newspapers cost 7 pesos daily in 2004, about 65 cents (U.S.). Prices for a liter of pasteurized milk ranged from 6.8 pesos for a bag to 8.65 pesos for a carton, according to lists compiled by the Attorney General's Office for Consumer Affairs. See http:// www.profeco.gob.mx/html/precios/df/lacteos.htm.

13. Only two of twenty articles mentioning Slim from October 13 through November 12, 1999, in the business section of *Reforma* referred to something negative. Both columns were about the possible investment of the Salinas brothers in Telmex and Telmex's legal maneuvering to maintain high connection fees for long-distance telephone companies tapping into Telmex's local network. Articles were retrieved November 12, 1999, through the Internet search mechanism at www.reforma .com.mx.

14. For example, the following nine articles mentioning Slim, two of which contained a critical focus, appeared in *El Universal* between June 25 and July 26, 2003: Nicholas Benequista, "'Más gasto público para crecer más': Slim" ["More public spend-

ing to grow more": Slim], June 14, 2003, p. A1, A20; "Detallan el proyecto empresarial del Centro" [Details provided about the downtown business project], June 26, 2003, p. 1A; "Construcción de Acuerdos" [Building agreements], June 25, 2003, p. A1, A12; Horoshi Takahashi, "Frenan expansión de Slim en EU" [They block Slim's expansion in the U.S.], June 27, 2003, p. B1; Roberto Aguilar, "Aprovecha Slim ajuste en tasas" [Slim takes advantage of interest rate adjustment], July 15, 2003, p. B1; Angelina Mejía Guerrero, "Muestra Telmex debilidad" [Telmex demonstrates weakness], July 15, 2003, p. B3; Mónica Archundia, "Pedirán a Slim para rescatar Xochimilco" [They will ask Slim to rescue Xochimilco], July 21, 2003, p. B1; Orquídea Soto and Ella Grajeda, "Slim cuestiona la ideología económica del gobierno" [Slim questions the government's economic ideology], July 24, 2003, p. A9, B1; Orquídea Soto and Ella Grajeda, "Apoyará Slim un Presidente de izquierda o de derecha" [Slim will support a president from the left or the right], July 24, 2003, p. A9.

15. I have removed the name of the magazine and newspaper to protect the confidentiality of the informant, but I verified the incident with other employees and by looking at a copy of the magazine edition in question.

16. Name of the reporter withheld by the author. The reporter was nineteen years old when I interviewed him in 1999. He had recently left the financial publication.

17. The cost of the program, created to prevent a banking system breakdown following the peso devaluation of 1994–1995, had reached $137.4 billion pesos as of January 2004. See Teherán and Jiménez (2003).

18. Author interview with *El Universal* editor, June 10, 2003, Mexico City. Name withheld by author, per University of Miami regulation.

19. Author interviews with editors at *La Jornada* and *Reforma*, June 12 and June 18, 2003, Mexico City. Names withheld by author. Banamex, mentioned as one of the advertisers that did not return to *La Jornada,* is now owned by Citibank.

20. The most complete work on the church in Mexican politics in English is Camp (1997).

21. Author confidential interviews, June 10 and June 18, 2003, Mexico City.

22. The Inter-American Press Association's allegations are made in an online article by the association's director. See Ricardo Trotti, "Mexico: The Case of Víctor Manuel Oropreza," *Impunity,* November 1999. http://www.impunidad.com/cases/victorE.htm (accessed November 21, 2005).

23. Barraza (1998). See also Xanic (2001) and Anderson (1997).

24. Statement made in a focus group of seven reporters from seven Mexico City newspapers, July 23, 1999, Mexico City. Names withheld by the author. The focus group was sponsored by the Dallas Morning News and run by Morde México (now MUND Américas). Participants came from *Reforma, El Universal, La Jornada, El Economista, El Financiero, Crónica,* and *Novedades.*

25. I also asked, in a number of ways, whether journalists would accept payments or favors in exchange for coverage. The response was overwhelmingly negative. Because the acceptance of payoffs, called *"chayote,"* or squash, had become so socially unacceptable in Mexico by 1999, I decided to omit the question in favor or a more nuanced line of inquiry.

26. A Pearson's R test found a weak-to-moderate positive correlation between an age under forty and support for working for a candidate (.203) that was significant at the .03 level.

Chapter 6: How Institutional Entrepreneurs Created Civic Newsrooms

1. The emergence period, or first wave, runs roughly from the transfer of leadership at *El Norte* to Alejandro Junco in 1971 through the implementation of ethics regulations increasing newspaper autonomy at *El Imparcial* in 1986. The year 1986 was also the year when competitive elections in Chihuahua and the intention to enter the General Agreement on Tariffs and Trade signal the beginning of a gradual liberalization trend in politics and the economy. The environment during the first wave was characterized by a statist economy and political authoritarianism. The second wave, diffusion, begins in 1986 with the decision to change the economic model and the initial push for political liberalization.

2. One case was the closure of *ABC* in Tijuana in 1979. State Governor Roberto de Lamadrid promoted a labor strike that eventually caused the dismissal of editor Jesús Blancornelas and twenty-six reporters from the newspaper. De Lamadrid offered Blancornelas his job back if he fired critical columnist Héctor Félix Miranda, but Blancornelas refused. Enrique Gómez, publisher and executive editor of *A.M.*, reported that business owners boycotted his newspaper in 1982 because they did not like its coverage. See Rodríguez-Castañeda (1993, 198). Data was also collected via a written questionnaire from Enrique Gómez, April 1999.

3. See also Fernández (1999). Reporters and editors discussed the importance of friendship ties in order to get information during two focus group discussions on July 23 and 30, 1999, Mexico City.

4. This statement is based on informants' reporting in the survey and in interviews about education abroad, contact with foreign reporters, participation in exchange programs, knowledge of foreign newspapers on the Internet, and new international journalism associations that include reporters and midlevel editors. In the 1970s, the long-standing Inter-American Press Association was largely limited to publishers and editors in chief. In the early 2000s it extended its training and outreach.

5. Scherer (1990) provides a detailed description of payments given to top publishers, reporters, and columnists during the administration of President José López Portillo (1976–1982). His work is based upon original documents provided by the head of the rural development bank, Banrural, through which the payments were channeled.

6. This happened during both the ouster of editor Julio Scherer from *Excélsior* in 1976 and the government-promoted strike that shut down *ABC* in Tijuana in 1979. See Levy and Székely (1987, 99, 102).

7. As noted in chapter 4, President Luis Echeverría cut *El Norte*'s state-subsidized paper supply by 83 percent because he did not like the newspaper's coverage of the kidnapping of Eugenio Garza Sada. In 1979, President José López Portillo made a similar cut, forcing young publisher Alejandro Junco to find alternate supplies and end his dependence on government newsprint subsidies. President Miguel de la Madrid cut government advertising in *El Financiero* because he did not like the way the newspaper covered debt negotiations in the mid-1980s. The newspaper survived on private sector advertising and the ad ban was later lifted. Also disgruntled, President Carlos Salinas limited reporters' access on presidential excursions. The government has had to turn to more Byzantine measures to oust famous editors. Julio Scherer of *Excélsior* faced an advertising boycott and a revolt by members of the newspaper's cooperative of owners in

1976. He and his followers left the paper and gave birth to the newsmagazines *Proceso* and *Unomásuno,* and later *La Jornada.* Jesús Blancornelas faced a government-inspired labor strike at *ABC* in 1979, which eventually closed the newspaper. It reopened as *Zeta* in 1980. Manuel Becerra Acosta, editor of *Unomásuno,* was reportedly forced to sell the newspaper to a government ally in 1989 after insulting the incoming president, Carlos Salinas. See Fromson (1996, 131);. Levy and Székely (1988); Riva Palacio (1991, 9; 1994); Torres (1997, 131, 134).

8. Francisco Javier Ortíz Franco (editor, *Zeta*), response to written questionnaire by author, June 1999. See also Levy and Székely (1998, 99).

9. Samuel García (editor, *Reforma*), interview by author, August 19, 1999, Mexico City; Author interview, finance section editor, May 26, 1999, Mexico City. Name withheld by request.

10. José Santiago Healy (publisher and executive editor, *El Imparcial*) and Enrique Gómez (publisher, *A.M.*), responses written questionnaires by author, March and April l999. Healy facts checked with Ricardo Moreno (assistant to the publisher, *Frontera*), interview by author, March 10, 2000, by telephone, Tijuana/San Diego. Alejandro Junco (CEO, *Grupo Reforma* newspapers), interview by author, Mexico City, June 2, 1999.

11. Alejandro Junco, interview, June 2, 1999.

12. Author interview with editor at *La Jornada*, June 12, 2003, Mexico City, name withheld by request; Manuel Meneses (former managing editor, *La Jornada*) interview by author, March 13, 2000, via telephone, Mexico City/San Diego. Meneses said *El País* inspired the journalists at *La Jornada* to urge Mexico's civil society to fight against the country's own particular brand of authoritarianism.

13. *El Universal,* "Lineaje de enero a junio de 1999 de 7 periódicos." Mimeograph.

14. Diego Peterson, *Público* publisher, personal interview with author, 20 Sept. 1999, Guadalajara.

15. Source material for table 6.2 is as follows:

1991: *El Universal* Estudio Enero–Febrero 1991, reprinted in AMAP (1992, 72).

1992: Moctezuma y Asociados, "Press Measurement Report," reprinted in AMAP (1992, 73).

1993: Moctezuma y Asociados, October 1993, reprinted in AMAP (1994, 71).

1994: Wilbert Sierra y Asociados, S.A., mimeograph sheet provided by Luis Felipe Enríquez Torres (market research coordinator, *El Universal*), March 22, 1999.

1995: Figures come from comparing two studies. Moctzezuma y Asociados, "Mediaflash," mimeograph sheet provided by Luis Felipe Enríquez Torres, March 22, 1999; and Wilbert Sierra y Asociados, S.A., mimeograph sheet provided by Luis Felipe Enríquez Torres, March 22, 1999.

1997: Nexus/Gallup de México, "Estudio media max 1997 y sus resultados definitivos," mimeograph sheet provided by Luis Felipe Enríquez Torres, April 1999.

1999: "Media Max 99," Gallup de México. 2000: Results of Media Max 2000, provided by Roberto Rock (executive editor, *El Universal*), July 25, 2003.

16. Ricardo Moreno (assistant to the publisher, *Frontera*), interviews by author, October 2000 and November 2001, Tijuana.

17. Sergio López (managing director of the Mexican Advertising Agency Association), interview by author, November 26, 1999, Mexico City.

18. Jorge Zepeda (former executive editor, *Siglo 21* and *Público*), interview by author, October 19–20, 1999.

19. Informal query at the Third Summit of Partners in the Americas, San Antonio, Texas, August 11–13, 1999.

20. Alejandro Paez (assistant finance editor, *Reforma*), interview by author, August 3, 1999, Mexico City.

21. Author interview with financial page editorMay 26, 1999, Mexico City. Name withheld by request.

22. Author interview with journalist, April 1999. Name changed to protect confidentiality. All quotes in this section, unless otherwise noted, come from this interview.

23. Roberto Rock (editor, *El Universal*), interview by author, March 19, 1999, Mexico City.

24. Sources include: 1999 Nexus/Gallup de México and 1999 Media Max (see note 15 to this chapter); Ricardo Moreno (assistant to the publisher, *Frontera*), interviews by author, October and November 2001, Tijuana; Diego Petersen (publisher, *Público*), interview by author, September 20, 1999, Guadalajara.

Chapter 7: Alternatives to the Civic Newsroom

1. Press figures in 1982 are based on the author's analysis of two constructed weeks of front-page electoral coverage (January 4, January 19, February 10, February 25, March 5, March 20, April 4, April 19, May 4, May 12, June 3, June 11, June 19, and June 27). *Unomásuno* represented civic-oriented newspapers. *El Universal* represented traditional newspapers. Traditional press data in 1988 and 1994 comes from analyses of *Excélsior, El Nacional,* and *El Universal* on sixteen and eighteen random campaign dates, respectively, considering three viable parties only. The figures were reported in Trejo (1994). Civic press coverage in 1988 responds to Trejo's analysis of coverage of the top parties in *La Jornada* and *Unomásuno*, and in 1994 responds to Trejo's analysis of top parties in *La Jornada* and *Reforma*. The 2000 figures for traditional newspapers correspond to author's content analysis of front-page stories in March in *Excélsior*. Civic newspaper figures correspond to an analysis of front pages in *El Universal, Reforma,* and four civic regional newspapers from January through March in Fernández (2000).

2. The careful panel study by Lawson (1999) during the 1997 congressional campaign supports this point.

3. Contributions from abroad are illegal in Mexican campaigns. See Rojas Cruz (2000).

4. See Tuynman (2001); Ruth Urry (assistant national editor of *Novedades*'s English-language publication, the *Mexico City News*), communication with author, June 2000, San Diego/Mexico City.

5. Rafael Cardona, interview, and Rafael Cardona to Manuel Alonso, July 3, 2000, quoted in Albarrán de Alba (2001). *Proceso* published these documents just days after Cardona resigned from *Unomásuno* on April 8, 2001.

6. Juan Francisco Ealy Ortiz (owner and publisher, *El Universal*), March 15, 2004, en route from an Inter-American Press Association meeting in Los Cabos, Mexico, to Mexico City.

7. Focus group interviews with six PRI press officers, December 2, 1999, Mexico City. The guide was written by the author. Independent journalist Claudia Fernández moderated the group, which was sponsored by the *Dallas Morning News*.

8. Antonio Gutiérrez (reporter, *Novedades*), interview by author, October 26, 1999, Mexico City. *Novedades* closed operations in January 2003. Its original owners retain control of 35 percent of *Novedades de Acapulco* and 15 percent of *Novedades de Yucatán*.

9. Ariadna Bermeo (reporter, *Reforma*) interview by author, Mexico City, August 3, 1999.

10. Author interviews, Mexico City, March 1999, names withheld by request. See also Tuynman (2000) and Staub (1995).

11. There were twenty-four newspapers in Mexico City in 1994 according to the advertising trade directory *Directorio de Medios Electrónicos* (2001). Only three—*La Jornada, El Financiero,* and *Reforma*—can be considered civic in orientation. This count does not include publications dedicated only to sports or advertising, but I included the publication *Esto* because it contains both news and sports coverage.

12. Ricardo Pascoe (Mexico City Delegation Director), December 1, 1999, in a focus group of PRD press officials. Pascoe used to be the party's chief spokesman and later became Fox's ambassador to Cuba.

13. Ealy, interview, March 15, 2004. In addition to the following sources, I read many of Ealy's speeches, which are available online at www.el-universal.com.mx: Ferráez and Ferráez (2003); *El Universal* (1994); *El Universal* (1998); Corro (2003); Fiestejan a Ángel Trinidad Ferreira (2003); Presenta Ealy La Revista (2004); Scherer (1990); La censura de El Universal (2005); Montes (2005).

14. See Jáquez (2000). The information about the purchase of *El Independiente* in Sonora comes from Roberto Rock (editor, *El Universal*), interview by author, March 19, 1999, Mexico City. The newspaper, the *Independent*, folded after Colosio's death.

15. Ealy, interview, March 15, 2004; Roberto Rock, interview, March 19, 1999.

16. Ealy, interview, March 15, 2004.

17. Statements in this and the following paragraphs from Roberto Rock, interviews by author, March 19 and 22 and April 7, 1999, Mexico City.

18. José Carreño (Washington DC correspondent, *El Universal*), interview by author, September 8, 2001, Washington DC; Ismael Romero (former assistant managing editor, *El Universal*) interviews by author, April–May 1999, Mexico City.

19. Claudia Fernández (former investigative reporter, *El Universal*), interview by author, April 9, 1999, Mexico City.

20. Pedro Enrique Armendares (director of Periodistas de Investigación), communication with author, Mexico City, March 18, 2004. On deleting the story involving friend and businessman Olegario Vázquez Raña, see "La censura del El Universal" (2005) and Montes (2005).

21. Greater detail on the quantitative analysis and cases reviewed in this section can be found in Hughes and Lawson (2004).

22. Elsewhere, my quantitative analysis with Chappell Lawson found that previous voter preferences moderated but did not preclude partisan news biases, so something beyond media response to audience preferences was at work. See Hughes and Lawson (2004).

23. Romeo Peña Silva (station manager, Televisión de Tlaxcala), interview by author, March 26, 2002, Tlaxcala. The president of the state's autonomous electoral institute, which monitors news programming during state elections, repeated this

version of events. Patricio Lima Gutiérrez, interview by author, Tlaxcala, March 25 and 26, 2002.

24. This information comes from a synthesis of information from several sources. Anonymous informant, interview, March 21, 2002, Villahermosa, Tabasco; Raúl Ojeda, (former PRD candidate for governor), interview by author, March 19, 2002, Villahermosa, Tabasco; *Directorio de Medios Electrónicos* (2001); Special Rapporteur for Freedom of Expression (2002); Weissert (2002); Rockwell and Janus (2003).

25. Author interview, March 21, 2002, Villahermosa, Tabasco. Name withheld by request.

26. Leonel Noguera (CEO, Televisa del Bajio), interview by author, June 2, 2002, León, Guanajuato.

27. Luis Arnoldo Cabada Alvídez (station owner and CEO, Intermedio de Mexicali), interview by author, Mexicali, Baja California, April 12, 2002. See also Mejía Barquera (1995).

Chapter 8: Market-Driven Journalism

1. Emilio Azcárraga Jean (CEO, Televisa), quoted in *La Jornada,* November 25, 1998, and reprinted in Alva de la Selva (1999).

2. *Reforma* newspaper media use surveys. See Orozco (1999, 2004). Survey results are for Mexico City only.

3. Author interview with Televisa news executive, July 23, 2003, Mexico City. Name withheld by author, per University of Miami regulation. This anecdote has been repeated throughout the company, according to Leopoldo Gómez (executive vice president for news, Televisa), interview by author, March 17, 2004, Mexico City.

4. The panel study conducted by Lawson (2002, chap. 9) during the 1997 campaign found strong evidence for the influence of balanced news coverage on voter decisions to support the opposition.

5. Author interview with *Hechos de la Noche* journalist, July 3, 2003, Mexico City. Name withheld by author, per University of Miami regulation.

6. Limites y responsibilidades de los medios en las campañas electorales [Limits and responsibilities of the media in the election campaigns], conference sponsored by Sociedad de Periodistas, Académica Mexicana de Derechos Humanos and The Freedom Forum, November 12–13, 1999, Mexico City.

7. Author interview with *Hechos* journalist, July 3, 2003. During my content study in 2003, images of burned children and a nanny hitting a toddler were featured in several sequential episodes of *Hechos.*

8. For a discussion on Americanization and globalization in comparative political communication studies, see the chapters by Pfetsch and Esser (2004) and Hallin and Mancini (2004).

9. Source material for table 8.1 is as follows. Analysis from 1994 and 1998–1999 come from Hallin (2000b). Hallin's analysis considered two weekly broadcasts between Dec. 3 and Aug. 26 (total of sixty-one) from Televisa's flagship newscast *24 Horas* in 1994 and five randomly selected newscasts each for Televisa's *El Noticiero* and TV Azteca's *Hechos* in 1998–1999. My content analysis with Jesús Arroyave in 2003 included fifteen randomly selected newscasts each for *El Noticiero* and *Hechos.* Twelve dates spanned the official April through June campaign season and were selected to

represent composite weeks on each network. In addition, three dates were selected randomly for each newscast during the pre-campaign season in January and February. The level of analysis was the news item. In total, 703 news items were coded. Reliability controlling for chance (Cohen's Kappa) was 0.971 for politics, crime, and all other. When considering all fifty-seven category codes, Kappa was 0.782. For more information on the samples, see Arroyave and Hughes (2004); Hallin (1994).

10. Unfortunately, I do not have comparative data for the 1997 congressional races. Only TV Azteca would open its archives back that far. However, Hallin (2000b) conducted content analyses during the 1994 presidential election and a nonelectoral season in 1998–1999.

11. Author interview with anchor of *Hechos*, July 3, 2003

12. See McLeod, Kosicki, and McLeod (2002) for a useful discussion of media effects on turnout at the individual and systemic level. Gross and Aday (2003) were able to disentangle real and TV effects, but in a situation where television grossly exaggerated crime levels. This does not appear to be the case in Mexico City, where crime is a serious problem.

13. Based on IBOPE market share scores for 2002, for Mexico, Brazil, Chile, and Argentina. A Herfindahl index measuring concentration in the Mexican television market is 5,672, more than 2,000 points higher than the second-most-concentrated Latin American television market, Brazil. Herfindahl indices represent the sum of the squares of the market shares of each company; higher scores indicate more concentration. The potential score ranges from 0 to 10,000. The only exception may be Guatemala, where a single owner, Ángel González, holds a monopoly on national broadcast television. See Lawson and Hughes (2005).

14. Adrian Angel Muñoz (director of research, National Radio and Television Chamber [CIRT]), interview by author, March 18, 2002, Mexico City.

15. Muñoz, interview, March 18, 2002.

16. Television executive Miguel Alemán Velasco called this "the Mexican system." See Sinclair (1999) and Molina (1987).

17. Miguel Alemán Velasco (acting president, Televisa), quoted in Corro (1994).

18. Author interview with Televisa news executive, July 23, 2003. Name withheld by author, per University of Miami regulations.

19. For the case of a star who went too far, see Fernández and Paxman (2000: 330–31).

20. This is part of what Adler (1993a, 155) describes as a ritual of crowning the candidate with king-like qualities.

21. The author was present on the stage as a reporter at the Cárdenas rally.

22. Author interview with founding member of *Hechos de la Noche,* July 1, 2003, Mexico City. Name withheld by author, per University of Miami regulation.

23. Author interview with anchor of *Hechos*, July 3, 2003.

24. See also accounts by Alemán and Delgado.

25. Coverage time was distributed in the following manner from March 16 to July 3, 1997, on commercial, cable, and state-run networks in Mexico City, considering only the top three parties: 34.14 percent for the PRD, 33.04 percent for the PRI, and 32.82 percent for the PAN. See Instituto Federal Electoral (1997).

26. IBOPE's historical data is available at www.ibope.com.mx/hgxpp001.aspx?1,1,8 ,0,5,0,MNU;E;1;3;MNU;,.

27. Author interview with Televisa executive, July 23, 2003, Mexico City. Name withheld by author, per University of Miami regulation.

28. Author interview with Televisa executive, July 23, 2003.

29. One analyst stated that this was more continuous coverage than what the networks had dedicated to the assassination of the PRI's presidential candidate in 1994. See Turcott (1999).

30. TV Azteca President Ricardo Salinas Pliego, quoted in Báez Rodríguez (1999, 11), and Mejía Barquera (1999, 10). See also Villamil Rodríguez (1999, 119).

31. César Yáñez (city press officer), in a mini-focus group of press officers from the PRD and affiliated governments sponsored by the *Dallas Morning News,* December 1, 1999, Mexico City. His precise institutional affiliation was withheld by request.

32. While ratings drove news at TV Azteca, a free-market orientation was a litmus test for favorable coverage from the network. TV Azteca's vice president for news, Sergio Sarmiento (1995–1998), said the company had made a decision to defend the government's policy of market liberalization, including free trade and the privatization of state retirement funds. Cárdenas had opposed these policies. See Albarrán de Alba (1994, 18, 20).

33. Although TV Azteca apparently ran the response, only Sarmiento's critique appeared in the primetime newscast. Salinas Pliego said his network did nothing wrong by airing an unpopular commentary. See Cisneros Morales (1999); Fernández and Paxman (2000: 3, 325–27, 330–31); Molina (1987); Turati (1999).

34. *Reforma* media use surveys, 1997–1999.

35. The data from this study were generously shared by the *Reforma* Newspaper Group and its chief pollster, Alejandro Moreno.

36. This is based on an analysis of eight episodes of five programs aired on TV Azteca during the last two weeks of the 2003 congressional campaigns: The profile program *Un Día con . . .* (A Day with . . .), the quiz show *Entre lo Público y lo Privado* (Between the Public and the Private), the newsmagazine *Reporte 13* (Report 13), and the roundtable programs *El Debate* (The Debate) and *En Contexto* (In Context). For more information on the method and findings, see Hughes (2005).

37. Leopoldo Gómez (Televisa vice president for news) interview by author, March 17, 2004, Mexico City.

38. Bejarano was stripped of his immunity as a public official and charged with money laundering. A judge ordered the charges dropped for lack of evidence on July 6, 2005.

Chapter 9: The Durability of Civic Journalism

1. For this content analysis, I used the same coding instrument as that described in chapter 3 and presented in the Appendix.

2. High inter-coder reliability means that the coding instrument is measuring what the researcher intends for it to measure since two coders reach the same conclusion about how to code a case (in this case a newscast segment). Perfect inter-coder reliability would be 0.1. Research with inter-coder reliability of less than 0.85 is rarely reported. For this test, I used the Gamma statistic, which controls for chance. For more on this methodology, see Riffe, Lacy, and Fico (1998). University of Miami School of Communication doctoral student Jesús Arroyave, a native Spanish speaker, conducted the coding. The author coded 10 percent of the data a second time, constructed the

coding instrument, and supervised data cleaning. The simple agreement (percent) and controlled agreement (Cohen's Kappa) for the television measures are as follows: tone of treatment of the actor (90.1%, 0.822); reporting assertiveness (97.6%; 0.964); and framing assertiveness (91.5%; 0.975).

3. To judge positive or negative treatment of an actor, I considered the language used to describe the actor, whether or not the actor's version of events was accepted unquestioningly as truth, and whether or not there was an implied criticism in the meaning of the language. An article containing an equivalent amount and distribution of positive and negative information about an actor was coded as "balanced." An article presenting neither positive nor negative information was coded as "neutral."

4. Quantitative assessments from earlier years are not available. Comparative data from 1994 come from Hallin (2000a). Foreign news was excluded in the calculation.

5. I used the same definition of passive and assertive coverage as in the longitudinal press analysis presented in chapter 3. I defined as examples of passive reporting news items based upon staged events, press conferences, group interviews, press releases, and letters to the editor. A mixed category included breaking news that did not come to light as part of staged interviews, reporting from public documents such as a government budget or a police report, and articles by newsmakers that were requested by the newspaper on a specific issue. Assertive reporting was defined as items that used multiple sources of information and polls conducted by newspapers.

6. News organizations interpreted the event when journalists identified issues as important and published or broadcast information about them, or when they changed the message set by a newsmaker who convoked the media to a press conference or a staged event. Similarly, they changed the frame by seeking out perspectives other than that pushed by the newsmaker, or by changing the message offered by the newsmaker. On the other hand, news organizations let outsiders determine the interpretation of an event when they followed the frame set down by newsmakers or did not take coverage of breaking news beyond the most readily available account.

7. Lara Klahr (2005) discussed *La Jornada*'s coverage of López Obrador in detail.

8. Roberto Rock and Ernesto Villanueva, personal communications with author, June 10, 2003, Mexico City. See also Escobedo (2003).

9. Roberto Rock, personal communication with author, October 30, 2003, Mexico City.

10. Statistics on the type of information requested run from June 12, 2003, through December 31, 2003. Information about petitions runs through November 24, 2003. Maria Marván (director, Federal Access to Information Institute), mimeograph given to author during interview, March 17, 2004, Mexico City.

11. Author interview with *El Universal* journalist, June 12, 2003, Mexico City. Name withheld by author, per University of Miami regulation.

12. The main attraction of *El Gráfico* prior to the redesign of the newspaper was a nude model on page 3. The model was later moved to an inside page, and a bit of clothing was added in an attempt to attract more family-oriented advertisers. While the tabloid's cover usually features a dramatic news photograph, articles focus intensely on city services and government as well as crime. The sports section is also highlighted.

13. Author interview with *La Jornada* editor, June 12, 2003, Mexico City. Name withheld by author, per University of Miami regulation.

14. I conducted the editor interviews in March 1999, June 1999, and June and July 2003, all in Mexico City. These were confidential in accordance with University of Miami policy. University of Miami doctoral student Juliet Gill conducted the reporter interviews in June and July 2003 in Mexico City. These were also confidential.

Chapter 10: Media Transformation in Comparative Perspective

1. The largest pro-Allende newspaper, *Clarín*, was quickly confiscated and shut down by the dictatorship. Its owner, Victor Pey, who spent the dictatorship in exile, filed a suit for millions of dollars in compensation once he returned in 1990. His claim included two downtown buildings and printing presses used by the *El Mercurio* chain. See León Dermota (2003, 5, 6, 59).

2. León Dermota (2003) provides a detailed account of the regime's financial and philosophical overlap with the two companies that now dominate Chilean newspapers, *El Mercurio* and *La Tercera*.

3. Germani reports circulation at 55,000 one month after the opening. Alves puts *La Epoca*'s circulation at 25,000 on weekdays at the end of the dictatorship. Vanden Heuvel and Dennis place circulation at 50,000 in 1994, but by then the *La Tercera* chain COPESA owned 50 percent of the newspaper. See Alves (1997) and Vanden Heuvel and Dennis (1995, 123).

4. Other publications that opposed the regime but were weekly or had lower circulation included *Hoy, Apsi, Cauce, Análisis*, and the working-class newspaper *Fortín Mapocho*. Alves identifies some of these publications as more openly ideological than *La Epoca*, but all were oppositional and several produced hard-hitting investigations that would astound Chilean journalism today. *Cauce*'s circulation rose to 25,000 near the end of the dictatorship when it produced exposés on Pinochet's posh mansions and his wife's business deals. *Cauce* reporter Mónica Gónzalez described the Pinochet mansion at El Melocotón with detail after sixty interviews. She was jailed repeatedly for her reporting. Diplomats and journalists believed in 1987 that all opposition publications together reached 100,000, about the same as the daily circulation of *El Mercurio*'s flagship newspaper. The company owned fourteen newspapers in 1999, up from eight before the coup. See Léon Dermota (2003, 23–33, 55), Bridges (1987b), Alves (1997), and Ungar (1988).

5. Alejandra Matus, interview by author, July 20, 2005, via telephone, Santiago/Miami.

6. See also Alves (1997), Bresnahan (2003), and Otano and Sunkel (2003).

7. Matus, interview, July 20, 2005.

8. Matus, interview, July 20, 2005. See also "Diario Siete" (2005).

9. Matus, interview, July 20, 2005.

10. See also Vincent (1992), Millman (1992), and Alves (1997).

11. The quote attributed to Saint-Jean, the military governor of Buenos Aires during the dictatorship, appears in several sources. *The Columbia World of Citations* attributes it to a bulletin of the Mothers of the Plaza de Mayo, vol. 1, no. 4 (May 1985). See Andrews, Biggs, and Seidel (1996). Also quoted in Knudson (1997, 93).

12. The upward adjustment was made after *Página/12* exposés in March 1995 on military teams dumping drugged prisoners out of aircraft into the ocean. The interviews are republished in Verbitsky (1996).

13. A fifty-thousand-page report by the National Commission on the Disappearance of Persons led to the successful prosecution of five junta members in 1985. They were later pardoned. The quote, from page 367 of the report, is cited in Knudson (1997). See also Ward (1983); CONADEP (1984).

14. *Clarín*, October 23, 1982, cited in Knudson (1997, 101).

15. Jorge Lanata (founder, *Página/12*), interviews by author, July 27, 2005 and August 2, 2005, via e-mail, Buenos Aires/Miami. All statements by Lanata in the following paragraphs are taken from these interviews.

16. Lanata, interview, July 27, 2005. See also Wiñazki (2005).

17. Lanata, interview, July 27, 2005.

18. José Rubén Zamora, interview by author, October 7, 2004, Guatemala City.

19. Zamora, interview, October 7, 2004.

REFERENCES

Academia Mexicana de Derechos Humanos. 1994. *Imágines intencionadas: Las elecciones de 1994* [Intentional images: The 1994 elections]. Mexico City: Mexican Human Rights Academy.

Acosta Valverde, M. 1996. Equidad en TV [Equity on TV]. *La Jornada,* May 5, 1996. http://www.jornada.unam.mx/1996/may96/960510/VALVEPOP-067.html (accessed July 5, 2004).

———. 1998. Television coverage of the 1994 and 1997 elections: A new attitude? Paper presented at the conference "Mexican Media in Transition," sponsored by the Roger Thayer Stone Center for Latin American Studies, Tulane University, New Orleans, January.

Adler, I. 1993a. The Mexican case: The media in the 1988 presidential election. In *Television, politics, and the transition to democracy in Latin America,* ed. T. Skidmore, 158–62. Baltimore: The Johns Hopkins University Press.

———. 1993b. Press-government relations in Mexico: A study of freedom of the Mexican press and press criticism of government institutions. *Studies in Latin American Popular Culture* 12:1–30.

Adler Lomnitz, L., C. Lomnitz, and I. Adler. 1990. El fondo de la forma: La campaña presidencial del PRI en 1988 [The foundation of the form: The PRI presidential campaign in 1988]. *Nueva Antropología* XI (38): 45–82.

Aguayo, S. 1995. A Mexican milestone. *Journal of Democracy* 6 (2): 157–67.

Aguayo, S., and M. Acosta. 1995. *Urnas y pantallas: La batalla por la información* [Ballot boxes and televisión screens: The battle for information]. México, D.F.: Oceano.

Agüero, F. 2003. Chile. Unfinished transition and increased political competition. In *Constructing democratic governance in Latin America,* 2nd ed., ed. J. I. Dominguez and M. Shifter. Baltimore: The Johns Hopkins University Press.

Aguilar, R. 2002. Disputa Coca vs. Pepsi por mercado mexicano [Coke fights Pepsi for the Mexican market]. *El Universal,* December 30. http://www.eluniversal.com.mx (accessed January 17, 2004).

Aguilar Zinser, A. 1995. *¡Vamos a ganar! La pugna de Cuauhtémoc Cárdenas por el poder* [We're going to win! Cuauhtémoc Cárdenas's struggle for power]. México, D.F.: Oceano.

Albarrán de Alba, G. 1994. Zabludovsky pone a "24 horas" al servicio de la 'promoción accelerada' de la imagen de Zedillo [Zabludovsky puts "24 hours" at the service of the "accelerated promotion" of Zedillo's image]. *Proceso,* July 2.

———. 1997. Frente a las elecciones, las grandes televisoras oscilan entre la equidad y la manipulación para beneficiar al PRI [With elections looming, the big networks oscillate between equity and manipulation to benefit the PRI]. *Proceso,* June 22.

———. 2001. Rafael Cardona, la exdirector de "Unomásuno", denuncia los intereses extraperiodísticos de Manuel Alonso [Rafael Cardona, former editor of *Unomásuno,* denounces the extra-journalistic interests of Manuel Alonso]. *Proceso,* April 14. www.proceso.com.mx (accessed December 18, 2005).

Alemán Alemán, R. 1996. Conflicto en Televisa por el video de Aguas Blancas. ¿Incomoda al gobierno el nuevo concepto informativo? [Conflict in Televisa for the Aguas Blancas video. Does the new concept make the government uncomfortable?] *La Jornada,* March 15. www.jornada.unam.mx (accessed May 1, 1999).

Altheide, D. 1996. *Qualitative media analysis.* Qualitative Research Methods Series. Thousand Oaks, CA: Sage Publications.

Altschull, J. H. 1984. *Agents of power: The role of the news media in human affairs.* New York: Longman.

Alva de la Selva, A. R. 1999. Panorama de la TV Mexicana durante 1998. Entre la crisis financiera y la guerra de los ratings televisivos [Panorama of Mexican TV during 1998. Between the financial crisis and the television ratings wars]. *Revista Mexicana de la Comunicación* 57 (1). www.fundacionbuendia.org.mx (accessed May 26, 2001).

Alves, R. 1997. Democracy's vanguard newspapers in Latin America. Paper presented at the 47th annual conference of the International Communication Association, Montreal, May 22–26.

Anderson, L. 1997. He got the story and then the story got him. *New York Times Sunday Magazine,* December 21.

Andrews, R., M. Biggs, and M. Seidel. 1996. *The Columbia world of citations.* New York: Columbia University Press.

Ansolobehere, S., R. Behr, and S. Iyengar. 1993. *The media game: American politics in the television age.* New York: Allyn and Bacon.

Aponte, D. 2005. Abrió Creel a Televisa negocio de apuestas [Creel opened the gambling business to Televisa]. *El Universal,* June 10.

Arredondo Ramírez, P. 1990. Los noticieros de televisión y la sucesión presidencial de 1988 [The television news and the presidential succession of 1988]. In *Medios, Democracia y Fines,* 47–79. México, D.F.: UNAM.

Arreola, F. 2000. Busco hacer de Televisa un líder mundial [I seek to make Televisa a world leader]. *Milenio Semanal,* June 25. http://www.milenio.com/semanal/146/en2 .htm (accessed July 9, 2004).

Arroyave, J., and S. Hughes. 2004. Wither the public sphere? The tabloidization of Mexican television news. Paper presented at the Broadcast Education Association National Conference, Las Vegas, Nevada, April 15–18.

Asociación Mexicana de Agencias de Publicidad [AMAP]. 1992, 1994. *Media data México.* México D.F.: Asociación Mexicana de Agencias de Publicidad.

Assant, C. E. 1997. *Press freedom and development. A research guide and selected bibliography.* Westport, CT.: Greenwood Press.

Audiffred, M. 2005. El reality show de concesionarios [The concessionaires' reality show]. *La Revista/El Universal,* February 21.

Avritzer, L. 1997. Introduction: The meaning and employment of "civil society" in Latin America. *Constellations* 4 (1): 88–93.

Ayala, A. 1999. Novedades de colores [Novedades in color]. *Adcebra* 8 (92): 1.

Báez Rodríguez, F. 1999. Difusiones. Stanley y el quinto poder [Diffusions: Stanley and the fifth power]. *Etcétera*, June 17.

Bailey, J. 1988. *Governing Mexico: The statecraft of crisis management*. New York: St. Martin's Press.

Barajas, A. 2005. Exonera la SFP a Vidal [SFP exonerates Vidal]. *Reforma*, August 27. www.reforma.com.mx (accessed September 2, 2005).

Barham, J. 1992. Survey of Argentina. *Financial Times*, May 14.

Barraza, J. 1998. El periodista y el narco. Los retos que enfrontamos cuando cubrimos la corrupción narco-política. [The journalist and the drug trafficker. The challenges we face when we cover narco-political corruption]. Paper presented at the conference "Mexican Media in Transition," sponsored by the Roger Thayer Stone Center for Latin American Studies, Tulane University, New Orleans, January 1998.

Barrera, E. 2004. Mexico. In *The Encyclopedia of Television,* 2nd ed. Edited by Horace Newcomb. The Museum of Broadcasting/Fitzroy Dearborn Publishers. http://www .museum.tv/archives/etv/M/htmlM/mexico/mexico.htm (accessed December 19, 2005).

Bass, D. J., and M. E. Burkhardt. 1992. Centrality and power in organizations. In *Networks and organizations: Structure, form and action*, ed. N. Nohria and R. G. Eccles, 191–215. Boston: Harvard Business School Press.

Bennett, W. L. 1998. The media and democratic development: The social basis of political communication. In *Communication democracy: The media and political transitions*, ed. P. H. O'Neil, 195–207. Boulder: Lynne Rienner.

———. 2004. *News: The politics of illusion*. New York: Pearson/Longman.

Blancornelas, J. J. 2004. Los sospechosos [The suspects]. *Zeta*, June 25. http://www .zetatijuana.com/edicion/edicion.html (accessed July 1, 2004).

Boas, T. 2005. Television and neopopulism in Latin America: Media effects in Brazil and Peru. *Latin American Research Review* 40 (2): 27–49.

Bohmann, K. 1989. Medios de comunicación y sistemas informativos en México [Communication media and information systems in Mexico]. Trans. A. Zenker. México, D.F.: Alianza Editorial.

Bordon, A. and É. Hernández. 2004. Justifica Provida gasto con facturas alteradas [Provida justifies expenses with altered receipts]. *Reforma*, July 14.

Bourdieu, P. 1977. *Outline of a theory of practice*. New York: Cambridge University Press.

Bresnahan, R. 2003. The media and democracy in Chile: Democratic promise unfulfilled. *Latin American Perspectives* 30 (6): 39–68.

Bridges, T. 1987a. Pinochet seen to relax some control by allowing new play on torture. *Christian Science Monitor*, October 27.

———. 1987b. Political apathy may put Chilean opposition paper out of business. *Washington Post*, November 17.

Brint, S., and J. Karabel. 1991. The institutional origins and transformations: The case of American community colleges. In Powell and DiMaggio 1991, 337–360.

Bruhn, K. 1997. *Taking on Goliath: The emergence of a new Left party and the struggle for democracy in Mexico*. University Park: Pennsylvania State University Press.

Bucio, E. P. 2004. Arturo Pérez Reverte: 'Prefiero ser lúcido a imbécil' [Arturo Pérez Reverte: I prefer to be lucid than an imbecile]. *Reforma*, March 9.

Bureau for International Narcotics and Law Enforcement Affairs. U.S. Department of State. 2003. *International Narcotics Control Strategy Report 2002.* Washington DC.

Bureau of Western Hemisphere Affairs. U.S. Department of State. 2004. *Background Note: Guatemala.* Washington DC.

Butler, E. W., and J. A. Bustamante, eds. 1991. *Sucesión presidencial: The 1988 Mexican presidential election.* Boulder: Westview Press.

Camp, R. A. 1986. *Intellectuals and the state in twentieth century Mexico.* Latin American Monographs 65. Austin: University of Texas Press.

———. 1997. *Crossing swords: Politics and religion in Mexico.* New York: Oxford University Press.

———. 2002a. *Mexico's mandarins, crafting a power elite for the 21st century.* Berkeley: University of California Press.

———. 2002b. *Politics in Mexico. The democratic transformation.* New York: Oxford University Press.

Carter Center. 1994. *Elections in Mexico: Third report.* Atlanta: Carter Center.

Casas Zamora, K. 2004. Media discounts for politicians: Examples from Latin America. In *Global Corruption Report,* 49–50: London: Transparency International.

Casillas Bermúdez, K. M., and S. Frausto Crotte. 1998. Parcialidad en el manejo informativo del noticiero 24 horas en los procesos electorales de 1988 y 1994 [Partiality in the information management of 24 hour news in electoral processes of 1988 and 1994]. Bachelor's thesis, Universidad Tecnológica de México.

Casteñeda, S. 2003. Spots políticos impulsan gasto en TV y radio [Political spots stimulate spending on TV and radio]. *Advertising Age en español/ El Asesor,* June. www.elasesor.com.mx/adage1/noticia2.html (accessed January 15, 2004).

Castillo, A. 2003. "Es mejor, he, he, mejor", comenta Vicente Fox a mujeres que le dijeron que no sabían leer ["It's better, ha, ha," Vicente Fox tells women who told him they don't know how to read]. *La Crónica,* February 12. www.cronica.com.mx (accessed July 28, 2004).

Centeno, M. A., and P. Silva. 1997. *The politics of expertise in Latin America.* New York: St. Martin's Press.

Chand, V. K. 2001. *Mexico's political awakening.* Notre Dame, IN: University of Notre Dame Press.

Christian, S. 1987. Opposition paper launches in Chile. *New York Times,* March 19.

Christie, M. 1999. Mexican newspapers face overdue shake-up. *Reuters News Wire,* November 23.

Cisneros Morales, J. 1999. Un "error", el reproche de Guillermo Ortega a Medina Plascencia, admite Azcárraga. Televisa apuesta al cambio y se compromete a alentar la pluralidad, asegura el empresario [An "error," Guillermo Ortega's rebuke of Medina Plascencia, Azcárraga admits. Televisa bets on change and promises to promote pluralism, assures the businessman]. *La Jornada,* September 7. http://www.jornada.unam.mx/1999/sep99/990907/azcarraga.html (accessed June 1, 2000).

Committee to Protect Journalists. 2005. *Attacks on the press in 2004: Argentina.* New York: Committee to Protect Journalists.

CONADEP (Comisión nacional sobre la desaparicion de personas). 1984. *Nunca más. Informe de la Comisión nacional sobre la desaparición de personas* [Never again. Report of the National commision on the disappearance of persons]. Buenos Aires: Editorial Universitaria de Buenos Aires.

Cook, L., K. Middlebrook, and J. Molinar. 1994. The politics of economic restructuring in Mexico: Actors, sequencing and coalitional change. In *The politics of economic restructuring: State-Society relations and regime change in Mexico*, ed. L. Cook, K. Middlebrook, and J. Molinar, 1–45. La Jolla: Center for U.S.-Mexico Studies, University of California, San Diego.

Cook, T. E. 1998. *Governing with the news: The news media as a political institution.* Chicago: The University of Chicago Press.

Cornelius, W. A. 1987. Political liberalization in an authoritarian regime: Mexico, 1976–1985. In *Mexican politics in transition*, ed. J. Gentleman, 15–40. Boulder: Westview Press.

———. 1996. *Mexican politics in transition: The breakdown of a one-party dominant regime.* La Jolla: Center for U.S.-Mexico Studies, University of California, San Diego.

Cornelius, W. A., A. L. Craig, and J. Fox., eds. 1994. *Transforming state-society relations in Mexico: The national solidarity strategy.* La Jolla: Center for U.S.-Mexico Studies, University of California, San Diego.

Corro, S. 1994. De los gobiernos Priístas, Emilio Azcárraga ha recibido todos los favores y, como Priísta confeso, sabe ser agradecido [From the PRI governments, Emilio Azcárrage has received all the favors, and as a PRI member confesses he knows how to be appreciative]. *Proceso*, July 2.

———. 2003. Ealy Ortiz supervisará a la PGR [Ealy Ortiz will supervise the Attorney General's office]. *Proceso*, July 13.

Curran, J. 2000. Rethinking media and democracy. In *Mass media and society*, 3rd ed., ed. J. Curran and M. Gurevitch, 120–53. New York: Oxford University Press.

Curran, J., and M. Park. 2000a. Beyond globalization theory. In Curran and Park 2000b, 3–18.

———. eds. 2000b. *De-westernizing media studies.* London: Routledge.

Delgado, Á. 1996. La 'primavera de Televisa', Efímera: Azcárraga se plegó y Burillo dijo adíos [Ephemeral "springtime for Televisa": Azcárraga retreated and Burillo said goodbye]. *Proceso*, March 25.

De Uriarte, M. L. 2003. Diversity disconnects: From classroom to newsroom. A research report funded by the Ford Foundation. With Cristina Bodinger de Uriarte and Jose Luis Benevides. www.journalism.utexas.edu/faculty/deuriarte/diversity_disconnects.pdf (accessed December 19, 2005).

Diamond, L. 1992. Introduction: Civil society and the struggle for democracy. In *The Democratic Revolution: Struggles for Freedom and Pluralism*, ed. L. Diamond, 1–25. New York: Freedom House.

———. 1999. *Developing democracy: Toward consolidation.* Baltimore: The Johns Hopkins University Press.

"Diario Siete" debuta manana en los kioskos de jaguarlandia ["Diario Siete" debuts tomorrow in the kiosks of jaguarlandia]. 2005. *La Cuarta*, January 20. http://www.lacuarta.cl/diario/2005/01/20/20.06.4a.CRO.DIARIO.html.

Díaz Redondo, R. 2002. *La gran mentira ocurrió en Excélsior* [The big lie happened in *Excélsior*]. México, D.F.: Libros Para Todos.

DiMaggio, P. J. and W. W. Powell. 1991a. Introduction. In Powell and DiMaggio 1991, 1–38.

———. 1991b. The iron cage revisited: Institutional isomorphism and collective rationality in organizational fields. In Powell and DiMaggio 1991, 41–62.

Dinges, J. 2005. Letter from Caracas. Soul Search. *Columbia Journalism Review* 44 (2): 52–58. http://www.cjr.org/issues/2005/4/dinges.asp (accessed September 5, 2005).

Directorio de Medios Electrónicos. 2001. México, D.F.: Medios Publicitarios.

Domínguez, J. I., ed. 1997. *Technopols, free politics and markets in Latin American in the 1990s.* University Park: Penn State University Press.

Dresser, D. 1994. Bringing the poor back in: National solidarity as a strategy of regime legitimation. In *Transforming state-society relations in Mexico: The national solidarity strategy,* ed. W. A. Cornelius, A. L. Craig, and J. Fox, 143–65. La Jolla, CA: Center for U.S.-Mexico Studies, University of California, San Diego.

Dzur, A. W. 2002. Public Journalism and deliberative democracy. *Polity* 34 (3): 313–24.

Edición Conmemorativa 1951–2001. 2001. *Prensa Libre,* August 20.

Eisenstadt, S. N. 1968. Social institutions. In *International encyclopedia of the social sciences,* ed. David Sills, vol. 14, 409–41. New York: MacMillan Company.

El Universal, Compañía Periodística Nacional, SA de CV. 1994. *Los designos del futuro. El Universal. 25 años decisivos* [Designs for the future: El Universal. 25 decisive years]. Mexico: El Universal.

El Universal. 1998. 82 Aniversario [82nd anniversary]. Pamphlet.

Entman, R. 1989. *Democracy without citizens: The media and the decay of American politics.* New York: Oxford University Press.

Epstein, E. J. 1973. *News from nowhere: Television and the news.* New York: Random House.

Escobedo, J. F. 2003. Movilización de opinión pública en México: El caso del Grupo Oaxaca y de la ley federal de acceso a la información pública [Mobilization of Mexican public opinion: The case of the Oaxaca Group and the Federal Access to Public Information Law]. *Felafacs: Diálogos de la Comunicación* 66 (June): 16–28.

Fernández, C. 1998. Media ethics in Mexico: Constructing a new culture. Paper presented at the conference "Mexican Media in Transition," sponsored by the Roger Thayer Stone Center for Latin American Studies, Tulane University, New Orleans, January.

———. 1999. Más allá de la filtración [Beyond leaks]. Paper presented at the Third Summit of Partners in the Americas, San Antonio, TX, August 18–21.

———. 2000. ¿Qué tan derecha es la prensa Mexicana? Un análisis sobre los detonadores, los marcos y los mensajes en la cobertura periodística en México [How fair is the Mexican press? An analysis of the detonators, frames and messages in news coverage in Mexico]. Report prepared for the Fourth Summit of Partners in the Americas conference, Puerto Vallarta, Mexico, August 9–12.

———. 2001. Emilio Azcárraga Jean. *Revista Poder,* August 21.

Fernández, C., and A. Paxman. 2000. *El tigre: Emilio Azcárraga y su imperio Televisa* [The tiger: Emilio Azcárraga and his Televisa empire]. México, D.F.: Editorial Grijalbo.

Fernández Christlieb, F. 1985. *Los medios de difusión masivos en México* [The mass communication media in Mexico]. México, D.F.: Juan Pablos Editor.

Ferráez, J., and R. Ferráez. 2003. En la rotativa con Juan Francisco Ealy Ortiz [On the press floor with Juan Francisco Ealy Ortiz]. *Líderes Mexicanos* 12 (68): 59–64.

Fiestejan a Ángel Trinidad Ferreira [They celebrate Ángel Trinidad Ferreira]. 2003. *El Universal,* July 6.

Fligstein, N. 1991. The structural transformation of American industry: An institutional account of the causes of diversification in the largest firms, 1919–1979. In Powell and DiMaggio 1991, 311–35.

Flor Zapler, E. 2005. La inversión en el periodismo de investigación en America Latina [The investment in investigative journalism in Latin America]. University of Miami, School of Communication.

Foweraker, J., and R. Krznaric. 2002. The uneven performance of third wave democracies: Electoral politics and the imperfect rule of law in Latin America. *Latin American Politics and Society* 44 (3): 29–60.

Fox, E., and S. Waisbord, eds. 2002. *Latin politics, global media.* Austin: University of Texas Press.

Fox, J. 1994. The difficult transition from clientelism to citizenship: Lessons from Mexico. *World Politics* 46 (2): 151–84.

Fox, V. 2000. Presidential inaugural address. December 1. http://www.presidencia.gob. mx (accessed November 31, 2000).

Fromson, M. 1996. Mexico's struggle for a free press. In *Communication in Latin America: Journalism, mass media and society,* ed. R. Cole, 115–37. Wilmington, DE: Jaguar.

Fuentes, V. 2004. Abren al acceso a casos judiciales [They open access to judicial cases]. *Reforma,* July 18. www.reforma.com (accessed July 18, 2004).

Gallo, D. 2004a. Amor por encargo: El gobierno usa 80 millones en avisos para presionar a medios y conseguir oficialismo [Love by order: The government uses 80 million in ads to pressure the media and obtain *oficialismo*]. *Noticias,* March 7.

———. 2004b. Domesticados: Por qué los rebeldes de ayer se volvieron dóceles con el kirschnerismo [Domesticated: Why yesterday's rebels have become docile under Kirschner]. *Noticias,* October 16.

Gans, H. J. 1979. *Deciding what's news: A study of CBS Evening News, NBC Nightly News, Time and Newsweek.* New York: Vintage.

Garcia, J. E. 1993. Crackdown on press continues in Guatemala. *New Orleans Times-Picayune,* May 29.

Germani, C. 1987. Chile's new paper risks "opposition" labor by printing all the news. *Christian Science Monitor,* April 10.

Giddens, Anthony. 1984. *The constitution of society: Outline of a theory of structuration.* Berkeley: University of California Press.

Gil Olmos, J. 2003. 'Marketing' electoral: El 2000 al revés [Electoral "marketing": 2000 reversed]. *Proceso,* July 13. http://www.proceso.com.mx/archivocomint. html?nid=4265 (accessed October 19, 2000).

Giménez, R., and V. Romero. 1997a. Mantiene Cárdenas paso hacia el triunfo [Cárdenas maintains path towards triumph]. *Reforma,* June 18. www.reforma.com (accessed June 25, 2004).

———. 1997b. Se despega Cárdenas en DF [Cárdenas takes off in the DF]. *Reforma,* April 24. www.reforma.com (accessed June 25, 2004).

———. 1997c. Aventaja el PRD por imágen de Cárdenas [PRD advantage because of Cárdenas' image]. *Reforma,* April 24. www.reforma.com (accessed June 25, 2004).

———. 1997d. Revierte PRD tendencia [PRD tendency comes back]. *Reforma,* March 6. www.reforma.com (accessed July 11, 2004).

Glasser, T. L., ed. 1999. *The idea of public journalism*. New York: The Guilford Press.

Glasser, T. L., and F. L. F. Lee. 2002. Repositioning the newsroom: The American experience with 'public journalism'. In *Political journalism. New challenges, new practices*, ed. Raymund Kuhn and Erik Neveu, 203–24. London: Routledge.

Goldman, F. 2003. Guatemala's fictional democracy. *New York Times*, November 3.

Gómez, F., and J. Martínez. 2004. Caso Ortiz Franco: Blancornelas duda que el gobierno aclare crimen [The Ortiz Franco Case: Blancornelas doubts that the government will clear up the crime]. *El Universal*, July 1.

González, R. 2000. 'Chato' Ochoa: La crisis tiene nombres. Hoy, hondradez. El diario saldrá adelante. Apoya la sociedad su rescate, manifiesta ['Chato' Ochoa: The crisis has names. Today, honor. The newspaper will go forward. Society manifests support]. *Excélsior*, October 23.

Grabe, M. E. 1997. Tabloid and traditional television news magazine crime stories: Crime lessons and reaffirmation of social class distinctions. *Journalism & Mass Communication Quarterly* 73:926–946.

Grabe, M. E., S. Zhou, and B. Barnett. 2001. Explicating sensationalism in television news: Content and the bells and whistles of form. *Journal of Broadcasting & Electronic Media* 45 (4): 635–55.

Grabe, M. E., S. Zhou, A. Lang, and P. Bolls. 2000. Packaging television news: The effects of tabloid on information processing and evaluative responses. *Journal of Broadcasting & Electronic Media* 44 (4): 581–598.

Graber, D. 2004. Mediated politics and citizenship in the twenty-first century. *Annual Review of Psychology*: 545–571.

Graham, B. 1987. Despite liberalization, free speech severely restricted in Chile. *Washington Post*, December 5.

Gramsci, A. 1975. *Letters from prison*. New York: Harper and Row.

Gross, K., and S. Aday. 2003. The scary world in your living room and neighborhood: Using local broadcast news, neighborhood crime rates, and personal experience to test agenda setting and cultivation. *Journal of Communication* 53 (3): 411–26.

Guillermoprieto, A. 1991. Letter from Buenos Aires. *New Yorker* (July 15): 64–78.

Gutiérrez, M. 1998. *Violencia en Guerrero* [Violence in Guerrero]. México D.F.: La Jornada Ediciones.

Haas, T. 1999. What's 'public' about public journalism? Public journalism and the lack of a coherent public philosophy. *Communication Theory* 9 (3): 346–364.

Haber, P. L. 1994. The art and implications of political restructuring in Mexico: The case of urban popular movements. In *The politics of economic restructuring: State-society relations and regime change in Mexico*, ed. L. Cook, K. Middlebrook, and J. Molinar, 277–303. La Jolla: Center for U.S.-Mexico Studies, University of California, San Diego.

Habermas, J. 1989a. The public sphere. In *Critical theory and society: A reader*, ed. S. E. Bronner and D. M. Kellner, 136–44. New York: Routledge.

———. 1989b. *The structural transformation of the public sphere. An inquiry into a category of bourgeois society*. Trans. T. Burger. Cambridge, MA: MIT Press.

Hachten, W. A., and H. Hachten. 1996. *The world news prism: Changing media of international communication*. Ames: Iowa University Press.

Hall, P. A., and R. Taylor. 1996. Political science and the three new institutionalisms. *Political Studies* XLIV:936–57.

Hallin, D. C. 1994a. Dos instituciones, un camino: Television and the state in the 1994 Mexican election. Paper presented at the XIX Annual Congress of the Latin American Studies Association, Washington DC, September.

———. 1994b. *We keep America on top of the world. Television journalism and the public sphere.* New York: Routledge.

———. 2000a. Commercialism and professionalism in the American news media. In *Mass media and society*, 2nd ed., ed. J. Curran and M. Gurevitch, 218–37. New York: St. Martin's Press.

———. 2000b. *La nota roja:* Popular journalism and the transition to democracy in Mexico. In *Tabloid tales: Global debates and media standards*, ed. C. Sparks and J. Tulloch, 267–82. New York: Rowman and Littlefield.

Hallin, D. C., and P. Mancini. 2004. Americanization, globalization, and secularization: Understanding the convergence of media systems and political communication. In *Comparing political communication: Theories, cases and challenges*, ed. Pfetsch and Esser 2004, 25–44.

Hannon, M. T., and J. Freeman. 1987. The ecology of organizational founding: American labor unions, 1836–1985. *American Sociological Review* 49:149–64.

Hernández, Anabel, and Areli Quíntero. 2005. *La familia presidencial. El gobierno de cambio bajo sospecha de corrupción* [The presidential family. The government of change under suspicion of corruption]. Mexico, D.F.: Grijalbo.

Hewlett Foundation. 1998. Visión latinoamericana de la democracia: Encuestas de opinion pública en Mexico, Chile y Costa Rica. Reporte final [Latin American vision of democracy: Public opinion surveys in Mexico, Chile and Costa Rica. Final Report], October 20. Hewlett Foundation: R. Camp.

Hughes, S. 1994. Shackled together: Biased campaign coverage highlights government control of media. *El Financiero International Edition*, July 11–17.

———. 1995a. A family's value: Huge bank deposits further blacken the Salinas name. *Maclean's*, December 11.

———. 1995b. Feeding the rich: How a government food program meant to benefit the poor was used and abused by the Salinas administration and big business. *Mexico Business* (September): 62–67.

———. 1995c. Irate Mexican voters hand ruling party a stinging loss. *Miami Herald*, February 14.

———. 2003. From the inside out: How institutional entrepreneurs transformed Mexican journalism. *Harvard International Journal of Press/Politics* 8 (3): 87–117.

———. 2005. The politician in prime-time: Democratic accountability, journalistic verification and the rise of infotainment programming on Mexican broadcast television. Paper presented at the 55th Annual Conference of the International Communication Association, New York City, May 26–30.

———. 2006. The role of the Latin American news media in the policymaking process. Working paper produced for *The 2006 Report on Economic and Social Progress in Latin America*. Washington DC: Inter-American Development Bank.

Hughes, S., and C. Lawson. 2004. Propaganda and crony capitalism: Partisan bias in Mexican television news. *Latin American Research Review* 39 (3): 81–105.

Imágenes intencionadas [Intentional images]. 1997. Mexico City: Mexican Academy of Human Rights.

Instituto Federal Electoral. Comisión de Radiodifusión. 1997. *Monitoreo de las campañas de los partidos políticos en noticiarios de radio y televisión. Acumulado total* [Monitor of campaigns of political parties in radio and television news. Total tally]. México D.F.: Instituto Federal Electoral.

———. 2000. "Elección de diputados federales por el principio de mayoría relativa" [Election of federal deputies by the principle of relative majority]. http://www.ife.org.mx/wwworge/esta2000/inidemr.htm (accessed November 1, 2001).

Intentó SG censurar spot que critica al tricolor, denuncia el PAN [SG tried to censor a spot that criticized the tricolor, the PAN denounces]. 1999. *La Jornada*, November 9.

Inter-American Press Association. 2004. *Conclusion of first meeting of working group to review Héctor Felix Miranda case.* Inter-American Press Association, April 28. http://www.impunidad.com/pressreleases/news_english_28abril2004.htm (accessed July 1, 2004).

———. 2005. *Informe preliminar de la misión de la SIP en Argentina* [Preliminary report of the IAPA mission in Argentina]. Miami: Inter-American Press Association.

Iyengar, S. 1991. *Is anyone responsible? How television frames political issues.* Chicago: University of Chicago Press.

Jakubowicz, K. 1998/99. Normative models of media and journalism and broadcasting regulation in central and eastern Europe. *International Journal of Communications Law and Policy* 2:1–32.

Jáquez, A. 2000. Testimonios desde la cúpula del régimen salinista. Alrededor del asesinato de Colosio: Intrigas, golpes bajos, chismes, insidias . . .[Testimonies from the inner circle of the Salinista regime. Around the Colosio assassination: Intrigue, low blows, rumors and malice . . .]. *Proceso*, October 21. www.proceso.com.mx (accessed October 21, 2000).

Jepperson, R. L. 1991. Institutions, Institutional Effects, and Institutionalism. In Powell and DiMaggio 1991, 143–63.

Karlekar, K. D. 2003. *Freedom of the press 2003: A global survey of media independence.* New York: Freedom House/Lanham, MA: Rowman and Littlefield.

———. 2004. *Freedom of the press 2004: A global survey of media independence.* New York: Freedom House/Lanham, MA: Rowman and Littlefield.

Knudson, J. W. 1997. Veil of silence: The Argentine press and the dirty war, 1976–1983. *Latin American Perspectives* 24 (6): 93–112.

Kurpius, D. D. 2002. Sources and civic journalism: Changing patterns of reporting? *Journalism and Mass Communication Quarterly* 79 (4): 853–866.

La censura de *El Universal* [The censorship at *El Universal*]. 2005. *Etcétera*, September. http://www.etcetera.com.mx/contene59.asp (accessed September 10, 2005).

La pregunta del millón. ¿Quién es el dueño de Página 12? [The million-dollar question: Who owns Página 12?]. 2005. La Vaca, March 3. http://www.lavaca.org/seccion/actualidad/0/301.shtml (accessed July 19, 2005).

Lara Klahr, F. 2005. *Diarísmo. Cultura e industria del periodismo impreso en México y el mundo* [Daily newspapers. Culture and industry of print journalism in Mexico and the world]. Mexico City: Editorial E.

Lawson, C. 1999. Why Cárdenas won: The 1997 elections in Mexico City. In *Mexico's democratization. Parties, campaigns, elections, and public opinion,* ed. J. I. Domínguez and A. Poiré, 147–73. New York: Routledge.

———. 2001. Television coverage, media effects, and Mexico's 2000 elections. Paper prepared for the Midwest Political Science Association conference, Chicago, April 19.

———. 2002. *Building the fourth estate: Democratization and the rise of a free press in Mexico*. Berkeley: University of California Press.

Lawson, C., and J. A. McCann. 2004. Television news, Mexico's 2000 election and media effects in emerging democracies. *British Journal of Political Science* 35:1–30.

Lawson, C., and S. Hughes. 2005. Latin America's post authoritarian media. In *Uncivil societies: Human rights and democratic transitions in Eastern Europe and Latin America*, ed. A. K. Milton and R. May, 151–86. Lanham, MD: Lexington Books.

Leñero, V. 1978. *Los periodistas* [The journalists]. México, D.F.: Joaquín Mortiz.

León Dermota, K. 2003. *And well tied down: Chile's press under democracy*. Westport, CT: Praeger.

Levario Turcott, M. L. 1999. Primera plana: El último show con Paco Stanley [Front-page: Paco Stanley's last show]. *Etcétera*, June 17. http://www.etcetera.com. mx/mlt333ne3.asp (accessed October 20, 2005).

Levitsky, S. 2003. Argentina: From crisis to consolidation (and back). In *Constructing democratic governance in Latin America*, ed. J. I. Domínguez and M. Shifter, 244–68. Baltimore: The Johns Hopkins University Press.

Levy, D. C. and Bruhn, K. 2002. *Mexico: The struggle for democratic development*. Berkeley: University of California Press.

Levy, D. C. and Székely, G. 1987. *Mexico: Paradoxes of stability and change*. Boulder: Westview Press.

Lira, C. 1999. Periodismo y poder [Journalism and power]. *La Jornada*, September 20. www.jornada.unam.mx (accessed October 1, 2000).

López, L. E. 1996. Televisión: Sí, aún hay más [Television: Yes, there's still more]. *Reforma*, January 22. www.reforma.com (accessed June 21, 2004).

López, Mayolo. 2005. Dan en la TV rebaja a Creel [They give Creel a discount on TV]. *Reforma*, July 22.

López Obrador, A. M. 1995. *Entre la historia y la esperanza: Corrupción y lucha democrática en Tabasco* [Between history and hope: Corruption and the democratic fight in Tabasco]. México, D.F.: Grijalbo.

Lukes, S. 1974. *Power: A radical view*. New York: Macmillan.

Lustig, N. 1992. *Mexico: The remaking of an economy*. Washington DC: The Brookings Institution.

Mainwaring, S. 1999. Democratic survivability in Latin America. In *Democracy and its limits: Lessons from Asia, Latin America, and the Middle East*, ed. H. Handelman and M. Tessler, 11–68. Notre Dame, IN: University of Notre Dame Press.

Martínez, S., and F. Ortega Pizarro. 2000. Inversión estimada en 10 millones de dólares: Mansión de Díaz Redondo, en la zona más cara de Madrid [Investment estimated at 10 million dollars: Díaz Redondo's mansion, in Madrid's most expensive zone]. *Proceso*, November 26. www.proceso.com.mx (accessed November 27, 2000).

Martínez, V. T., A. Pineda, and O. R. Martínez. 1999. *Recuento de daños a las libertades de expresión e información durante 1998* [Review of damage to freedom of expression and information during 1998]. México, D.F.: Fundación Manuel Buendía, A.C.

Martínez, V. T., M. Soto, and O. R. Martínez. 2004. *Recuento de daños a las libertades de expresión e información durante 2003* [Review of damage to free expression and information during 2003]. México, D.F.: Fundación Manuel Buendía, A.C. http://mexicanadecomunicacion.com.mx (accessed July 28, 2004).

McAdam, D. 1982. *Political process and the development of Black insurgency, 1930–1970.* Chicago: University of Chicago Press.

McChesney, R. W. 2000. *Rich media, poor democracy: Communication politics in dubious times.* New York: The New Press.

McDevitt, M. 2003. In defense of autonomy: A critique of the public journalism critique. *Journal of Communication* 53 (1): 155–64.

McLeod, D., G. M. Kosicki, and J. M. McLeod. 2002. Resurveying the boundaries of political communication effects. In *Media effects: Advances in theory and research*, 2nd ed., ed. J. Bryan and D. Zillman, 215–67. Mahwah, NJ: Lawrence Erlbaum Associates.

McManus, J. H. 1994. *Market-driven journalism: Let the citizen beware?* Thousand Oaks, CA: Sage.

McNair, B. 1998. *The sociology of journalism.* London: Arnold.

McQuail, D. 1987. *Mass communication theory: An introduction.* London: Sage

———. 2000. *McQuail's mass communication theory.* London: Sage.

Medina, H. 1995a. The Americas. *Forbes* 164 (1): 202.

———. 1995b. Lugar en ventas: 447; en rentabilidad: 2 [Sales ranking: 447, in profits: 2]. *Reforma*, July 20. www.reforma.com.mx (accessed January 15, 2004).

Mejía Barquera, F. 1995. Echoes of Mexican media in 1993. *Mexican Journal of Communication* 2. www.mexicanadecomunicacion.com.mx (accessed February 15, 2006).

———. 1999. Intermedios [Intermission]. *Etcétera*, June 17, 1999. http://www.etcetera.com.mx/2000/391/fmb391.html (accessed October 19, 2005).

———. 2003. Concesiones de radio y TV: 2004, año crucial [Radio and TV concessions: 2004, a crucial year]. *Etcétera*, September 12. http://www.etcetera.com.mx/pagmejia1ne35.asp (accessed July 28, 2004).

Meraz, C., and T. C. del Rio. 1995. '24 horas.' 25 años de marcar el tiempo ["24 hours": 25 years of marking time]. *Reforma*, September 7.

Middlebrook, K. J., ed. 2002. *Party politics and the struggle for democracy in Mexico.* La Jolla: Center for U.S.-Mexico Studies, University of California, San Diego.

Millman, J. 1992. Argentina: A fix on corruption. *Columbia Journalism Review* 31 (1): 52–53.

Milton, A. K. 2001. Bound but not gagged: Media reform in democratic transitions. *Comparative Political Studies* 34 (5): 493–526.

Molina, G. 1987. Mexican television news: The imperatives of corporate rationale. *Media, Culture and Society* 8 (2): 159–87

Monsiváis, C. 2003. Señor presidente: A usted no le da vergüenza su grandeza? [Mr. President: Doesn't your grandeur shame you?] In *Tiempo de saber. Prensa y poder en México*, ed. J. Scherer García and C. Monsiváis, 99–337. México, D.F.: Nuevo Siglo/Aguilar.

Montalbano, W. D. 1987. Young newspaper tests limits of Chile's dictatorship. *Los Angeles Times*, May 17.

Montes, G. I. 2005. El semanario de El Universal censura reportajes. *Zócala: Comunicación, Política, Sociedad,* September. http://www.periodicozocalo.com.mx/ (accessed September 9, 2005).

Moreno, A. 2001. The effects of negative campaigns on Mexican voters. Paper prepared for the Congress the Latin American Studies Association, Washington DC, September 6.

———. 2003. *El votante mexicano: Democracia, actitudes políticas y conducta electoral* [The Mexican voter: Democracy, political attitudes and electoral behavior]. México, D.F.: Fonda de Cultura Económica.

Moreno Garavilla, J. 1993. Jorge Castañeda Gutman: ¿Académico o provocador del PRD y organizador de campañas contra México en Estados Unidos? [Jorge Castañeda Gutman: Academic or PRD provocateur and organizer of anti-Mexico campaigns in the United States?]. *El Financiero*, October 26.

Morris, S. D. 1995. *Political reformism in Mexico: An overview of contemporary Mexican politics*. Boulder: Lynne Rienner Publishers.

MUND Américas. 2003. Latinobarometer: Results from Latin America and Mexico. Opinion Report 3 (12): 1–2. www.mundamericas.com (accessed June 27, 2004).

Ochoa, E. C., and T. D. Wilson. 2001. Introduction. *Latin American Perspectives* 28 (118): 5–6.

O'Donnell, G. 1998. Horizontal accountability in new democracies. *Journal of Democracy* 9 (3): 112–26.

O'Donnell, G., and P. Schmitter. 1986. *Transitions from authoritarian rule: Tentative conclusions about uncertain democracies. Themes and Issues*. Baltimore: Johns Hopkins University Press.

Olivera, A. J. 1997. Civil society and the political transition in Mexico. *Constellations* 4 (1): 105–23.

Omiten noticieros de TV la respuesta de Medina: Rechaza panista haber injuriado al presidente [Medina's response was omitted from TV news: PAN member rejects having injured the president]. 1999. *Reforma*, September 2.

Orozco, G. 1999. Encuesta/Television: Info-entretenimiento [Television survey: Infotainment]. *Reforma*, March 9.

———. 2004. Encuesta/Bajan noticieros estelares [Survey/Stellar newscasts decline]. *Reforma*, May 14. www.reforma.com (accessed June 21, 2004).

Ortega Pizarro, F. 2001. Vazquez Raña desnuda a Díaz Redondo. La fallida venta de 'Excélsior' [Vazquez Raña unmasks Díaz Redondo. The failed sale of *Excélsior*]. *Proceso*, April 29. www.proceso.com.mx. (accessed April 30, 2000).

Ortiz Pinchetti, F. 1982. La democracia—ficción de México, en seis frentes [Democracy: Fiction in Mexico, on six fronts]. *Proceso*, February 20.

Otano, R., and G. Sunkel. 2003. Libertad de los periodistas en los medios. *Revista Comunicación y Medios* 14. http://www.icei.uchile.cl/comunicacionymedios/ 14otanoysunkel.html (accessed October 14, 2005).

Otero, S. 2004. Ha recibido la PGR 24 quejas de periodistas. [The PGR has received 24 complaints from journalists.] *El Universal*, August 12. http://www.eluniversal.com. mx/pls/impreso/noticia.html?id_nota=114337&tabla=NACION (accessed August 12, 2004).

———. 2005. Exigen aclarar crímenes contra los periodistas [They demand that crimes against journalists be solved]. *El Universal*, August 31. www.eluniversal.com.mx (accessed August 31, 2005).

Parisi, P. 1998. Toward a philosophy of framing: News narratives for public journalism. *Journalism and Mass Communication Quarterly* 74:673–86.

Payán, C. 1999. Credibilidad, nuestro capital [Credibility, our capital]. *La Jornada*, September 20. www.jornada.unam.mx (accessed October 1, 2000).

Pérez Liñán, A. 2003. Presidential crises and political accountability in Latin America (1990–1997). In *What justice? Whose justice? Fighting for fairness in Latin America*, ed. Susan Eva Eckstein and Timothy P. Wickham-Crowley, 98–129. Berkeley: University of California Press.

Pérez Silva, C. 2004. Lamenta la CNDH que autoridades socaven la libertad de expresión [The CNDH laments that authorities suffocate freedom of expression]. *La Jornada*, August 10. http://www.jornada.unam.mx/2004/ago04/040810/003n1pol. php?origen=politica.php&fly=1 (accessed August 10, 2004).

Periodistas: Asociación para la defensa del periodismo independiente. 1998. Ernesto Tiffenberg. April. http://www.netizen.com.ar/periodistas/integrantes/e_tiffenberg. htm (accessed December 22, 2005).

Pfetsch, B., and F. Esser., eds. 2004. *Comparing political communication: Theories, cases and challenges.* New York: Cambridge University Press.

Poder Ciudadano. 2004. Planillas oficiales de la Secretaría de Medios. Distribución de la publicidad oficial por medio [Official Media Secretariat lists. Distribution of official advertising by media]. http://www.infocivica.org/nota.asp?ID=1677&Ultimo=0 (accessed December 22, 2005).

Powell, W. W. 1991. Expanding the scope of institutional analysis. In Powell and DiMaggio, 184–203.

Powell, W. W., and P. J. DiMaggio, eds. *The new institutionalism in organizational analysis.* Chicago: University of Chicago Press.

Presenta Ealy La Revista [Ealy presents La Revista]. *El Universal,* March 2. www. el-universal.com.mx. (accessed December 16, 2005).

Preston, J. 1996a. Mexico's elite caught in scandal's harsh glare. *New York Times,* July 13.

———. 1996b. An upstart Mexican network gets a bit personal. *New York Times,* July 22.

Proa Fundación. 2003. Escenas de los ochentas [Scenes of the eighties]. Exhibition. http://www.proa.org/exhibicion/80s/indice.html (accessed August 15, 2005).

Puig, C. 1997. La historia de Televisa: el aplauso sumiso al gobierno en turno [The history of Televisa: Submissive applause to the government in turn]. *Proceso,* April 19.

Ravelo, R., and R. Vera. 1993. El gobierno veracruzano: 'Pago a los travestis, porros y teporochos que hostilizaron a Cuauhtémoc' [The Veracruz government: "I pay the transvestites, thugs and thieves that threaten Cuauhtémoc"]. *Proceso,* October 2.

Reid, M. 1993. Guatemala's press fights return to the dark ages. *Guardian,* June 23.

Reporters Without Borders. 2005. *Mexico: Authority, impunity and self-censorship: Frontier journalists in a pitiless landscape.* Reporters without Borders, June. http:// www.rsf.org/article.php3?id_article=14153 (accessed September 2, 2005).

Riffe, D., S. Lacy, and F. G. Fico. 1998. *Analyzing Media Messages. Using Quantitative Content Analysis in Research.* Mahwah, NJ: Lawrence Erlbaum Associates.

Riva Palacio, R. 1991. Mexican press on the take? Unpublished paper. Cambridge, MA.

———. 1994. Mexican press on the take? A case study of the Mexico City press. *Neiman Reports* 48 (2): 76–77.

———. 1996. Fuera mascaras [Take off the masks]. *Reforma*, September 16. www. reforma.com (accessed January 23, 2004).

———. 1997. A culture of collusion: The ties that bind the press and the PRI. In *A culture of collusion: An insider's look at the Mexican press*, ed. W. A. Orme, 21–32. Miami: North-South Center Press, University of Miami.

Rockwell, R., and N. Janus. 2003. *Media power in Central America*. Chicago: University of Illinois Press.

Rodríguez Castañeda, R. 1993. *Prensa vendida: Una historia del periodismo mexicano y su vínculo con el poder* [Sold-out press: A history of Mexican journalism and its link with power]. México, D.F.: Grijalbo.

Rodríguez Yebra, M. 2005. *El perro no ladra: Ocaso del periodismo de investigación en Argentina*. [The dog does not bark: Decline of the investigative journalism in Argentina]. University of Miami, School of Communication.

Rojas Cruz, M. 2000. Lista de amigos y empresas que financian la campaña de Fox [List of friends and businesses that finance Fox's campaign]. *Excélsior*, June 7.

Rosen, J., and D. Merritt. 1994. *Public Journalism: Theory and Practice*. Dayton, Ohio: Kettering Foundation.

Rosenberg, T. 2001. The monochromatic media of Latin America. *New York Times*, May 7.

Russell, J. W. 1997. Mexico's rising inequality. *Monthly Review* 49 (7): 28–33.

Salas, N., and M. Olivos. 1999. Relación de actos contra el ejercicio periodistico ocurridos en México de enero a diciembre de 1999 [History of acts against journalism in Mexico from January to December 1999]. Fraternidad de Reporteros de Mexico. www.fremac.org.mx/obs/inf99/recue3.html (accessed July 15, 2002).

Salas Mar, B. 2004. Una resolución del IFAI favorece la seguridad en Laguna Verde [An IFAI resolution in favor of security at Laguna Verde]. *Proceso*, June 13.

Schein, E. H. 1985. *Organizational culture and leadership*. San Francisco: Jossey-Bass Publishers.

Scherer, J. 1990. *El poder: historias de familia* [Power: Family histories]. México D.F.: Grijalbo.

———. 1995. *Estos años* [These years]. México, D.F.: Oceano.

Schmitter, P. C. 1992. The consolidation of democracy and representation of social groups. *American Behavioral Scientist* 35 (4/5): 442–49.

Schudson, M. 1999. What public journalism knows about journalism, but doesn't know about "public." In *The idea of public journalism*, ed. T. L. Glasser, 118–33. New York: The Guilford Press.

———. 2000. The sociology of news production revisited (again). In *Mass Media and Society*, 3rd ed., ed. J. Curran and M. Gurevitch, 175–200. London: Edward Arnold.

Scott, J. C. 1990. *Domination and the arts of resistance: Hidden transcripts*. New Haven: Yale University Press.

Scott, R. W. 1995. *Institutions and organizations*. Thousand Oaks, CA: Sage.

———. 1998. *Organizations: Rational, natural and open systems*. 4th ed. Upper Saddle River, NJ: Prentice Hall.

Semo, I., ed. 1993. *La transición interrumpida: México 1968–1988* [The interrupted transition: Mexico 1968–1988]. México, D.F.: Universidad Iberoamericana/Nueva Imagen.

Senge, P. M. 1994. *The fifth discipline: The art and practice of the learning organization.* New York: Currency Doubleday.

Shirk, D. A. 2004. *Mexico's new politics. The PAN and democratic change.* Boulder: Lynne Rienner Publishers.

Siebert, S. F., T. Peterson, and W. Schramm. 1956. *Four theories of the press.* Urbana: University of Illinois Press.

Simón G, J. L. 1999. The Paraguayan press is threatening freedom of expression. Pulso del periodismo, July 18. http://www.pulso.org/English/Archives/Paraguayan%20Press-%20freedom.htm (accessed October 19, 2005).

Sims, C. 1995. Argentine reporter shot in back: Failed assasination try seen as latest bid to silence press. *New York Times,* June 14.

Sinclair, J. 1999. *Television in Latin America: A global view.* London: Oxford University Press.

Singh, J. V., D. J. Tucker, and A. G. Meinhard. 1991. Institutional change and ecological dynamics. In Powell and DiMaggio 1991, 390–422.

Sistema Internet de la Presidencia. 2001. Fox en vivo, Fox contigo [Fox live, Fox with you]. November 3. www.presidencia.gob.mx/?P=2&orden=Leer&tipo=PP&art=2080 (accessed November 7, 2001).

Skidmore, T. 1993. *Television, politics, and the transition to democracy in Latin America.* Baltimore: The Johns Hopkins University Press.

Skidmore, T., and P. Smith. 2001. *Modern Latin America.* 5th ed. New York: Oxford University Press.

Smith, P. H., ed. *Latin America in comparative perspective: New approaches to methods and analysis.* Boulder: Westview Press.

Smulovitz, C., and E. Peruzzotti. 2000. Societal accountability in Latin America. *Journal of Democracy* 11 (4): 147–58.

Sparks, C. 1998. Introduction. *Javnost: The Public* 5 (3): 5–9.

Sparks, C., and J. Tulloch, eds. 2000. *Tabloid tales: Global debates over media practices.* Lanhham, MA: Rowman and Littlefield.

Special Rapporteur for Freedom of Expression. 2002. Preliminary evaluation of freedom of expression in Guatemala. Press release, PREN/24/00. Guatemala City, Guatemala: Organization of American States.

Splichal, S. 1994. *Media beyond socialism: Theory and practice in East Central Europe.* Boulder: Westview Press.

Staub, J. 1995. Self-censorship and the Mexican press. www.cs.uwaterloo.ca/~alopez~o/politics/selfcens.html (accessed December 16, 2005).

Straubhaar, J., O. Olsen, and M. C. Nunes. 1992. The Brazilian case: Influencing the voter. In *Television, politics and the transition to democracy in Latin America,* ed. Thomas Skidmore, 118–36. Baltimore: The Johns Hopkins University Press.

Sussman, L. R., and K. D. Karlekar. 2003. *The annual survey of press freedom 2002.* New York: New York: Freedom House/Lanham, MA: Rowman and Littlefield.

Swanson, D. L. 2004. Transnational trends in political communication: Conventional views and new realities. In *Comparing political communication: Theories, cases and challenges,* ed. Pfetsch and Esser 2004, 45–63.

Teherán, J., and S. J. Jiménez. 2003. Asciende rescate bancario a más de un billon de pesos [Bank bailout climbs to more than one billion pesos]. *El Universal,* January 22. www.eluniversal.com.mx (accessed January 22, 2004).

Thomson, A. 2005. The improbable hero: Man in the news. Nestor Kirchner: Argentina's president has achieved the biggest reduction of developing nation debt. *Financial Times*, March 5.

Timerman, J. 1981. *Prisoner without a name, cell without a number.* Trans. T. Talbot. New York: Knopf.

Torow, J. 1992. *Media systems in society: Understanding industries, strategies, and power.* New York: Longman.

Torres A., F. J. 1997. *El periodismo mexicano: Ardua lucha por su integridad* [Mexican journalism: Arduous fight for its integrity]. México, D.F.: Ediciones Coyoacán.

Trejo, R. 1991. La prensa y los partidos [The press and the parties]. *Nexos,* August 1.

———. 1994. 1994: El voto en la prensa [1994: The vote in the press]. *Nexos,* December 1.

Turati, M. 1999. Admiten televisoras error en cobertura del informe [Telecasts admit error in coverage]. *Reforma,* September 9.

Tuynman, J. 2001. Free press Mexico: News of the freedom of the Mexican press. www.geocities.com/freepressmexico/index.html (accessed June 1, 2001).

Underwood, D. 1993. *When MBAs run the newsroom: How the marketers and managers are reshaping today's media.* New York: Columbia University Press.

Ungar, S. J. 1988. How Chile muzzles its press: In Santiago, only the bravest fight repression and apathy. *Washington Post,* January 3.

Uribe, H. 1998. Prensa y periodismo político en los años 60/70 [The press and political journalisms in the 60s/70s]. In *Morir es la noticia* [To die in the news], ed. E. Carmona. Santiago: J & C Productores Gráficos.

U.S. Drug Enforcement Administration. 2003. *Country Profile for 2003: Mexico.* Washington DC: DEA, DEA Intelligence Report (DEA-03047), November.

Valenzuela, J. S. 1992. Democratic consolidation in post-transitional settings: Notion, process and facilitating conditions. In *Issues in democratic consolidation: The new South American democracies in comparative perspective,* ed. S. Mainwaring, G. O'Donnell, and J. S. Valenzuela, 57–63. Notre Dame: University of Notre Dame Press.

Vanden Heuvel, J., and E. E. Dennis. 1995. *Changing patterns: Latin America's vital media.* New York: The Freedom Forum Media Studies Center, Columbia University.

Venegas, J.M. 2003. Gira de Fox con sabor a acto de campaña [Fox's tour has the flavor of a campaign event]. *La Jornada,* February 12. www.jornada.unam.mx (accessed July 28, 2003).

Verbitsky, H. 1995. Time to discuss the 'dirty war'. *World Press Review.* 42(7): 47–48.

———. 1996. *The flight. Confessions of an Argentine dirty warrior.* Trans. Esther Allen. New York: New Press.

———. 1997. *Un mundo sin periodistas: Las tortuosas relaciones de Menem con la ley, la justicia y la verdad* [A world without journalists: Menem's torturous relations with law, justice, and truth]. Buenos Aires: Planeta.

Vilas, C. 1997. Inequality and the dismantling of citizenship in Latin America. *NACLA Report on the Americas* (July/August): 57–63.

Villamil Rodríguez, J. 1999. El caso Stanley y los medios: El rating manda [The Stanley case and the media: The ratings matter]. *Bucareli* 83 (119): 18–19.

———. 2005a. Televisa. El verdadero poder. [Televisa. The real power.] *Proceso,* December 10. http://www.proceso.com.mx/hemerotecaint.html?arv=137410 (accessed December 21, 2005).

———. 2005b. Frenazo. [Stopped.] *Proceso*, December 18. http://www.proceso.com. mx/hemerotecaint.html?arv=137453 (accessed December 21, 2005).

Villanueva, E. 2003. Derecho de acceso a la información y organización ciudadana en México [The right to access to information and civic organization in Mexico]. *Derecho Comparado de la Información* 1 (January–June): 145–58.

Vincent, I. 1992. An Argentine gadfly. *World Press Review* 55.

Vinelli, N. 2002. *ANCLA: Una experiencia de comunicación clandestina orientada por Rodolfo Walsh* [ANCLA: An experience of clandestine information inspired by Rodolfo Walsh]. Buenos Aires: Editorial La Rosa Blindada.

Wager, S. G., and D. E. Schulz. 1995. Civil-military relations in Mexico: The Zapatista revolt and its implications. *Journal of Interamerican Studies and World Affairs* 37 (1): 1–42.

Waisbord, S. 1994. Knocking on newsroom doors: The press and political scandals in Argentina. *Political Communication* 11:19–33.

———. 1998. The unfinished project of media democratization in Argentina. In *Communicating democracy: The media and political transitions*, ed. P. H. O'Neil, 41–62. Boulder: Lynne Rienner Publishers.

———. 2000. *Watchdog journalism in South America: News, accountability and democracy*. New York: Columbia University Press.

Ward, O. 1983. When press freedom dies: Repression, Latin American style. *World Press Review* 56 (November): 56.

Weissert, W. 2002. Miami-based businessman controls big chunk of Latin American airwaves, looks to extend reach. *Associated Press*, June 5.

Williams, H. 2001. Of free trade and debt bondage: Fighting banks and the state in Mexico. *Latin American Perspectives* 28 (119): 30–51.

Wiñazki, N. 2005. El perro vuelve a ladrar [The dog returns to bark]. *Noticias*, June 18.

World Bank. 2005a. ICT at a glance. http://www.worldbank.org/cgi-bin/sendoff.cgi ?page=%2Fdata%2Fcountrydata%2Fict%2Farg_ict.pdf (accessed August 17, 2005).

———. 2005b. World development indicators database. The World Bank Institute. http://www.worldbank.org/data/wdi2005/wditext/index2.htm (accessed October 20, 2005).

Xanic, A. 2001. One acquitted, three sentenced to 25 years for murder of Benjamín Flores González. *Impunity*, May 2. http://www.impunidad.com/pressreleases/iapa _news5_04_01E.html (accessed July 1, 2004).

Zacarías, M. 2000. Es Juan Aguilera director de RTG [Juan Aguilera is the director of RTG]. *A.M.*, January 7. www.am.com.mx (accessed March 1, 2002).

Zamora, J. R. 2004. La teología financiera: Agonía diaria detrás del éxito [Financial theology: Daily agony behind success]. Paper presented at the World Association of Newspaper, 57th World Newspaper Congress, Istanbul.

INDEX

ABC, 106, 113, 250n2, 250n6, 251n7. *See also
Zeta*
Acapulco, 14, 120, 174
access to information law. *See* Federal Law for
Transparency and Access to Information
adaptive authoritarianism: defined, 12;
development of, 133; and local television
stations, 131, 135, 148, 150–51, 154; and
newsroom leaders, 19, 137; as part of
Mexican media system, 10, 44, 131, 196. *See
also* inertial authoritarianism
advertising: and the 2003 congressional
campaign, 163–64; in Argentina, 223, 225,
226, 230; in Chile, 211, 214, 217; at civic
newspapers, 105, 109, 118, 204–5; and corporations, 94–95, 248n10; at *El Financiero*,
79, 115–16, 118, 250n7; at *El Universal*, 89,
116, 118, 141, 204–5; at *Excélsior*, 118, 137, 142,
250n7; government, 137, 165; influence of,
97–98, 99, 112, 164; at *La Jornada*, 89, 115,
118, 204–5, 249n19; and the market-driven
news model, 14, 54, 157; at *Página/12*, 23,
225, 229, 231–32; and the private sector, 11,
40, 84, 115–16, 135, 155; at *Reforma*, 15, 89,
116, 118, 141, 204–5; television, 156, 169, 171,
177–78, 182
advocacy journalism, 5–6
Alemán, Ricardo, 126, 144, 174
Alemán Valdes, Miguel, 165, 166, 194
Alemán Velasco, Miguel, 167, 255n16
Alfonsín, Raúl, 224–25
Alianza Cívica, 8, 170, 172
Allende, Salvador, 50, 211, 213, 214, 216, 258n1
Alonso, Manuel, 44, 136, 138. *See also
Unomásuno*
Alves, Rosental, 210, 234, 258nn3–4
A.M., 114, 115, 250n2

Análisis, 219, 258n4
Argentina, assertive journalism in, 224–26,
230–32; democratic consolidation in, 210,
225; military rule in, 220–21, 223–24; news
production under dictatorship in, 221–24;
postauthoritarian media system in, 209,
229–30, 239. *See also Clarín*; Menem, Carlos; *Nación, La*; National Commission on
the Disappearance of Persons; *Página/12*;
Saint-Jean, Ibérico
assertiveness in newsgathering: in Argentina,
222, 224–32; and authoritarian journalism,
51; in Chile, 216–17; and civic-oriented
journalism, 13, 16, 41, 69, 83, 93, 112,
115, 134, 137, 208, 211; in coverage of the
president, 76–79, 193; definition of, 63–64;
as element of alternative model of news
production, *14*; in Guatemala, 233–36;
importance of, 4, 30; laws to protect, 202–3,
206; and market-driven journalism, 11, 54;
measurement of, *64*, 65–66, *68*; models of
outside of Mexico, 112; and press treatment
of powerful figures, 85, 92
authoritarian news model: as alternative to
civic-oriented model, 27, 38, 69, 133; as
alternative to market-driven model, 27,
161; defined, 4, 14, 55; and democratization,
132–33, 134; in Mexico, 47–48, 50–53; in
newspaper coverage, 66–67; and the PRI,
7, 10, 51, 53, 69; and television, 156, 165,
179–82, 184; theories of, 49–50; transformation of, 10, 132, 197
autonomy in newsgathering: in Argentina,
222, 226, 230, 232; and the authoritarian
model of journalism, 4, 12, 13, 134; in Chile,
217, 219–20; and the civic model of journalism, 4, 13, 19, 41, 69, 83, 112, 115, 126, 137,

279